D1521995

THE PRAGMATIST TURN

STUDIES IN RELIGION AND CULTURE

John D. Barbour and Gary L. Ebersole, Editors

THE PRAGMATIST TURN

Religion, the Enlightenment, and the Formation of American Literature

GILES GUNN

University of Virginia Press

CHARLOTTESVILLE AND LONDON

University of Virginia Press
© 2017 by the Rector and Visitors of the University of Virginia
All rights reserved
Printed in the United States of America on acid-free paper

First published 2017

1 3 5 7 9 8 6 4 2

Library of Congress Cataloging-in-Publication Data

Names: Gunn, Giles B., author.
Title: The pragmatist turn : religion, the Enlightenment, and the formation of
  American literature / Giles Gunn.
Description: Charlottesville : University of Virginia Press, 2017. | Series: Studies in
  religion and culture | Includes bibliographical references and index.
Identifiers: LCCN 2017025190 | ISBN 9780813940809 (cloth : acid-free paper) |
  ISBN 9780813940816 (pbk. : acid-free paper) | ISBN 9780813940823 (e-book)
Subjects: LCSH: American literature—History and criticism. | Religion and literature—
  United States. | Enlightenment—Influence. | Religion in literature.
Classification: LCC PS166 .G84 2017 | DDC 810.9/382—dc23
LC record available at https://lccn.loc.gov/2017025190

Cover art: Detail from *In the Sierras,* Albert Bierstadt, 1868. (Harvard Art Museums/
Fogg Museum, Gift of Mr. and Mrs. Frederic Haines Curtiss)

For Barbra, Adam, and Abigail

We thank thee, Father, for these strange minds that enamor us against thee.

—Emily Dickinson

I feel along the edges of life for a way that leads to open land.

—David Ignatow

CONTENTS

ACKNOWLEDGMENTS

Though I have spent the greatest portion of my career writing about religion, literature, and American culture and ideas, I have devoted the better part of the last twenty years attempting to widen my focus to address normative questions across a more global field. In books like *Beyond Solidarity: Pragmatism and Difference in a Globalized World* (Chicago, 2001), *America and the Misshaping of a New World Order* (California, 2010), *Ideas to Die For: The Cosmopolitan Challenge* (Routledge, 2013), and, most recently, *Ideas to Live For: Toward a Global Ethics* (Virginia, 2015), I have sought to use admittedly American and Western perspectives for the sake of trying to see, if I could, beyond them, to, in Ngũgĩ wa Thiong'o's terms, "move the center." But this has inevitably prompted questions about where, at least in my case, some of these perspectives actually came from; how deeply inflected they were by the history of American religion and the American Enlightenment; what enabled those perspectives to survive as spiritual and moral imaginaries long after they had lost their identities as more specific creeds and codes of behavior; how the development of a distinctive pragmatist temperament and intellectual method of inquiry in the nineteenth century influenced this process; and whether such imaginaries can still prove a moral and spiritual resource in an era of increasing absolutisms of nationalistic as well as global kinds—and thus the rationale for *The Pragmatism Turn* was eventually born.

Such questions as these make it obvious that this book possesses a personal as well as a professional dimension. It has been written very self-consciously with a general audience in mind even where it takes up issues of a somewhat more specialized nature. What has chiefly motivated me to write it is a desire to turn some of what I have learned from looking abroad at normative questions raised by many of the more vexing global issues of our time back, as it were, on America itself. My principal concern has been to track the two most important sources of American principles and values as they have contributed intellectually and aesthetically to the formation of American literary culture, not for their own sake alone but for the sake of determining their unspent potential in the present and the future. This book is not, then, simply a history of literary texts and ideas but also an assessment of a complex spiritual legacy that has been kept alive through its pragmatic adaptations and critical revisions over many years. Since it also results from reflections of my own over many years that have carried me across several different academic fields, from religious and literary to cultural, philosophical, and global studies, this book also presents particular difficulties when it comes to the task of making acknowledgments.

While its earliest roots go back to several courses I took in college that first aroused my interests in American literature and American pragmatism, the first on the philosophical background of American Romanticism from the great American studies scholar Leo Marx, the second a seminar on Marx, Freud, and Dewey from the pragmatist scholar Gail Kennedy, it wasn't until graduate school in a program on religion and literature that I began to put some of these interests together in a dissertation that was eventually to become an intellectual biography of the distinguished American literary historian and critic F. O. Matthiessen. Matthiessen's way of relating literature with philosophy and religion was most vividly expressed by the strange marriage of Christianity and democracy that he thought he found at the center of the work of the writers of the American Renaissance, even in authors like Hawthorne and Melville, who clearly discerned the tragic gap between America's professions of belief and its practices, but I was myself more clearly drawn to the intellectual grounds for their literary expressions of religious dissent, and thus found myself more sympathetic with their religious skepticism than with their spiritual affirmations.

While it would take me a number of years to work out some of my ideas about their problems with belief and the way those problems echoed down the years into the twentieth century, it is to an exceptional group of graduate students that I began working with as a young instructor at the University of Chicago that I owe my interest in how important an emergent American spirit of pragmatic questioning in the nineteenth century had become in keeping some of these concerns alive. Thus it is to Peter Vasile, the late Rowland Sherrill, Lynn Ross-Bryant, James Mosely, Errol McGuirre, Frank Scafella, and, in special ways, David Carrasco, as much as to colleagues like Nathan A. Scott Jr., Preston T. Roberts Jr., James E. Miller Jr., Wayne C. Booth, and Charles H. Long, that I owed my interest in balancing the literary with the philosophical and the religious. But these concerns were to be supported in later years by the example as well as the work and friendship of Joy and John Kasson, Alan Trachtenberg, Stephen Mailloux, John Carlos Rowe, John J. McDermott, David Chidester, David Hollinger, Edward Linenthal, the late Gunther Lenz, Winifrid Fluck, and Carl Gutiérrez-Jones.

There are others to whom my debt is still more personal. They begin with my wife, Barbra, to whom, yet again, I dedicate my book. She has as always in these recent years been my rock and inspiration and, in the very best sense, my enabler. It is she who has urged me to make my thinking more publicly useful, in this instance by employing American literary and intellectual experience as a lens through which to attempt to discern the outlines of a more humane future for America itself and the world. But they also include my children, Adam and Abigail, my own "new worlds" and continuous fellow travelers, whose support along the way has been indispensable. So, too, has been the encouragement I have received not only from DeAnn Gunn, Charles Gunn, Alexander Gunn, and the other members of our extended immediate family, who go by the names Sprafkin and Lannin, but also friends and colleagues of long standing, who include Peter and Kathy Vasile, David Carrasco, Jack Moxley, Mark Juergensmeyer, and Esther Lezra.

The essay on which this book is based was originally published as "The Pragmatist Turn: Religion and the Enlightenment in Nineteenth- and Twentieth-Century American Letters" in my *Thinking across the American Grain: Ideology, Intellect, and the New Pragmatism,* 119–51 (Chicago: University of Chicago Press, 1992. Copyright © by the University of Chicago. All rights reserved). Permission from the University of Chicago Press to reprint portions of it is gratefully acknowledged. The book for which it was prepared, though published later under the title of "Enamored against Thee by These Strange Minds: Recovering the Relations between Religion and the Enlightenment in Nineteenth-Century and Twentieth-Century American Literary Culture," is *Knowledge and Belief in America: Enlightenment Traditions and Modern Religious Thought,* edited by William M. Shea and Peter A. Huff, 52–87 (New York and London: Woodrow Wilson Center Press and Cambridge University Press, 1995. Copyright © The Woodrow Wilson International Center for Scholars).

I want to thank two chairs of the Department of Global Studies, Eve Darian-Smith and Alison Brysk, for helping me arrange sabbatical leaves to work on this book; the University of California, Santa Barbara, for granting those sabbatical leaves; and former dean Melvin Oliver and Dean Leila Rupp for supporting them. I also thank Kim Coonen for expert assistance in obtaining a small research grant, and Tymotuez Chajdas for generous support as my research assistant. The University of Virginia Press has again provided all that an author could wish for in moving this book through the process of acceptance and production.

John Barbour, one of the editors of this series Studies in Religion and Culture, expressed a generous interest in this book when I first proposed the idea of it to him, and he quickly brought it to the attention of the press's new editor in chief, Eric Brandt. Eric Brandt, who admitted to reading me as a doctoral student in philosophy in the 1980s, then took over its development with the kind of collaborative support that an author can only hope for, providing me with sage advice, thoughtful criticism, and warm support that saw the manuscript through two substantially different versions. I owe him a special debt of gratitude not only for his gracious counsel but also for his shared commitment to this project. I also owe a similar debt of gratitude to two readers who understood what I was up to but were exceptionally helpful in encouraging me to bring it out.

Once completed, this book has, like most my recent, profited from Ellen Satrom's expert and thoughtful management of the production process, which enables the writer to feel like the press is as much an indispensable ally as a necessary partner. Ruth Melville has smoothed out my sentences and clarified my ideas as only a masterful editor can, and Enid Zafran is to be thanked for the provision of an index that will make the book more fully accessible to the reader.

THE PRAGMATIST TURN

Introduction

This book possesses a somewhat unusual genealogy. Its origin goes back to a conference organized by the Woodrow Wilson Center two decades ago where I was asked to contribute to a volume of essays on the general subject of belief and reason in America. My specific assignment was to discuss how their relations had later found expression in nineteenth- and twentieth-century American literary culture. Initially assuming that I was being asked to explain the influence of two different traditions of faith and practice associated, on the one hand, with seventeenth-century American religion, and particularly its Protestantism branch, and, on the other, with the eighteenth-century American Enlightenment, I quickly realized that these two complex traditions had survived in modern American writing, to the degree that they had, less as organized systems of belief and morality or creed and conduct than as something more like frames of reference, conceptual mindsets, moral dispositions, even structures of feeling. They persisted, that is to say, less as confessional, dogmatic, or ideological constructs to which one gives assent and owes obedience than as different "visions and ways," to borrow William James's description of the entire history of philosophy, "of feeling the whole push, and seeing the whole drift of life."[1]

What I discovered, then, is that if seventeenth-century American religion and the eighteenth-century American Enlightenment had managed to influence nineteenth- and twentieth-century American writing, they had succeeded in doing so less by generating wholly distinctive, much less easily discriminable, strains of thought or emotion than by undergoing what might be called a kind of pragmatist refashioning or, better, refiguration in their literary employment. This pragmatist refiguration resulted neither in their respective persistence under new names nor in their recombination as some new species of theological conviction and commitment. They had survived as modes of consciousness, as styles of sense and sensibility, or as what we would now call spiritual imaginaries.

The term *imaginary* has often been associated with fantasy, dream, fabulation, make-believe, illusion, or the unreal and associated with specialized precincts of life culturally set aside for it in art, myth, and ritual, but this is to forget that it has rarely been content to remain sequestered in such sanctuaries and has recurrently broken free of them to become a significant force in the shaping of personal, social, political, and historical life as a whole.[2] One need merely consider such ideas as "race," "ethnicity," "gender," "class," or "country" to realize how deeply the agency of the imagination has insinuated itself into their special logics and subjectivities. The term has acquired enhanced intellectual currency ever since Cornelius Castoriadis identified it as one of the principal constitutive factors in the creation of society itself. Benedict Anderson then applied it to the construction of the political notion of the nation, Arjun Appadurai extended it to the postelectronic world of the global, and Charles Taylor eventually associated it with the multiple modernities that have resulted from the different ways that a given people imagines its collective social life.[3]

By imaginaries, then, I refer to symbolic formations composed of metaphors, images, narratives, legends, and other discursive and figurative material that constitute the notional and affective schemata by which people define their collective sense of life or lifeworld. Conferring intelligibility and legitimacy on social practices, these symbolic matrices help shape collective subjectivities and install them in a normative framework.[4] Occupying a kind of subjective middle ground between embodied practices and explicit doctrines, these symbolic matrices of meaning are thus imaginary in a double sense. They are imaginary not only because their cognitive utility and influence cannot be dissociated from their suggestive power but also because their suggestive power is closely tied to what might be called their "buzz and hum of implication." This last phrase was famously used by the American cultural critic Lionel Trilling to describe what he meant by a culture's manners, "the whole evanescent context in which its explicit statements are made, . . . that part of a culture which is made up of half-uttered or unuttered or unutterable expressions of value."[5]

But I want to employ this phrase still more broadly to indicate how imaginaries of various kinds, often in relation to, or in potential conflict with, others, actually find their way into lived or potentially livable experience. Such imaginaries make themselves felt not as direct expressions of any of the more formalized departments of culture, such as religion, politics, morality, or even art, as Trilling originally noted, but rather as the adhesive that threads these more institutionalized, sometimes ideational, configurations of meaning together, however loosely, into a structure that can be experienced as opposed to merely conceived, inhabited as opposed to merely contemplated.

But seventeenth-century religion and the eighteenth-century Enlightenment were by no means the only spiritual imaginaries vying for the control of religious space in what was to become the "United States of America." Long before Protestantism or the Enlightenment ever reached the shores of North America, sway over that imaginary space had already been claimed by the idea of "America" itself. In this sense, the origins of "America" as an imaginary idea go back to a period long before the creation of the first European settlements on the North American continent, to the beginning of the early modern era and what is now referred to as the oceanic discovery of the world, and, more exactly, to the religious and philosophical aspirations that fueled those oceanic voyages and the spiritual reactions that followed in their wake. What entered history was the ocean itself and the new worlds it suddenly opened to the imagination, one of which was given the name for Europeans of "America."[6]

American history thus properly begins not with the history of American colonization but rather with the creation of the idea of "America" itself. "America" came into existence as a compelling symbol long before it became an empirical fact, and the symbol or image of America was inseparable from the hopes, dreams, fears, and dreads it inspired among those first drawn to it. Whatever America was destined to become socially or politically, or, for that matter, economically or religiously, the nature, though not the substance, of its spiritual composition was already in a fair measure fixed. Idea and actuality, image and reality, would thereafter consort together, and the historical and spiritual reality of America, as of American literature, would eventually emerge from their continuous union and conflict. The only question, then as now, was what to make of this American imaginary, or, as Ralph Waldo Emerson was later to call it, "this new yet unapproachable America I have found in the West."[7]

Emerson's pregnant phrase comes from his essay entitled "Experience" in which he attempts to wrestle with the tragic loss of his beloved son Waldo. The "America" Emerson found in the figurative "West" of his spiritual experience seemed, precisely because of its inspirational capacity, to provide the only possible compensation for the loss of this cherished symbol of his patrimony, of his parenthood, perhaps of his creative agency. But the "America" Emerson identifies in this essay suggests that we have not, as one would expect from the experience of unappeasable loss, arrived "at a wall, but," as he reimagines it in the metaphor of its European discovery, "at indeterminate oceans. Our life seems not present so much as prospective. . . . So in accepting the leading of the sentiments," Emerson consoles himself, "it is not what we believe concerning the immortality of the soul or the like, but *the universal desire to believe,* that is the material circumstance and is the principal fact in the history of the globe" (italics Emerson's).[8]

If Emerson turned his imagination of "this new yet unapproachable America" into what might be considered a kind of compensatory belief or "God-term" for his loss, he was neither the last American writer to do this nor, more importantly, the first; he was simply the most successful in capturing what as symbol as well as fact made the spiritual imaginary of America itself, whether as inspiration, enigma, or warning, so bewitching and bedeviling. It would be up to Emerson's literary and intellectual descendants to work through these alternative implications of "the universal desire to believe" with, as we will see, the assistance of what was left and still usable in America's religious and Enlightenment legacies.

Thus *The Pragmatist Turn* has not been constructed as a study in intellectual influence, nor as an examination of the marriage of two traditions of reflection and sentiment in individual moments, sites, or institutions where their affiliation, asymmetries, disjunctions, and refashionings are most evident. Much less is it intended to be a study of how these two traditions were effectively merged in the thought of William James himself, or how the traces of his philosophical or methodological interests are reflected in the work of later imaginative writers. Still less is it an attempt to convert the history of American literature into a "site" for the testing of a theory called pragmatism. It is rather an inquiry into how two different, but not wholly discrete or unrelated, spiritual imaginaries were able to remain consequential in the development of later American writing through their pragmatist refashioning as instruments designed to come to terms in part with the spiritual imaginary of America itself, an imaginary that still remains for various reasons unapproachable not simply to others but also, as far as many American writers are concerned, to itself.

While this volume takes the form of a history, then, its structure will be far from linear. The flow of ideas and habits of mind that I am concerned to understand is anything but successive, since such processes of reflection and revision often move in directions more varied than literary histories sometimes allow, and the more obvious lines of literary influence, direct and indirect, have already been mapped countless times before. My interest is not in tracking sequences of thought and literary practice so much as in understanding how constellations of ideas and aesthetic formations—what Walter Benjamin and Theodor Adorno referred to as "a juxtaposed rather than integrated cluster of changing elements that resist reduction to a common denominator, essential core, or generative first principle"—could be transformed into cognitive and affective components of a felt sense of life.[9]

Such a history might well have attempted to resituate these texts, and the constellation of ideas that inform them, in the sociopolitical and economic contexts of their creation and reception, or in relation to the material and other empirical conditions that shaped their formation, or in terms of their connections with systems of historical practice from sorcery to science with which they have extensive affinities and affiliations, but my own purpose here has been to pursue an inquiry of a somewhat different nature.[10] My interest has been principally concerned with tracking the persistence of modes of spirituality under conditions of experience and possibility for which they were never originally designed in order to explore what later thinkers and writers made of them, how useful they found them both epistemologically and morally. In other words, my focus is not simply on what has survived of religion and the Enlightenment in some of the more characteristic literature and thought of American Romanticism, modernism, and late modernism or postmodernism but on its still unexhausted potential at once spiritual and critical.

With some qualifications, then, one might describe this book, after Pierre Bourdieu, as a literary and cultural study of spiritual embodiment, since it focuses on religion and the Enlightenment not as fixed structures of abstract thought and commitment but as structuring formations of significance and sentiment, or what Bourdieu referred to as forms of *habitus* that predispose us to think and act—and rethink and react—in certain ways. Known as deeply in our bodies as our minds, such imaginary formations may thus be thought of as dispositional rather than diagnostic or prescriptive constructs whose purpose is less to define or regulate thought and behavior than to generate the improvisational possibilities for adapting them to new conditions.

In this more affective and agentic model of understanding systems of belief and practice, religion and the Enlightenment might otherwise be described as forms of symbolic capital that not only help to configure the literary and cultural field but to determine its power relations. Since such fields normally contain more than one kind or system of symbolic capital in play, the relations between symbolic systems cannot be determined by which one has the most capital but rather by how different symbol systems relate to one another based on the kind of capital they control. The object is not simply to accumulate as much symbolic capital of a particular kind as possible but to be able to reproduce it, which often requires, according to Bourdieu, converting it, or, as I call it, symbolically refiguring it, across different literary, cultural, or social fields. A complex maneuver, this is by no means an unusual one, and it is frequently assisted by what Bourdieu calls "virtuosos"—in this book, poets, novelists, essayists, social thinkers, philosophers, scientists, and theologians—whose "scheme of thought and expression . . . are the basis for the *intentionless invention* of regulated improvisation." As Bourdieu continues, "Endlessly overtaken by [their] own words, with which [they] maintain a relation of 'carry and be carried,'" the virtuoso finds in the operations of his or her own discourse new triggers for further discourse, "so that his [or her] discourse continuously feeds off itself like a train bringing along its own rails."[11]

Bourdieu's language gives us a new way of thinking about how the seventeenth- and eighteenth-century spiritual systems associated with belief and reason, respectively, might have continued to have something to do with one another even after they lost their normative force when their symbolic relations were pragmatically refigured in the nineteenth and twentieth centuries on behalf of understanding how the third spiritual imaginary known as America could continue to remain, in Emerson's language, both new and still unapproachable. This is a story whose underlying plot has been discerned before, but it has never been told from the point of view I wish to tell it or associated with the kinds of meanings I wish to give it.

That point of view is unconventional in several senses. To begin with, this story derives as much from the American Enlightenment, or at least from certain selective and extended emphases within it, as from American religion, and specifically its Protestant background. Moreover, it assumes that the emphases within the American Enlightenment that mattered most to the formation of later American writing were not rational or didactic but skeptical, critical, and sometimes disbelieving. They were more focused on questioning authority, liberating criticism, and illuminating darkness than on intellectually consolidating or applying the scientific heritage of the seventeenth century or expanding the eighteenth-century defense of rationality, moderation, and progress. Contrary to conventional understanding, it also assumes that these more suspicious, self-reflexive, even at times more cynical, sides of Enlightenment thinking—the elements reflected in René Descartes's assumption that doubt is the key to belief, or Immanuel Kant's association of the Enlightenment with daring to know, or Voltaire's conviction that "those who can make you believe absurdities can make you commit atrocities," or David Hume's belief that "reason is and ought only to be a slave of the passions"—crossed the Atlantic not in the later seventeenth and eighteenth centuries but rather in the nineteenth century and have intermittently but persistently continued this emigration ever since. This narrative represents that part of the Enlightenment that was as committed to overcoming ignorance, resisting intolerance, challenging parochialism, and generating criticism as it was to creating a new society built around the separation of powers and organized by law that gave broad authority to citizens, or at least to white male citizens with property, claiming specific human rights.[12]

What is not understood as well as it should be is that this more intellectually self-reflexive side of the American Enlightenment would never have acquired the influence it did in the creation of an emergent American literature if it had not been able to accommodate itself to, and learn to utilize for its own purposes, certain residual concerns of the American religious heritage. The synergistic agent in this case, as already stated, was the development in the nineteenth century of a new intellectual disposition and theory of inquiry known as pragmatism whose own frame of mind and critical self-consciousness was born of a long, and indeed venerable, tradition of reflection in America rooted both in the seventeenth century's absorption with the spiritual problematics of personal regeneration and community renewal and also in the eighteenth century's more worldly preoccupations with the creation of viable social and political institutions and the science of governance. In this sense, the intellectual task that pragmatism set for itself was twofold: not just to investigate those dimensions of experience that lay within the more discernible borders of the collective, the civic, and the commercial, and thus susceptible to rational exploration, public deliberation, and empirical verification, but also to investigate those dimensions of experience that lay, as it were, beyond such ostensible borders, in the realm of the subjective, the subjunctive, the imaginary, or what James simply referred to as "the More."[13]

The convergence of James's theory of pragmatism and the aesthetic project of so much modern American writing was thus no coincidence. Each was part of the same collective effort to release the energies of the imagination from the confines of its own inherited boundaries and inhibitions so that they might become freer to discover whatever spiritual possibilities and liabilities might lie beyond them. But before attempting to delineate how currents of seventeenth-century American religion and the eighteenth-century American Enlightenment were to be absorbed—and at the same time transformed—in subsequent American writing and thought by means of a kind of pragmatist turn, we need to take careful note of how they each evolved historically in America, which spiritual needs they seemed respectively to address or allay, how such spiritual projects overlapped or interacted, and what kinds of literary and intellectual creations they generated.

No adequate estimate can be made of the impact or fate of these two spiritual imaginaries, much less of the aspirational forms that the original European—and not just English—explorers, conquistadors, colonists, and settlers brought with them, without making at least two acknowledgments at the outset. The first is that seventeenth-century religion and the eighteenth-century Enlightenment both flourished in an emergent society in which slaveholding was at once an accepted institution in parts of the North as well as the South and also an indispensable source for legitimating as well as sustaining them, "part of the res itself," to refer to a famous formulation, "and not about it."[14] The second is that these same spiritual imaginaries also continuously offered massive support and justification for the violent displacement and essential erasure of the indigenous people who already inhabited the American landscape. While it will not be possible at every point in this narrative to draw attention to the hypocritical use to which these two spiritual imaginaries could be put, it should never be forgotten that the history they produced was for many of America's citizens or potential citizens one of world rending as much as of world making, of devastation as of mondialization—of depredations and ravages as of awakenings and redemptions. What made Emerson's America new yet unapproachable for some is clearly not what made it so for others. Indeed, whatever America has or has not become for others, including its own "others," Emerson's phrase leaves open the question whether it has ever become fully approachable, much less intelligible, to itself.

One of the dangers of pursuing issues like these is that it risks the appearance of presuming that while the story of American literature obviously possesses more than one narrative, there is a figure to be found in the carpet of its history that, however variously expressed, can still be recognized as culturally distinctive and in that sense unique. But this would be to forget how much we have learned over a number of decades about the referential instability of such terms as *history, literature,* and *culture.* Just as we have learned how deeply terms like literature and history are implicated in the meanings of the other—how the figurative, the generic, and the tropological shape our understanding of the historical, and how narrativity, historicity, and temporality influence our conception of the literary—so we also have come to appreciate how both are arranged and organized within much larger networks of meaning, at once symbolic, interpretive, and legible that we call culture.

Culture is, of course, composed of many things besides discourse—signs, sounds, sights, gestures, actions, material objects, ideas, institutions, rituals, and, above all, imaginaries—but discourse of a certain breadth and complexity is exactly what enables us to comprehend how diverse voices striving to speak both from within and sometimes from without one national framework can together shape a comprehensible dialogue, or at least an intelligible conversation. Such a conversation need not be assumed to possess a common set of subjects, or recurrent set of themes, or even a consistent set of features. But if this conversation is to be understood as in any sense shared as well as sharable, it must be perceived as one whose points of difference and even disagreement still bear at least enough of a family resemblance to each other to be construed as alternative and, at the same time, responsive ways of speaking within an ever-expanding range of discursive possibilities. In short, it must be conceived as a series of individual literary *parole* springing from some sort of shared cultural *langue* that can be imagined as in some sense answerable to one another, part of the same discussion.

In such terms as these, this volume seeks to explore the range and implications of one such conversation concerning versions of Protestantism and the Enlightenment in the formation of American writing. But it attempts to do so without forgetting that this discussion has been susceptible to many uses, some of which have been employed to legitimate or excuse the nation's imperialist and racist expansionism in the later nineteenth, twentieth, and now twenty-first centuries. This is an expansionism that for millions around the world, no less than many in the United States, has turned what was ideally symbolized by Emerson's "new yet unapproachable America" into something unrecognizable to itself but all too familiar to the victims of its predations as a repressive, rapacious, reactionary "Amerika." While this symbolic transformation of the national imaginary does not constitute the primary subject of this book, there can be little doubt that its refiguration shadows those spiritual imaginaries that are.

Chapter 1 introduces some of the difficulties of defining these two spiritual traditions, then considers several of the more traditional ways of interpreting them that have restricted our contemporary understanding of their availability for modern literary use, and, finally, takes account of the two alternative spiritual imaginaries that long predated the arrival of Christianity and the Enlightenment to North American shores but have rarely been given sufficient credit for their contribution to the former's respective development. The first spiritual imaginary is associated with Native American traditions and the significant contributions they made (and still do), not just in oppositional terms but also in constructive ones, to Protestant and Enlightenment thinking about the so-called New World. The second alternative spiritual imaginary is associated with early modern European thinking about that "New World" and centered on the symbolic notion of "America" itself. These alternative spiritual imaginaries, and their contributions to the development of literary practice in the United States, need to be included in any history of American writing if that subject is ever to become more than a provincial story of how American literature has contributed to the myths of national consensus even when criticizing them. This is another way of saying that the history of American writing, like the history of the United States itself, can only be understood from a more global perspective.

Chapter 2 will then pick up the narrative of development by exploring the somewhat complex grammar of religious and other motives that led to the settlement principally of the New England colonies. The intention here is not to provide a detailed history of movements, peoples, and ideas but rather to identify some of those individuals, and the literary forms they employed, who made distinctive contributions to the unfolding of the Puritan "errand," as it was termed, "in the wilderness."[15] That errand was dogged from the start by temptations to hubris that its leaders so often railed against in their followers but seldom escaped exhibiting themselves, but the reasons these temptations spiraled so rapidly into a situation that imperiled the Puritan experiment itself were far beyond the ability of Puritanism's own theological resources to address. Those problems lay as much in alterations to the fabric of social, political, and material life as they did in the inability of Puritanism's disciples to live up to the demands of their new covenant with God, but they were to require a spiritual flexibility and moral resourcefulness and compromise virtually unknown among New England's first leaders.

The third chapter takes up the alternative set of spiritual forces set in motion by those developments and associated with the European Enlightenment which subsequently altered the sacred canopy and established some of the building blocks of a new nation. While the spiritual fervor of Puritanism was to break out in two great religious awakenings that swept through the colonies in the middle of the seventeenth century and at the beginning of the eighteenth, its descendants were already living in a country growing increasingly restive under the hand of continued British rule and more pre-occupied with political debates about the creation of a new state than with theological debates about the present state of the soul. Though their inter-ests in revolution and nation building were backed by a religious belief that they were still doing God's work, that work had much less to do with the pu-rity of the heart than with the order of Nature and Nature's God. Just as their leaders' faith was becoming increasingly Deistic rather than Christocentric, so their political aim was shifting from a desire to build a new world where, as in the theocratic model, church and state are one to a new world where, as in the republican model, they are kept separate.

With this as background, we will then be prepared in chapter 4 to move into the nineteenth century, which opened on the note sounded by "the rising glory" poems of Hugh Henry Brackenbridge, Phillip Freneau, and John Trumbull, along with assorted others, and closed on the note recorded by Henry Adams in his *Education* that the constellation of spiritual forces had now been irrevocably transformed. The movement was from a world of rational order and benign prospect assured by a benevolent deity to a world of disorder and chaos produced by the explosion of industrial power. The problem was not only to determine what to make of this new idea of order but also how to manage and survive its exactions when the coordi-nates of experience had changed from the nineteenth century's triumvirate of Nature, God, and Self to force, dynamism, and potency. This was the task taken up by male and female narratives in the nineteenth century, and in various ways significantly extended in African American slave narratives by writers like Frederick Douglass and Harriet Jacobs, but the struggle to re-configure the spiritual legacies of the past was most profoundly undertaken in fiction by Herman Melville and in poetry by Emily Dickinson.

To explore more deeply the process of symbolic refiguration that enabled these two spiritual imaginaries to be reappropriated in the twentieth as well as twenty-first centuries, chapter 5 will then turn back to the later nine-teenth century for a more extended examination of the writings of William James. After explaining why his writing as a philosopher and public intellec-tual could be repossessed in different eras for such different reasons, we will examine the relations between the pragmatic method and the nature of tem-perament or disposition, why this made James's notion of truth so radical, and how that radicality is related to his theory of consciousness and mean-ing. The aim of this chapter is to show why a pragmatic disposition could prove so useful to American writers in a world in which all of the old gods apparently have disappeared and the new ones, if such there are, offer less comfort than alarm. The key was to loosen the emotional and evaluational as well as intellectual and spiritual restraints placed on consciousness by an increasingly moralistic and sanctimonious bourgeois culture and replace it, if William and Henry James were any guide, with a more relaxed and at the same time probing curiosity and receptivity desirous of comprehending the shifting, enigmatic, contradictory, and continuously disruptive contours of experience itself.

This will then prepare us to return in chapter 6 to American writing in the twentieth century to consider what happened when the modern absorption with flux, mobility, and fluidity was put under pressure by a late or postmodern obsession with indeterminacy, relativity, and recursivity. In a world where the Internet and its technologies not only constitute so much of experience itself but also promise, through their own ineffabilities, their own version of the sublime, America continues to remain somehow suspended between these two spiritual imaginaries. The story this book tells, then, is not about modern American literature's pragmatic conversations with earlier spiritual imaginaries but rather about how those imaginaries, through their pragmatist refigurations in critical, comic, or uncanny forms, have managed to keep alive a sense of what is both new and yet unapproachable about America itself.

Like all narratives, mine is inevitably a kind of selection, even a distortion, but a distortion created not to deform the truth so much as to try to detect a portion of it that has been obscured. My own narrative reflects the ambivalence expressed in both of my epigraphs, along with the tension between them. Like the passage from Emily Dickinson—"We thank thee, Father, for these strange minds than enamor us against thee"—those who seek to challenge the religious legacy of America must at the same time risk their exposure to the corrosive cynicism they have had to create in order to protect themselves from its ministrations, as though in that act of calculated rebellion "regret were in it / And were sacred."[16] Like the passage from David Ignatow—"I feel along the edges of life for a way that leads to open land"—those released from commitment to the conventional source or sources of religious insight who set off on antinomian quests of their own in hopes of finding a new idea of order, a new image of divinity, as Hart Crane thought he did when he petitioned the Brooklyn Bridge to "descend, and of the curveship lend a myth to God," can only imagine it in terms of the limitations they must overcome, the boundaries they must traverse, the horizons they must transcend to find what is yet unbounded, limitless, free. There is, moreover, an obvious tension between the retrospective disenchantment and disdain of the first passage from Emily Dickinson—who can fail to hear the note of defiant outrage in Captain Ahab's curses from Herman Melville's *Moby-Dick?*—and the prospective wariness and uncertainty of the second passage from David Ignatow's *Rescue the Dead*—who isn't afraid, like Melville's Ishmael, of the open independence of their sea?

ONE

The Difficulty of Beginnings

Provisional Definitions

This narrative must begin with the difficulty of beginning itself, or at least with the difficulty of beginning here. There are, in fact, at least four such difficulties that increase in ascending order. The first concerns the reference of the two constitutive terms of this inquiry, religion and the Enlightenment. Even if we set aside the fact that Roman Catholicism was not an inconsequential presence in some of the colonies, and that by the time of the American Revolution Judaism had also established a modest foothold in Rhode Island and South Carolina that did not miss the attention of George Washington, we are still confronted with a conundrum. Restricting what we mean in this case by religion to the basic tenets of American Protestantism in the first two centuries of colonial settlement, and of the Enlightenment to the core of epistemological, anthropological, and cosmological ideas shared by the Founding Fathers, we are still presented with considerable variation in the way such principles and axioms were interpreted by representative figures of each so-called camp.

The theological affirmations of the Synod of Dort—unconditional election, limited atonement, total depravity, irresistible grace, the perseverance of the saints—were by no means accepted by all Protestant Christians in the seventeenth and eighteenth centuries, any more than Voltaire's cynicism, Hume's skepticism, or Dugald Stewart's common sense can be flattened out into a characterization of the beliefs of all members of the Enlightenment. Just as colonial Christians differed greatly over their views on everything from the nature of God, the ineradicability of sin, the universality of redemption, and the order of worship to the proper organization of the church, so the American Enlightenment was composed of at least four discriminable traditions that ranged in ethos and method from the moderation, rationality, and balance of figures like Locke, Newton, and Franklin, through the skepticism and critique of Voltaire, Hume, and Holbach, to the utopian optimism and revolutionary millennialism that begins in Rousseau and continues through Jefferson, Paine, and Godwin, to, finally, the didacticism of Scottish Common Sense philosophy associated with Thomas Reid and Lord Kames.[1]

In addition, it must be noted that the Enlightenment did not constitute itself as a historical movement in reaction to religion, and thus by nature opposed to religion, but rather as itself an alternative to or substitute for religion.[2] Hence religion and reason, belief and doubt, faith and freedom, are never opposed, or at least opposed as absolutes, in the writings of the Founding Fathers but are opposed instead, particularly as one moves closer to the Revolution, to what Jonathan Mayhew described as "Tyranny, PRIEST-CRAFT, and Nonsense."[3]

Since so much of the concern about liberty and democracy in the eighteenth century, no less than the suspicions of authoritarianism, originated in debates about explicitly theological issues and were nourished by evangelical interests, this is, or should be, scarcely surprising.[4] The founders came by their ability to mix secular and religious rhetoric in their writing naturally, and they exploited that ability for reasons other than political expediency. As in the changes the signers of the Declaration of Independence made to Jefferson's initial draft, they felt that they could not convey their theological sense of the cosmic significance of the events in which they were participating unless they added to the phrase about "the laws of nature and of nature's God" an appeal "to the supreme judge of the world for the rectitude of our intentions." One can try to discount this kind of appeal as merely the hegemonic efforts of a dominant group to appropriate the theological language of its residual precursor, but the Founders' need for such discourse was anything but disingenuous or simply calculating: "Irrespective of belief, the frame of mind within which the Founders operated has a vital religious component, and that component is richly connotative. 'In God we trust' is more than just the motto of American republicanism; it points back in time to a central promise in the language of national creation."[5]

Nevertheless, there are important distinctions to be made between the spiritual legacy associated with the Protestant tradition of thought and feeling in America and that associated with the American Enlightenment, distinctions which, for purposes of discussion, can be formulated as follows. By "religion" I shall mean the predisposition to view all human problems not traceable to natural accidents as reducible to the corruptibility and depravity of human nature; to view the corruptibility and potential depravity of human nature as unamenable to satisfactory redress by any agencies such as reason, will, or feeling intrinsic to human nature itself; and to view access to any agencies of empowerment that are transcendent to human nature as possible only through faith rather than works, including the efforts of the human mind to secure through analysis, criticism, or imaginative projection relief from such problems. By the "Enlightenment" I shall mean, in contrast, the inclination to view all human problems amenable to any kind of redress, whether they derive from human nature or not, as dependent for such resolution as they can obtain on the human capacity to think about them critically and to critically validate the insights achieved by the intellect through appeal to human experience.[6]

These provisional definitions sometimes carry with them—though not necessarily always—certain other associations. Religion is often linked with belief in a sovereign God, dependence on a personal savior, the existence of original sin, the treachery of reason, the need for justification and absolution, the intercession of the sanctified, or the immortality of the soul. The Enlightenment is frequently related to convictions about historical progress, the beneficence of nature and its author, the reliability of ordinary human understanding, the salience of criticism, the existence of inalienable rights, the virtues of free inquiry, and the pursuit of happiness. But the key to the difference between Protestant Christianity and the Enlightenment, as I am defining them here, is the question whether relief of the human estate is dependent on powers that originate in, and derive their authority from, realms of experience beyond the boundaries of its own agencies and capacities or rather from realms of experience within, or at least accessible through, them.[7]

Previous Scholarly Consensus

The second difficulty that attends the problem of beginning an inquiry into the relations between religion and the Enlightenment in nineteenth- and twentieth-century American literature has to do with the state of much modern scholarship. The problem can be put simply. While elements of religion and the Enlightenment have both exerted a measurable—in fact, considerable—cultural pressure on the shape of literary life in the United States during the last two centuries, their comparative significance has not been assessed equally. Indeed, the presence of the Enlightenment, no less than an appreciation of the tension between Enlightenment and Protestant presences, has grown more and more invisible, or at least opaque, to recent generations of literary historians. This phenomenon is the more surprising just because traces of their dual presence beyond the confines of the eighteenth century are everywhere evident in subsequent American writing.

Evidence of those presences and the tension between them can readily be seen, for instance, in Poe's vacillation between experiments with the associationist psychology of David Hartley in nature poems like "Tamerlane," or his more radical commitment to reason in such "tales of ratiocination" as "The Murders in the Rue Morgue, "A Descent into the Maelstrom," and "The Gold Bug," and the residual religious gothicism of other tales like "The Fall of the House of Usher" or "The Cask of Amontillado" and poems such as "The Raven," "Ulalume," and "Annabel Lee." But marks of this tension between Enlightenment interests in reason, freedom, and individual fulfillment and Christian, really Protestant, commitments to faith, obedience, and self-renunciation are even more visible in a writer like Nathaniel Hawthorne. Often acknowledged as one of America's best historians of American Puritanism, Hawthorne was also a child of the eighteenth century who, for all of his anguished misgivings about the rights and responsibilities of the detached observer, was incapable of subordinating his quasi-scientific interest in the psychological complexities of human nature to any residual religious scruples about their moral impropriety or experiential belatedness. Employing ethical and religious allegory in his best work only to suspend and often deconstruct it, Hawthorne risked the "specular gaze," as it has come to be called, because in the last analysis he was as convinced as any of his Enlightenment forebears that the only way we can see at all is first by looking at the empirical facts of human behavior intently, remorselessly— even if, in a reflex action deferential to his own conscience, he quickly added that the act of looking out and looking at requires the ironic correction of an equally intense and unforgiving look within.

In a different and less tortured form, this tension is also present in the writings of Oliver Wendell Holmes, "the autocrat of the breakfast table." An early imitator of Lawrence Sterne and a devoted scientist as well as distinguished physician, Oliver Wendell Holmes could be adamant in his opposition to the harshness of Calvinist doctrines like predestination in *Elsie Venner,* and yet indulge in playful satire on the logic of Jonathan Edwards in "The Deacon's Masterpiece; or, The Wonderful 'One-Hoss Shay.'" But Holmes's more characteristic stance is expressed in poems like "The Chambered Nautilus" and "The Secret of Stars," where science and faith are shown to be perfectly compatible and religious and Enlightenment concerns can, like the lamb and lion of the book of Revelation, lie down together.

This more irenic position sometimes found a correspondent resonance in the work of several of Holmes's other contemporaries, such as Henry Wadsworth Longfellow and John Greenleaf Whittier. But it was not until after the War between the States that strong Enlightenment concerns, still colored by religious ideality but also chastened with a strong dose of Scottish Common Sense, found their way back into the center of literary culture and seemed to displace religion, or at least the religion of American Protestantism, altogether. The route back for the Enlightenment was mapped by a somewhat disparate group of writers that included the poet Edmund Clarence Stedman, novelist-editors like Thomas Bailey Aldrich and Charles Dudley Warner, and better-known figures such as William Dean Howells and even Henry James—men of letters who for all their diversity of talents and accomplishments helped create, in the second half of the nineteenth century, perhaps the closest thing the United States has ever achieved to "a coherent national literary culture."[8] Easily dismissed for its sometimes tepid spirituality, its latent didacticism, and its reliance, at least in writers like William Dean Howells, on common sense, the "Genteel tradition" not only gave new life to Enlightenment perspectives and postures but extended itself deep into the present century. Its descendants include the New Humanists of the 1920s, many of the Southern Agrarians and New Critics of the 1930s and 1940s, and even, it should be noted, several of the more prominent cultural critics of the 1940s and 1950s who, like Edmund Wilson and Lionel Trilling, were deeply suspicious of the Genteel tradition's overly optimistic assessment of human nature but no less indebted to some of the Enlightenment values it consistently emphasized of balance, variousness, complexity, possibility, modulation, and mind.

Other major writers in the later nineteenth century, however, worked to one side of the Genteel tradition and expended much of their energy puncturing its pretensions. In these authors—particularly Mark Twain and Henry Adams—the dialogue between what still existed of the Calvinist roots of American religion and what remained of the Enlightenment origins of American skepticism left an indelible imprint on later nineteenth-century American literary culture. Think only of *The Adventures of Huckleberry Finn,* which reduced the posturings of a debased and sentimentalized Calvinism to "soul butter and hogwash," or Mark Twain's most enigmatic novel, *Pudd'nhead Wilson,* in which he mounted a withering satire against the emergent religion of Jim Crowism through a defense of the empirical temper. All the more interesting, if not surprising, that in his last years the

Calvinism that Mark Twain had earlier spurned in its specious versions of racist sentimentality and spiritual soporifics tended to turn against him by darkening his view of humanity and generating the quiet but corrosive bitterness of "The War Prayer" and *The Mysterious Stranger.*

In Adams, it could be said, the Enlightenment confronted its old Calvinist antagonist more directly than it had for an entire century. But it was a confrontation that took place not in the realm of ideas so much as in the medium of temperament, when a child of New England resistance—"the atmosphere of education in which he lived was colonial, revolutionary, almost Cromwellian, as though he were steeped, from his greatest grandmother's birth, in the odor of political crime"—sought to measure the value of an eighteenth-century education for living in a nineteenth-century world.[9] *The Education of Henry Adams* is simultaneously one of the genuine masterworks of American literature and one of the few fully self-conscious assessments of the two moral, intellectual, and spiritual legacies that have shaped its past. In this, *The Education* not only sums up a century but seeks to rescue a divided past, or at least to assess what has been irretrievably lost to it.

Mention of Adams's central achievement in *The Education* returns us again to the puzzlement with which we began: Why has the Enlightenment disappeared so quickly and, seemingly, so irretrievably from our modern estimation of the religious meanings of nineteenth- and twentieth-century literary culture? Why has the Enlightenment been so often effaced in modern literary historiography, even when critics and scholars have continued to employ distinctions that reflect the difference between the American religious heritage and the American Enlightenment heritage, distinctions between piety and rationalism, or enthusiasm and skepticism, to structure their understanding of the past?[10]

The Erasure of the Enlightenment

Looming above all other reasons has to be the primacy we have given to the geographical region known as New England and to the experience of its seventeenth-century Protestant spokesmen in American literary history. Ever since the appearance in 1939 of the first volume of Perry Miller's *The New England Mind,* American literary historians have, with comparatively few, though notable, exceptions, maintained—often in the face of considerable counterevidence—that European colonization of America took most

fateful root around Massachusetts Bay, and that the most politically consequential as well as intellectually articulate colonists spoke, thought, and felt
almost exclusively in the language of a selective kind of Christian theology.
Moreover, by the time Miller had published the second volume of *The New
England Mind* in 1953 and complemented it in 1956 with the enormously
influential collection of essays that made his view of this "errand into the
wilderness" fully accessible to literary scholars, it had become possible to
see how this significant immigration of peoples and ideas across the Atlantic had also made its way not only spatially across the water but temporally
across the centuries.

Miller's case for the existence of Puritan continuities of experience capable of surviving the successive articulation of ideas for three centuries,
dated though it may now be, owed its credibility to the brilliant intellectual
and cultural links that he forged in various of his chapters between, say,
"the marrow of Puritan Divinity," or the federal theology of the seventeenth
century, and the eighteenth-century metaphysics of Jonathan Edwards, or
between Jonathan Edwards's latter-day Puritanism and the nineteenth-
century transcendentalism of Ralph Waldo Emerson, or between Emerson's
conversion of America into the trope of "Nature's nation" and modern mil-
lennialist expectations exacerbated by the threat of nuclear apocalypse in
the Cold War era.

Now it seems to matter little or at all that critics have shown many of
these associations to have been more rhetorical than historical, or that numerous later students of the period have found Miller's view of Puritanism,
indeed his interpretation of the whole legacy of early American spirituality,
to be highly intellectualistic and extremely selective.[11] Seventeenth-century
New England, and the theological precepts for which it became known,
have continued to hold priority of place and exert hegemonic authority for
too long. Listen to the way Kenneth Murdock, one of American Puritanism's first great modern students, and one of Miller's predecessors at Harvard University, dismisses the Enlightenment, even as he truncates it, in his
discussion of the "Puritan legacy" at the end of his important study of 1951
on *Literature and Theology in Colonial New England:*

> If . . . the phenomenon of religious experience is still real for some men; if
> there is a place for a faith transcending what unaided reason, logic, or science
> can supply; if there is still value in the prayer and worship which proceed
> from deep inward emotion, then scientific manuals, polite moral essays, and

popular novels will not suffice. There will be need for more intellectually incisive and more emotionally effective expression of contemporary religious
life; there will be need for some myth in which to symbolize and concretize
its values.[12]

With its grand themes of creation, damnation, election, and sanctifica-
tion, seventeenth-century American Protestantism clearly lent itself to the
provision of such a myth "to symbolize and concretize its values" in a way
that the Enlightenment's eighteenth-century preoccupation with rights,
reasons, and rectitude never could. Just as important, the central tenets of
early American religion were far more susceptible to demythologization
than those of the American Enlightenment in terms consonant with the
modernist-existentialist spirit of the immediate postwar age and even later.
To reduce Franklin's beliefs about a divine Providence whose rule guarantees the immortality of the soul, and whose service is to be found in "doing good" to others, to any set of precepts or prescriptions more elemental
than the terms in which they were expressed in Franklin's own prose was
to risk caricaturing them as wholly prudential and self-serving, or as what
Van Wyck Brooks and D. H. Lawrence called, respectively, "catchpenny realities" and moral machinery.[13] By contrast, Miller's identification of the
whole of seventeenth-century religion with what he called the "Augustinian
strain of piety" and his translation of the "Augustinian strain of piety" into
what he described as a subjective mood or frame of mind only succeeded in
rendering Puritan spirituality more rather than less intellectually attractive
in the postwar cultural climate. One could, of course, simply conclude that
Puritanism has been better served than the Enlightenment by its modern
interpreters, but this would be to gloss several other factors that have delim-
ited our historical ability to perceive the Enlightenment's aftereffects in the
last two centuries of literary expression.

One of these factors derives from the assessment literary and cultural historians have made of the different spiritual legacies that each of these traditions left to subsequent centuries. It is generally assumed, for example, that
American Protestantism, at least in its Calvinist form, has left as its chief
legacy in America something like an inherited penchant for self-criticism
that at its best is capable of correcting even its own excesses. This assessment
of the spiritual legacy of American Protestantism is often explained by reference to Herman Melville's famous review of Hawthorne's *Mosses from an
Old Manse,* where Melville attributes the force of Hawthorne's appeal to "a
blackness, ten times black" that shrouds, or at least casts into deep shadow,

the "Indian-summer sunlight" of Hawthorne's historical romances. Melville is not prepared to say whether Hawthorne has availed himself of this "mystic blackness" merely to secure his marvelous chiaroscuro effects or is really afflicted with "a touch of Puritanic gloom," but he is convinced that the power of this blackness in Hawthorne ultimately derives from its reference to an intuition that no deeply feeling, thoughtful person who attempts to "weigh this world" and "strike an uneven balance" can for long do without. This is an intuition of "something, somehow" like "that Calvinistic sense of Innate Depravity and Original Sin, from whose visitations, in some shape or other, no deeply thinking mind is always and wholly free."[14]

Melville's emphasis on the indefinite pronoun—"something, somehow"—is what makes all the difference in the way this statement has offered itself to later generations. Although it permits him to appropriate a sense of evil as a principle of moral and spiritual correction, it enables him at the same time to dissociate this sense from the necessity of any conscious assent to the theological doctrine in which it was first expressed. The cultural utility of the principle continues to engender respect for the tradition that generated it without requiring anyone to believe in the specific tenets of that tradition itself. Thus Melville and his cultural heirs can remain, and have remained, Puritans at heart while at the same time disavowing Puritanism as dogma.

By comparison, the cultural heirs of the Enlightenment have not been similarly favored. To embrace the Enlightenment in almost any form in the postwar period has been tantamount to affirming virtually all of the liberal republican ideals, from freedom, autonomy, individualism, and rationalism to the self-reliance, scientific mindset, secular predisposition, and free market capitalism in which they have been thought to issue. But to affirm as diverse, vague, and potentially conflicting a set of ideals as these has been to advocate something much like what America's editorial pundits, no less than historical scholars on both the extreme Right and the extreme Left, take to be America's official ideological version of itself. Thus where the Calvinist legacy has frequently been interpreted as the intellectual and spiritual source of whatever real cultural criticism has been produced in America, the Enlightenment legacy has as readily been dismissed as the moral and philosophical source of American cultural consensus and complacency.

Yet another factor contributing to the increasing opaqueness of the Enlightenment in twentieth-century literary scholarship is the fairly widespread conviction that its chief aesthetic assumptions exerted an influence on subsequent literary practice in the United States that was essentially negative. Their influence is held to have been essentially negative because it is still generally supposed that they derived from those Scottish Common Sense philosophers who restricted the creative arts, and particularly the writing of fiction, to the provision of moral exempla.[15] As the story goes, the effect of such strictures was to compel gifted young antebellum writers like Hawthorne and William Gilmore Simms to abandon the writing of novels altogether in favor of creating an alternative fictive form in reaction to the restraints of eighteenth-century Common Sense. This fictive form is known as the romance and came in time to be defined as a kind of counteraesthetic to the Enlightenment. This development would have made little difference, however, to any but a few historians of early nineteenth-century fiction if the romance had not in turn, following World War II and for many decades thereafter, come to be regarded as virtually the only authentic fictive form in America. Defining the romance in opposition to the more conventional form of the novel, this persuasion helped transform postwar nineteenth- and twentieth-century literary history into an outright repudiation of Enlightenment values.[16]

Discoveries vs. Inventions

But the greatest difficulty in knowing how to begin this narrative has to do with the problem of deciding where American writing itself begins. If the true sources of early American writing are now held to go back as far as the commencement of what we now call the early modern period and to include everything from European narratives of discovery to utopian fantasies about the creation or recovery of Paradise and Amerindian legends about the founding of the world, then it must be understood to extend far enough forward to encompass the emergence of the new nation-state in part wrested out of the tensions and conflicts associated with this earlier, presettlement legacy and to include some of the more consequential spiritual energies liberated by its early development. Where this literature was once thought to be the expression chiefly of men, we now realize that it was also shaped in significant ways by the different expressive talents of women. Where this literature was formerly considered the experiential record primarily of transplanted English citizens, we now know that Hispanic, French, African American, and Native American peoples played a not insubstantial role in its constitution and growth. And with an expanded sense of the various peoples who contributed to the complex formation of this literature has come as well a deepened understanding of the distinctive kinds of writing that the colonization of the United States produced. In other words, we now know that the "America" that was brought into existence by the practice of colonial writing was not "discovered," as the Mexican historian Edmundo O'Gorman has pointed out, so much as "invented," or "discovered" because it was "invented."[17]

This is not, of course, to claim that there was nothing to be found on the early morning of Friday, October 12, 1492, when Christopher Columbus made landfall on the island of what is now called San Salvador in the West Indies. It is only that Columbus was mistaken about what he had come upon that fateful morning and then compounded the problem by repeatedly resisting the corrections of experience. Looking for a sea passage to India and supposing that he had actually managed to reach Asia, he in fact never reached farther west on any of his three later voyages than the Paria Peninsula of Venezuela but failed to realize that this was part of a new land mass.

Columbus's mistake is largely to be attributed to the fact that he believed his discoveries were more the work of divine Providence than of navigational genius or any other element of good fortune. As he wrote to his patrons, King Ferdinand and Queen Isabella of Spain, in 1502, "Neither reason nor mathematics nor maps were any use to me: fully accomplished were the works of Isaiah." In Isaiah 11:10–12 it is prophesied that God will gather the dispersed faithful remnant of his people into a new redeemed community, and this sense of providential purpose was no doubt fed in part by the fact that Columbus arrived in Portugal after a miraculous escape from shipwreck that brought him ashore very close to the rock of Sacres, where Prince Henry the Navigator had established his famous academy of seamanship.

But the mental picture that Columbus had constructed in his head was derived not alone from his reading of the Bible or his own miraculous deliverance from death but also from his familiarity with the accounts of Marco Polo's overland journey to China and his prior knowledge of Ptolemaic geography. Ptolemy had postulated soon after the beginning of the Common Era that the earth was considerably smaller than we now know it to be and that the Asian landmass extended much farther into the ocean than it actually does. This mistaken theory nonetheless turned out to be admirably suited to Columbus's purposes, because it tended to confirm Marco Polo's speculations about the proximity of Japan's position relative to Portugal and was reinforced by certain additional claims made by scripture as well. The apocryphal book of Esdras (2:6) held that the world was six parts land and only one part water, and the book of Ezekiel (5:5) maintained that Jerusalem was at the center of the world. Such assertions not only persuaded Columbus that the sea voyage from Portugal to Asia was comparatively short

(2,700 miles, as opposed to the actual 12,000); they also assured him that in undertaking this expedition he was fulfilling the scriptural injunctions of the Bible and would consequently receive divine favor.

While these beliefs and fantasies allowed him to overcome all of the repeated rejections of his proposal to sail west in order to reach the east by means of a sea passage to the Indies—first by the king of Portugal, and then by Ferdinand and Isabella before they finally relented—they also put him in position to perpetuate another fiction by misnaming the native peoples he subsequently discovered. From this time forth the indigenous people of the Americas would pay the price of Columbus's failed search for the Indies by being viewed as primitives living in a state of nature and referred to as "Indians."

Columbus alone was scarcely responsible for the association of native peoples with such conditions, nor were descriptions of them to remain as idyllic in the reports of subsequent explorers and their chroniclers. Indeed, in his writings the Italian merchant and navigator Amerigo Vespucci, who claimed, as Columbus did not, to have actually discovered the landmass of a new world and to furnish that landmass, thanks to an obscure Dutch cartographer named Martin Waldseemüller, with his own name, painted a different and much less flattering picture of the native life he found on his supposedly four trans-Atlantic voyages. Whether Vespucci actually made the four voyages that he claimed, at least in one document, to have taken or only as few as two, his report of the discovery of a "mundus novus" in his *Quatro Americi Navigationis,* published in 1504, caught the attention of Waldseemüller just as the latter was preparing a new edition of Ptolemy. Deciding that the new continent should bear the name of its first discover, Waldseemüller saw no reason why it should not be named after Vespucci in the feminine form of his first name Amerigo, since both Europe and Asia had received their names from women. While Waldseemüller was soon to have second thoughts, and other interested parties like the Spanish and the Portuguese were to object to his decision for centuries, the new world delineated on Waldseemüller's planisphere, or world map, of 1507 (or, rather, only its southern half) was to be named forever more, and at the cost of no little misrepresentation, "America."

Both tales tell us something of what it means to say that America was invented rather than discovered. They suggest that from this moment forward that portion of the world that was known as "America" would be shaped as much by the energies of the imagination as by the substance of the actual; that it would be a world defined as much by the ambiguities of desire as by the structures of the empirical. The world, both north and south, named after Vespucci and not Columbus would henceforth be a world dominated and controlled by meanings as much as by facts, a world where fantasy, fabulation, and fiction would determine many of the contours and much of the substance of the so-called real.

Nothing demonstrates this more vividly than the way Europeans immediately took credit for what they referred to as America's "original" discovery. Whether Columbus reached the shores of this continent before Vespucci or Vespucci before Columbus, neither group of explorers, as even they could see for themselves, were America's first inhabitants. That title belonged instead to the ancestors of those singular and, as Columbus and Vespucci both reported, extraordinary human specimens that confronted them on the beaches of the Caribbean. Already in occupancy for millennia on lands that Columbus and Vespucci claimed to have "found" for the first time, these natives were descendants of nomadic peoples from Asia who first made their way across a land bridge in the Bering Strait nearly 22,000 years before the ocean voyages of Columbus and Vespucci. And whatever the motives of those first "American" discoverers, their descendants over time were to work their way down and settle almost the whole of the Northern and Southern Hemispheres, creating in the process some of the great civilizations of the ancient world: the Mayan in southern Mexico and Guatemala, the Incan in Peru, and the Aztec in Mexico. Indeed, so numerous had these disparate native descendants of America's first discoverers become by the time Columbus and Vespucci arrived at the end of the fifteenth century of the Common Era that there were then living in the two western hemispheres of the Americas, according to some estimates, anywhere between 60 and 100 million people speaking as many as 2,200 different languages.[18]

One can measure something of the sophistication and diversity of these various Native American peoples by the ruins of the many magnificent cities they left behind, when disease, famine, natural disaster, and the genocidal policies of many of the Europeans took their toll: cities such as Palenque, Tikal, Tula, Monte Albán, Uxmal, and Chichén Itzá. On entering the Aztec capital of Tenochtitlan with the invading army of Hernando Cortés, one of his sergeants, Bernal Díaz del Castillo—who eventually recorded the history of the Spanish conquest in his great *The Discovery and Conquest of Mexico* (1632)—likened the soldiers' amazement to the enchantments of a dream. Reflecting on the Aztec palaces, he could not help remarking the following:

How spacious and well built they were, of beautiful stone work and cedar wood, and the wood of other sweet scented trees, with great rooms and courts, wonderful to behold, covered with awnings of cotton cloth. . . . And all was cemented and very splendid with many kinds of stone (monuments) with pictures on them. . . . I say again that I stood looking at it and thought that never in the world would there be discovered other lands such as these, for at the time there was no Peru [or knowledge of the great cities of Cuzco and Machu Picchu], nor any thought of it. Of all these wonders that I then beheld, today all is overthrown and lost, nothing left standing.[19]

An even more dramatic indication of the achievements of Amerindian civilizations—in agriculture, economics, government, arts and crafts, and religion—is to be found in the way Europeans were in time to borrow so heavily from them. From Native American agriculture, the rest of the world's peoples acquired such staples as corn, potatoes, manioc, and sweet potatoes as well as peanuts, squash, peppers, tomatoes, pumpkins, pineapples, avocados, cacao, and various kinds of legumes, to say nothing of cotton, tobacco, and a host of medicinal herbs. From Native American crafts and technology, they obtained such useful items as hammocks, canoes, toboggans, snowshoes, kayaks, and parkas. From Native American politics, and particularly the Iroquois League, colonial leaders like Benjamin Franklin derived some of their best ideas for constitutional government. From Native American economies, early white settlers to the New World learned about the principles and practices of trade and barter, which often saved them from starvation. And not least, from Native American mythology and metaphysics, New World settlers heard, and sometimes learned, stories, poems, tales, and sayings that taught them, often for the very first time, about the ecological interdependence and unity of all natural, human, and heavenly life.

Yet for all the sophistication and heterogeneity of their societies and cultures—while some native Americans remained hunters and gatherers, others created written languages, became expert at engineering and astronomy, and even mastered the art of mathematical calculation—these infinitely various peoples were quickly, and often tragically, lumped together by the misnomer they received from Columbus when he mistook their homeland for Asia and thus called them "Indians" and assumed to be living in effect without history in a state of nature where, as reported by Vespucci, war was common and cannibalism an accepted practice. Such identifications were to prove as tenacious before the years of actual colonial settlement in the Americas as after it began and were fed by a thousand different motives, misunderstandings, misinterpretations, and misrepresentations.

Misinterpretations and Misrepresentations

Not least among the problems that affected relations between native peoples and Europeans was the different ways they made sense of themselves and their experience to themselves. Native peoples relied on myths and other metanarratives both to understand the meaning of their world and to define their place in it. Such forms pay less attention to the logics of cause and effect, or of premise and conclusion, than to those of possibility and probability that structure a given lifeworld hierarchically. To the mythic imagination, "there are more things in heaven and earth," as Shakespeare's Hamlet says to Horatio, "than are dreamt of in your philosophy." Hence it has been said that mythic structures function more like classificatory schemes than like historical or factual narratives, since their purpose is not simply to help define and organize the constituents of the thinkable but to arouse, channel, release, and sometimes contain the various sets of feelings associated with them.

But there is more to mythic practice than this. Because of the often schematic nature of the narratives by which they are composed, they are more easily employed not only for oral repetition and embellishment but for ritual expression and interaction, where the reiteration of the narrative they represent is used to sweep the auditor back into that sacred time—*in illo tempore*—of which the story is both record and template. Under such ritual circumstances, the listener may not only relocate him- or herself within the sacred sphere, as Mircea Eliade has written, but reactualize the power still potentially resident within that sphere and extend it forward over the more ephemeral world of the profane.[20]

This way of understanding and employing myth has often been assumed in modern times to be somehow foreign to the more rational dispositions of Europeans and their descendants and has thus been dismissed, as it typically was by America's earliest colonists, as primitive, infantile, degenerate, or even diabolical. To the first Western settlers in North America, and particularly the most determinedly religious among them, such communicative and communal practices undoubtedly appeared alien and unworldly despite the fact that they were themselves dependent on similar conceptual and notional structures. For among all the other cognitive and affective constructs that defined the expectations and ambitions of those first generations of pilgrims, it was not their explicit theological beliefs that proved indispensable to their spiritual errand but rather the larger mythic scaffolding they brought with them in which they could situate and restructure such beliefs. That is to say, the earliest European settlers to America were no less dependent on metanarrative structures for their understanding of themselves and the lifeworld they were seeking to create than, as it appeared to many of them, the primitive, alien, or subhuman people who confronted them on American shores. Those archetypal frameworks, which had antecedents in the very distant past, were essentially three in number and had most recently been reformulated in works of English literature in the years just preceding the first trans-Atlantic crossings.

The first of these archetypal structures derived from Greek and Roman mythology and centered on a pastoral people cut off from the corruptions and complications of the world around them who lived in an ideal state of peace and simplicity. Given more recent expression in Sir Philip Sidney's *Arcadia* as well as in Edmund Spenser's *Faerie Queene* and William Shakespeare's *The Tempest*, this myth, which was often linked with a lost golden age, gave credence to the belief, later encouraged by promoters of American expeditions like Captain John Smith, that America was the new land of milk and honey. The counter-narrative to this bucolic idyll had its origins in the Hebrew scriptures and the New Testament, and portrayed humankind as now fallen from divine grace and banished to a wilderness of woe and affliction. This was the anti-Arcadian myth which structured the experience of the Puritans and which stated, in literary texts like John Milton's *Paradise Lost* and John Bunyan's *Pilgrim's Progress,* that this exile could only be overcome through faith in the unmerited mercies of God as revealed in the sacrifice of his own son, Jesus Christ, to serve as atonement for human sin and iniquity. The third myth, which was eventually to provide a still different scaffolding for the hopes and convictions that followed European pilgrims to the New World, was drawn neither from the English pastoral, nor from English Protestantism, but rather from the English utopian tradition. In texts like Sir Thomas More's *Utopia* and Francis Bacon's *The New Atlantis,* as well as others drawn from the tradition of English country-house poems like Ben Jonson's poem "To Penshurst" and Andrew Marvell's "Upon Appleton House," a different spiritual possibility was entertained that nature and, by extension, humankind might be transformed by belief in the creation of a new Eden capable of being restored in the American wilderness.

Such metanarrative frameworks can rarely be understood for what they are by those who are subject to their power, because if they can be seen at all they are usually taken for truth. Yet this does not discount the irony of the fact that the European settlers to the New World inevitably took as the sign of their own superiority a kind of thinking that was no less dependent on mythical archetypes than the thinking they associated with native inferiority. Would that they could have been exposed to the balanced and humane perspective of the moralist and man of letters Michel de Montaigne, the French aristocrat who in his famous essay "On Cannibals" finds the reports about native inhabitants sent back by New World discoverers to be both deeply biased and radically unself-critical. Blinded by a sense of their spiritual superiority to their subjects, these European explorers and discovers were unable to provide a balanced view of native facts and comportment. Placing behavior held to epitomize the "primitive" against that assumed to represent "civility," Montaigne found that "civility" was exhibited precisely where Europeans expected to discover "barbarism," nobility exhibited in situations Europeans alleged to be savage, valor revealing itself in native behavior routinely reported by Europeans as cunning and deceitful.

What gives Montaigne's perceptions added authority is his unwillingness either to idealize or to sentimentalize native life. He is without illusions about its violence and cruelty. Otherwise, why would he be writing about cannibals and cannibalism? But for him it is the lens that this practice affords, if one uses it to look back at oneself, or at least at one's own cultural practices, that ultimately matters. Montesquieu sees the "barbarous horror" of cannibalism in the New World, but wants to use its reflective power to illumine the greater barbarism within those who would use its spectacle to cover their own inhumanity:

> I conceive there is more barbarity in eating a man alive, than when he is dead; in tearing a body limb from limb by racks and torments, that is yet in perfect sense; in roasting it by degrees, in causing it to be bitten and worried by dogs and swine (as we have not only read, but lately seen, not amongst inveterate and mortal enemies, but among neighbours and fellow-citizens, and, which is worse, under the colour of piety and religion), than to roast and eat him after he is dead.[21]

Yet one would be hard-pressed to find evidence of any such insistently balanced, morally self-reflexive, sentiments about social "others" exhibited in early American writing, at least by whites, much before the publication of the Quaker John Woolman's essay of 1754, "Some Considerations on the Keeping of Negroes," or the publication in 1784 of Benjamin Franklin's "Remarks Concerning the Savages of North America." On the other hand, the bulk of testimony furnished by Native American oratory, so much of which was concerned with Amerindian-white relations, tells a quite different story.

Given the violent history of those relations, what makes the oral record of it provided by Native Americans so revealing is that so much of it is not only dignified and restrained but also candid as well as magnanimous. Even when Indian orators are protesting the enormous injustices, deceptions, betrayals, and outrages committed against their people and their land, the tone is rarely shrill, accusatory, or self-pitying. The case they make on behalf of their people and against the injustices they have suffered at the hands of whites is consistently based on universal grounds of fairness and justice, and their appeal is always to the nobler side of their antagonists. It has sometimes been countered that the eloquence and restraint of Indian oratory derives from the fact that it was almost always transcribed by sympathetic whites who wanted to put the Indian cause in its most attractive light. But this is belied by the record itself, a record that leaves little doubt as to the large-mindedness and evenhandedness of so many of its practitioners.

Native American Presentiments and Displacements

That record begins, perhaps, with the words of Chief Powhatan, the father of Pocahontas, who presided over a confederacy of Algonquin tribes that occupied part of the territory of Virginia and Maryland at the time of the first English settlement at Jamestown in 1607. As reported by Captain John Smith, Chief Powhatan asked a group of whites in 1609, "Why will you take by force what you may obtain by love? Why will you destroy us who supply you with food? What can you get by war? . . . We are unarmed, and willing to give you what you ask, if you come in a friendly manner."[22] All too often that "manner" was anything but friendly, and the result was war.

One of the more famous of such exchanges, because of the praise the author of its resolution won from Thomas Jefferson, occurred in the upper Ohio River valley in 1774, when the Mingos decided to end their war of revenge against whites because of white atrocities committed against their people. The occasion was a council called by the colonial governor to end the hostilities at which Chief Logan was invited to speak. Chief Logan reminded his listeners that he had been a friend to his white brothers—"I appeal to any white man to say, if ever he entered Logan's cabin hungry, and he gave him not meat; if ever he came cold and naked, and he clothed him not"—until a white officer without provocation murdered all of Logan's family and relatives, including women and children. This cold-blooded act of violence called for retaliation, but once Logan's thirst for vengeance had been "fully glutted," he was once again prepared to embrace peace.[23] Of this speech Jefferson exclaimed in his *Notes on the State of Virginia*: "I may challenge the whole orations of Demosthenes and Cicero, and of any more eminent orator, if Europe has furnished more eminent, to produce a single passage, superior to the speech of Logan."[24]

There were reasons, however, why peace was often so far out of reach. Chief Pachgantschilias of the Delawares put the Native American case eloquently and succinctly when speaking to a group of Christianized natives in Pennsylvania in 1787:

> I admit that there are good white men, but they bear no proportion to the bad; the bad must be the strongest, for they rule. They do what they please. They enslave those who are not of their color, although created by the same Great Spirit who created them. They would make slaves of us if they could; but as they cannot do it, they kill us. There is no faith to be placed in their words. They are not like Indians, who are only enemies while at war, and are friends in peace. They will say to an Indian, "My friend; my brother!" They will take him by the hand, and, at the same moment, destroy him.[25]

Such duplicity was well known to Chief Tecumseh of the Shawnees, who was outraged by the sale of Indian lands in 1810 because whites purposely manipulated their Indian partners by striking a deal unfairly when the latter were inebriated. But Chief Tecumseh does not restrict the offense involved to treachery or deceit but sees it as an outrage against creation itself:

> The only way to stop this evil is for the red men to unite in claiming a common and equal right in the land, as it was at first, and should be now—for it was never divided, but belongs to all. No tribe has the right to sell, even to each other, much less to strangers. . . . *Sell a country! Why not sell the air, the great sea, as well as the earth?* Did not the Great Spirit make them all for the use of his children?[26]

Chief Tecumseh's question has echoed down through the years but was given a kind of definitive answer by Chief Seattle of the Dwamish who presided over all the tribes inhabiting Washington's Puget Sound. In a speech conceding that resistance to the Port Elliott Treaty that signed over the Washington territory to whites was futile, Chief Seattle suggested how his people, now facing extinction, might survive in, and as, the spiritual legacy of the American wilderness itself, their homeland:

> Every part of this soil is sacred in the estimation of my people. Every hillside, every valley, every plain and grove, has been hallowed by some sad or happy event in days long vanished. The very dust upon which you now stand re-

sponds more lovingly to their footsteps than to yours because it is rich with the blood of our ancestors and our bare feet are conscious of the sympathetic touch. Even the little children who lived here and rejoiced here for a brief season will love these somber solitudes and at eventide they greet shadowy returning spirits. And when the last Red Man shall have perished, and the memory of my tribe shall have become a myth among the white Men, these shores will swarm with the invisible dead of my tribe, and when your children's children think themselves alone in the field, the store, the shop, upon the highway, or in the silence of the pathless woods, they will not be alone. At night when the streets of your cities and villages are silent and you think them deserted, they will throng with the returning hosts that once filled and still love this beautiful land. The White Man will never be alone.

Let him be just and deal kindly with my people, for the dead are not powerless. Dead, did I say? There is not death, only a change of worlds.[27]

But Chief Seattle's prayer that the White Man be kindly and just was not fulfilled, except by a few, and thus the story of official United States abuse and disregard of the rights of its Native American populations, which continues down to the present day, needs to be balanced by the tragic history of the Nez Perce tribe, a history that didn't end until the early years of the twentieth century.

The Nez Perce people were first encountered by whites when in 1805 they provided shelter, supplies, and comfort to the Lewis and Clark expedition after its harrowing crossing of the Rocky Mountains. For fifty years thereafter, the tribe remained in the Wallowa Valley of the Oregon Territory and prided itself on its amicable relations with whites. As the progress of western settlement put increasing pressure on the Nez Perce to relinquish their lands and retire to a reservation, some complied, but others, led by Chief Joseph, refused. Chief Joseph's son by the same name appealed to President Ulysses S. Grant for protection and for a time received it. But by 1877 that peace had been revoked, and a military force was dispatched to remove the Nez Perce to a reservation. Chief Joseph was then compelled to submit, but the conditions for removal proved so difficult to meet that a small group of angry and desperate braves killed some whites, and the war between the United States and the Nez Perce then began in earnest.

Chief Joseph attempted to escape to Canada with the remainder of his tribe, but with four hundred women, children, and elderly people, together with two hundred and fifty warriors to transport, this proved impossible. Forced to surrender, the United States government then immediately betrayed the terms of the agreement by shipping the tribe off to Fort Leavenworth in Kansas rather than back to its reservation in Idaho. Many had already died in flight, and now many more would die in captivity.

Chief Joseph himself was finally permitted to travel from Fort Leavenworth to Washington, D.C., to plead the cause of his people, and while there he even managed to meet various government officials and publish an account of his people's sufferings in the prestigious *American Historical Review*. But all of these efforts proved unavailing. Chief Joseph was returned to Kansas, and only after further prolonged suffering were his people finally allowed to return to their reservation. But Chief Joseph himself, along with one hundred of his braves deemed too dangerous to accompany the tribe back to Idaho, were sent to another reservation hundreds of miles distant where, in 1904, separated forever from most of his people, Chief Joseph died of what the post physician diagnosed as a broken heart.

Native Americans were not, of course, the only people to have preceded Columbus and Vespucci to the New World. Earliest evidence of European discovery dates back to the beginning of the eleventh century, when Vikings landed on the shores of Newfoundland and possibly attempted to establish settlements there, though there is some reason to believe that still earlier Chinese expeditions may have reached the coast of California. Archaeological evidence also suggests that African explorers may have arrived in the Americas as early as the beginning of the fourteenth century, and we know for certain that English explorers sailed as far as North America at least a decade or more before Columbus's first voyage.

Nonetheless, it was eventually the Spanish, the sponsors of Columbus, who led the parade of European explorers to the Americas, followed closely by the French. Inspired not just by the excitement of discovery but also by dreams of conquest and wealth, Spanish explorers like Hernando Cortés, Francisco Pizarro, and Francisco Vásquez de Coronado penetrated deep into Mexico, South America, and the southwestern territory of the United States in the early sixteenth century, often destroying or subduing and enslaving native populations as they went. Their expeditions into Central and South America were paralleled by French expeditions mounted into North America, where explorers like Jacques Cartier, Samuel de Champlain, and Robert de La Salle opened up vast areas of Canada and the Mississippi valley to settlement. By such standards as these, the English were comparative latecomers to the Americas, and when they finally decided at the beginning of the seventeenth century to migrate in numbers, they came for a somewhat different purpose. Originally inspired, like the Spanish and the French, by imperial dreams of wealth, conquest, and religious conversion, they soon readjusted their ambitions in order to complement colonization with community building.

The cost of these multiple "discoveries of America" to the indigenous people who were so quickly displaced by them and so often threatened with destruction was unimaginably high. According to some calculations, somewhere close to 90 percent of the tens of millions of inhabitants of the Northern and Southern Hemispheres died before the beginning of the seventeenth century, either because of the genocidal policies of the Spanish conquistadors or because of the diseases that the Europeans brought with them. During the seventeenth century, the indigenous population of the Virginia colony declined from over 100,000 people to just 1,500 by 1697. In New England during the same period, there was a comparable decline of 95 percent of the native population, and similar figures can be found almost everywhere.

The full impact of this holocaust to native peoples and cultures only years after the conquest of the Americas had begun is registered in the great Mayan codex of prophecies, chronicles, and mystical speculations known as *The Book of Chilam Balam of Chumayel*. This extraordinary poem refers to the time preceding the arrival of the Spanish as the time before "the beginning of the sickness":

> There was no sin;
> in the holy faith their lives were passed.
> There was then no sickness;
> they had then no aching bones;
> they had then no high fever;
> they had then no smallpox;
> they had then no burning chest;
> they had then no abdominal pains;
> they had then no consumption;
> they had then no headache.
> At that time the course of humanity was orderly.

But when the Spanish arrived "from the east," then everything changed:

> Then Christianity also began. The fulfillment of its prophecy is
>   ascribed to the east . . .
> Then with the true God, the true *Dios*,
> came the beginning of our misery.
> It was the beginning of tribute,
> the beginning of church dues,

the beginning of strife by trampling on people,
the beginning of robbery with violence,
the beginning of forced debts,
the beginning of debts enforced by false testimony,
the beginning of individual strife,
a beginning of vexation.[28]

Early Modern Prefigurations and Premonitions

But what drove European dreams of conquest and colonization? Was it merely avarice, greed, trade, savagery, slavery, conversion? The literary record tells a more complex story that begins, if any accurate beginning there is, with *The Saga of Erik the Red* around the year 1000. Erik the Red was the father of Leif Erikson, who was presumably the first European to discover America. Erik himself is celebrated in legend as the founder in 985 of the earliest Scandinavian settlement in Greenland, but the saga suggests a number of motifs which were echoed in much of the literature of discovery that followed and which would eventually swell into a chorus of dominant themes in subsequent American writing: the sense of destiny attached to exploration and colonization; the high purpose of exploration and settlement associated with the religious errand of American Christianity; the imagination of the New World as a virgin paradise; the correlation of New World discovery with acts of deliverance and charity; and the underlying conviction that success in this missionary adventure was assured both by the beneficence of a favoring Providence and by the resourcefulness and courage of human beings.

Such dreams were in turn fed by a still larger body of writing at once utopian, promotional, and descriptive, such as Sir Thomas More's *Utopia,* published in 1551, which depicts an imaginary society governed entirely by reason. Inspired by descriptions of the New World provided by various sources including Amerigo Vespucci, which More combined with the social and political views of classical writers like Plato, Tacitus, and Pliny, More delineates a mode of life that was intended to present a stark contrast to the presiding conditions of English society. More identifies the source of all moral evil as egotism and suggests that the only alternative to a society governed by selfishness is a communist one in which all goods are shared and pleasure is never pursued at the expense of others.

More partially relied for his information about the New World on Peter Martyr, an Italian cleric who took up residence in Spain and made the acquaintance of many of the great New World explorers—Christopher Columbus, Vasco da Gama, Hernando Cortez, and Ferdinand Magellan. Martyr was deeply moved by their tales of discovery and decided to combine their information with official documents in order to compile a systematic account of what they had found. Martyr's letters were first published as *De Orbe Novo* in 1516 but came to be called, when they were expanded and translated by Richard Eden in 1555, *The Decades of the New World or West India*.

One of the many marvels of Martyr's book is its meditation on the color of the New World's native inhabitants. Arguing that diversity of color in human beings is a sign of divine omnipotence and wisdom, Martyr broke with the theological view that whiteness of skin represents some sort of divine preference. Martyr's belief that variety of color among New World peoples was—or should be—a source of religious wonder and gratitude was as novel as the assumption on which it was premised: that racial diversity is a blessing rather than a curse.

Eden's translation of *The Decades* also became for other reasons an important textual event in the history of New World discovery. Initially making available for English readers a coherent account of the voyages of Columbus and others, it was augmented in 1589 by Richard Hakluyt, an English clergyman, who compiled a more comprehensive record of all the English voyages of discovery known at the time. Published in 1589 as *Principal Navigations Voyages and Discoveries of the English Nation* (later expanded into three volumes in 1598–1600), Hakluyt's *Voyages* was in turn further expanded by Samuel Purchas from 1575 to 1626 into several books, including *Hakluyt's Posthumous* or *Purchas His Pilgrims* in 1625, all of these accounts furnishing material for still later chroniclers.

One of the most famous accounts of discovery included in Hakluyt's *Voyages* was Sir Walter Raleigh's record of an expedition he organized and led in 1595 to the Orinoco River in South America, an expedition that became the subject of his *The Discovery of Guiana* in 1595. In the history of American colonization, Raleigh is no doubt better known for the expedition he organized to America in 1584 to establish a colony on Roanoke Island off the coast of what is now North Carolina. This ill-fated settlement soon had to be abandoned, leaving its remaining settlers to be destroyed by the island's indigenous population, but not before Raleigh had conferred upon this country, in honor of his queen, the name "Virginia." Poet, courtier, adventurer, explorer, soldier, and statesman during the reign of Elizabeth I, Raleigh fell from favor when James I acceded to the throne after her death and was eventually tried for treason and beheaded. Neither his unjust condemnation, however, nor the memory of his failed exploits did much to diminish his reputation, which soon transformed him into a popular hero, even a figure of legend, and *The Discovery of Guiana* did nothing to lessen it.

While this book had largely failed to attract the financial support Raleigh hoped to secure for yet another expedition to America, it nevertheless helped to implant in the early modern imagination of his countrymen an image of the relationship between New World exploration and vast economic gain. Indeed, no work produced during the sixteenth century fused so powerfully the combination of glory and gold that dominated the English view of the Americas. If Raleigh cannot be said exactly to have founded the literature of the "American dream," he was nonetheless among the very first in a long line of writers that runs from Thomas Morton, in *New English Canaan,* to F. Scott Fitzgerald, in *The Great Gatsby,* to Thomas Pynchon, in *The Crying of Lot 49,* to Tom Wolfe, in *The Bonfire of the Vanities* who have associated the lust for material wealth with the symbolism of sexual fulfillment. He was also among the first to suggest that America's riches were particularly vulnerable to assault and exploitation precisely because they could be described in the imagery of a woman. Raleigh depicted the American continent as a virgin whose innocence still remains intact but whose virtue is ready to be violated by whichever nation first lays claims to her splendors. Little wonder, then, that this book helped inspire the conquistadores and set in motion the systematic plunder not only of the New World but also of its indigenous populations.

No one was more sensitive to the danger of the illusions aroused by these expeditions than William Shakespeare, who alluded to them in his "American fable" known as *The Tempest.* Sharing with many of his contemporaries a utopian perception of America as a site of Arcadian enchantment and possible spiritual regeneration, he also possessed a darker vision of this unknown, primitive, and vulnerable land. Although *The Tempest* depicts the American wilderness as a pastoral landscape or bucolic garden with Edenic properties, it also affords glimpses of another America that seems an anti-image of this first, a "hideous wilderness" and land of subjugation whose exploited native inhabitants, like its later enslaved subjects, must survive in a land of Prosperos, who can say of Caliban "this thing of darkness I acknowledge mine" while refusing accept that Caliban therefore belongs to the kind of being Prospero is.[29]

One of the earlier narratives of discovery that both confirmed but also complicated these images was provided by the Spanish author of *The Narra-*

tive of Álvar Núñez Cabeza de Vaca, which appeared in 1542. Cabeza de Vaca was a member of a colonizing expedition led by Pánfilo de Narváez to the west coast of Florida in 1528. Due to the hostility of the natives and the hazards of the Florida wilderness, the expedition proved disastrous. Forced to flee to Mexico, the expedition was shipwrecked off the coast of Texas near Galveston Island, and the survivors, now reduced from a company of three hundred to a group of only four individuals, were condemned to wander the Gulf Coast for eight years before finally making their way to Mexico City in 1536. Cabeza was frequently taken prisoner by various Indian tribes during this period, and his book constitutes, among other things, the first captivity narrative produced in the United States.

Like most captivity narratives, Cabeza's not only contains a wealth of information about natural as well as native conditions but also reflects an ambivalent attitude toward his various captors, ranging from fear of their strangeness, violence, and severity to respect for their fortitude and resourcefulness. Unlike many captivity narratives, however, Cabeza's refuses to diabolicize the natives even when, as a Christian, he was inclined to feel spiritually superior to them. A man of unusual candor as well as courage, he was most interested in understanding the indigenous people and in passing that understanding on to others.

Such advance heralds and recorders of New World discovery were extremely effective in creating a kind of American mythography of expectation and premonition. Michael Drayton, an otherwise minor English poet much taken with England's former literary glories, not only furnished a telling phrase for America's description, at least in the European imagination, as "Earth's onely paradise" in his 1607 poem "To the Virginian Voyage" but described its colonization as an opportunity to revive England's diminished sense of national destiny and pride. The fresh challenges presented by the New World, he believed, might serve to create a new generation of English heroes celebrated by American poets. On the other hand, in "The Church Militant" George Herbert, one of the great English poets of his time, portrayed religion fleeing the corruptions of the Old World to the unsullied purity of the New while simultaneously acknowledging that sin and darkness would inevitably follow the church into the West and corrupt it there. Yet he could find a measure of consolation in the realization that as the church moved west into the American wilderness, it also symbolically moved "east," where final redemption is promised.

Francis Bacon, philosopher, scientist, metaphysician, man of letters, and statesman, also identified America with the vanguard of the world, but he imagined that America would move it neither forward nor backward but in another direction altogether. Virtually no one living in his time understood as well as Bacon did that the Middle Ages had come to an end and that a new era of world history had been inaugurated. It was going to be a world in which the divinity that shapes our ends would no longer be transcendental but rather immanental. The supernatural would give way to the natural on the grounds that human beings can only understand what they have observed and can only observe with the assistance of the order and methods afforded them by Nature. This decidedly empirical outlook encouraged Bacon to construct a utopian society of his own in *The New Atlantis,* published in 1627, where the scientific spirit has displaced all others, the college of science, known as Salomon's House, has become its chief institution, and inquiry into the cause and motions of things for the sake of widening the boundaries of human knowledge and its empire is its chief work.

If it is difficult to imagine a more radical alternative to the world of the medieval Christian order that was then only beginning to undergo radical transformation, it is not at all difficult to detect the resemblance between Bacon's fantasies and the scientific utopianism of the eighteenth century. Either way, his imaginary prefigurations of the symbolic meaning of America, like those of so many others before him, would help contribute to the mental and emotional expectations that future settlers would carry with them on their transatlantic migration. And even where their own thinking was obliged to rely on more conventional religious and philosophical terminologies to express itself, much of their reflection and writing, even after the age of discovery had ended, would bear traces of these sometimes very un-Christian, un-Calvinist, un-Puritan imaginary constructs. People think and feel in figurative forms as much as they do in creedal or canonical ones even when, as we shall see throughout this book, they believe just the opposite. Such symbolic material not only furnishes much of the flavoring and texture of thought but also composes what might be called its ground base, the source of its timbre, gravity, and resonance.

We shall see in the next chapter how the mythological scaffolding of the Puritan project in the New World, and not just its theological architecture, was first built and then eventually began to splinter and subsequently deteriorate as problems of dissent began to reveal that its foundations no longer held in the subsoil of social and personal experience they were meant to inform and stabilize.

TWO

Puritan Ascendance and Decline

The Grammar of Religious Motives for Settlement

The earliest English experiments at settlement in the New World were fairly disastrous. The initial attempt made in 1584 on Roanoke Island off the coast of North Carolina and, as noted earlier, organized by Sir Walter Raleigh, was completely overrun and destroyed by the native population. When a relief operation reached the settlement in 1590, it found the colony in ruins and no trace of survivors. A second attempt was made roughly twenty years later at Jamestown, Virginia, in 1607, and this expedition was scarcely likely to be any more successful because in the words of its leader, the irrepressible Captain John Smith, the colony was composed of "poor gentlemen, tradesmen, serving-men, libertines, and such like ten times more fit to spoil a commonwealth than . . . to begin one." Smith helped rally his comrades against the threat of disease, weather, Indian attack, and near starvation by adopting the policy that "he who does not work shall not eat," but it was not the belated resilience of the colonists that finally helped the colony survive so much as the development of friendly relations with the neighboring natives. Members of the Algonkian confederation led by Chief Powhatan, the father of Pocahontas, they taught the colonists how to hunt and fish as well as how to grow corn and cultivate tobacco, thereby initiating a pattern of interracial contacts that would be repeated as long as relations between native peoples and European settlers remained amicable. This was the pattern where native American assistance to white settlers was secured and supported by the opportunity for interracial trade.

Through the English publication of his *Map of Virginia with a Description of the Country* in 1612 and his subsequent *Description of New England* in 1616, Captain John Smith was also instrumental, through his excited descriptions of its topography and landscape, in precipitating the next wave of English emigration to North America. But this third group of colonists also narrowly averted disaster when they missed their intended landfall in

Virginia and wound up on the barren coast of Massachusetts at Plymouth Rock, where they would never have survived their first winter without the support provided by neighboring tribes. Unlike the settlers drawn to James-town, these later colonists, known as the Pilgrims, and a subsequent group that followed them ten years later and settled thirty miles north on Massa-chusetts Bay, were quite different from the motley group of adventurers and others first drawn to Jamestown. The members of the original Jamestown expedition, however physically unprepared they were for the hardships they were to encounter, and however emotionally indisposed to meet the chal-lenges they were to face, were motivated chiefly by the desire for personal gain and advancement. By contrast, the members of the 1620 *Mayflower* migration to Plymouth Rock, and the later and much larger company of immigrants that settled in Massachusetts Bay in 1630, were drawn by mo-tives of a very different order. What the leaders of the Plymouth colony were seeking, like their neighbors surrounding Massachusetts Bay, was to satisfy not the desires of the flesh but the needs of the spirit. Their motives, in other words, were primarily religious and not secular. Their ultimate aim, which they sought without complete success to instill in all the members of their communities, was little less than the renewal of Western Christendom itself, and to this end they saw themselves as religious pilgrims journeying to what they hoped would be the Promised Land spoken of in the Hebrew scriptures and known to Christians from the Old Testament.

This is not to suggest that all or even most of the members of these early migrations to North America in the 1620s and 1630s shared the motives of their leaders. Since no more than approximately 30 percent of the company of the *Mayflower* were confessing Christians, it is clear that other factors fueled this third wave of English immigration as well. Chief among them were changes in the composition of English society itself, where a doubling of the population between 1530 and 1680 placed severe pressures on an al-ready shaky economy, and tensions between the lower and middling classes were increasing. Add to this the political turbulence caused by the afteref-fects of the English Reformation, and the imaginative vistas opened up by New World exploration, and one can begin to appreciate the complexity of factors that began to influence decisions to emigrate.

The literate, or at least socially advantaged, English of this era were in some sense citizens of two very different cultural worlds. One was the world of the Renaissance, which was associated with a revival of interest in the clas-sical ages of Greece and Rome, the dissemination of learning made possible by the invention of movable type, the geographical discovery of new lands and peoples, scientific advances in everything from mechanics to astronomy, commercial development that brought new classes into the economy, and, not least, the creation of new styles of dress, architecture, and painting that began to shift emphasis from preparation for fulfillment in the next life to the perfectibility of this life. That was a world capable of awakening appetites not easy to satisfy, of arousing curiosities not readily exhausted. This other world was defined by the Reformation, a world formally brought into being in 1517 when a German monk named Martin Luther nailed ninety-five theses to the door of a church in Wittenberg. Luther was seeking mainly to protest the sale of what were called indulgences by the Roman Catholic Church. Indulgences were originally designed as remissions of the temporal punishment for sins that the faithful could, under certain circumstances, petition to obtain from the church. Such indulgences were permissible to grant, so the church reasoned theologically, because the guilt for such sins had already been forgiven by Christ's sacrifice on the cross, and his crucifixion had thus created a spiritual Treasury of Merit on which the church could technically draw to provide special dispensations for deserving (and usually wealthy) communicants.

While some Roman Catholics justify the penitential use of indulgences to this day, it represented in medieval Christendom two serious problems. The first problem was implicitly the replacement of the notion of salvation by faith with the notion of salvation by works. The second problem, still more inflammatory, was the spectacle it created of priestly avarice that the sale of indulgences created in a time of smoldering conflict between church authorities and growing secular powers. Luther's protest in Wittenberg lit the match to a cascading chain of events that would quickly rend the entire body of Western Christendom into two separate and distinct parts, one still Roman Catholic, the other Protestant, and eventually force England, through what became known as the Anglican Compromise, to try to find a middle way between them.

The Protestant Reformation and Its Puritan Branches

As Roman Catholic resistance to Luther's original protest for reform solidified and turned militant, his protest itself expanded into a series of proposals for the complete renovation of Christian doctrine. These proposals, which would soon come to define much of the basic theological profile of Protestantism itself, were built around Luther's conviction that justification before God is never possible through the performance of good works but only through the act of faith in Jesus Christ as one's savior; that this faith, which is a function solely of divine grace rather than of human effort, cannot be mediated either by the church through its distribution of the sacraments or by tradition through its transmission of correct doctrine; that the sole authority for the spiritual deliverance that this faith brings to the practitioner is not the pope speaking for the Church Visible but Holy Scripture, or what Luther called the Word itself, representing the Church Invisible; that this faith turns all believers into de facto priests to themselves whether they have been episcopally consecrated or not; and that, as a result, the church is not a body of worshipers held together by apostolic authority but a communion of believers united in the belief that Christ is the Redeemer.

The Swiss theologian John Calvin was soon to systematize these beliefs and lend them further theological warrant in his two-volume *Institutes of the Christian Religion,* published in 1536, which reinforced the Reformation assertion of God's sovereignty, unknowability, and unpredictability through articulation of the related doctrines of Providence and Predestination. By the doctrine of Providence, Calvin meant to protect and strengthen the view that the whole of history is in God's control and that therefore nothing happens in the world that does not, in some mysterious but decisive way, express His will. By the doctrine of Predestination, Calvin intended to carry the doctrine of Providence to its logical conclusion by maintaining that if all of life is obedient to God's will, then everything that happens in life, including the separation of the elect from the unelect—or who is to be saved and who is to be damned—must be known in advance by God himself.

Such theological refinements were to have momentous consequences when Protestantism crossed the Atlantic to take its place in what the formidably orthodox Puritan preacher and writer Cotton Mather was to call "the American Strand," but they made almost no ripple at all when Protestantism merely traversed the English Channel. In England Protestantism itself became a major issue only when it provided King Henry VIII with an instrument to defy the pope in Rome so that he could proceed with plans to divorce his wife, Catherine of Aragon, because she was unable to provide him with a male heir, and marry Ann Boleyn. Thus the Protestantism established in England by Henry VIII bore only a faint resemblance to the Protestantism conceived by Luther or installed in Geneva by Calvin. Though the Church of England followed the Reformed tradition in severing all ties with Rome, suppressing all monasteries, abolishing prayers for the dead, replacing altars with tables, and rewriting the liturgy in English, it simply replaced the pope as its supreme head with the English monarch, reaffirmed the doctrine of apostolic succession, maintained the episcopal hierarchy of bishops, priests, deacons, and laity, retained the sacraments of baptism and holy communion, continued the practice of vesting the clergy, and otherwise insisted on doctrinal orthodoxy.

The retention of these remnants of Romanism, and the abuses of episcopal power to which they led, were soon to generate strong religious opposition. This opposition, which until the outbreak of the English Civil War in 1642 was forced to suppress itself in the face of increasing persecution, was centered on the attempt to purify the English national church of its continuing medieval corruptions. These corruptions involved, at the very least, the king's authority over the church, the hierarchy of the episcopate guaranteed by apostolic succession, the Book of Common Prayer, much church ritual, and even the celebration of Christmas. What the opposition or "Puritans," as they came to be called, wanted was a restoration of the kind of ecclesiastical and church order that was laid down in clear and decisive terms, so they insisted, in the New Testament. To the great majority of English Puritans, this meant a replacement of the Church of England with a new national church organized along different lines. Following the model of John Calvin's system in Geneva, which had also been adopted with modifications by the Church of Scotland, the majority of Puritans wanted to substitute for the episcopal organization of church order what they referred to as a Presbyterian form, where a group of ministers and elders of local churches constituted a presbytery, as it was termed, that was responsible to larger groups called synods, which then derived their authority from a national assembly.

Those Puritan settlers who came to the New World were of a still different persuasion. Insisting that each local church should be regarded as special and unique and composed of people calling themselves "visible saints" who had united through their confession of their faith in formally entering into a new covenant with God, they proposed an alternative form of church governance known as Congregationalism. In this form of church organization, there were to be no compelling agencies above the individual congregation and no class of acceptable believers besides them. Each congregation was to be self-governing—able to choose its own pastors, administer its own rites, and accept or reject it own members—and all were to enjoy the state's protection in discouraging competing heresies and keeping those who were "unchurched" in their place.

Lest it be concluded from this description that Congregationalism implied a more democratic form of church government than Presbyterian-ism, it should be remembered that the Puritans of New England, like those of Old England, possessed little sympathy for what we would now think of as representative governance. If their churches insisted on the right to select their own ministers, parishioners themselves never confused the freedom to elect their leaders with the duties those leaders were elected to perform. Church members might be free to select those by whom they were governed, but they were not free to alter the terms under which they were governed.

Among Congregationalists, there was a further doctrinal development that influenced the pattern of American colonization in the early seventeenth century. This was the dispute between those Puritans whose desire for congregational autonomy carried them to the point of wanting to separate themselves from the national church itself and those whose zeal clearly did not. The former group merely assumed that they were carrying to its inevitable conclusion the notion of a covenanted church organized congregationally and were immediately branded as "Separatists." Because the desire for separation from the national church struck the English Crown as seditious, some Separatists paid for this belief with their lives, and almost all Separatists in England suffered some form of persecution. One Separatist group in particular was so badly hounded by the ecclesiastical authorities that it fled to Holland, and when conditions there proved too difficult for it to remain, it then emigrated to the New World. This was the group known as Pilgrims that had landed by mistake at Plymouth Rock in New England. Ten years later in 1630 the Pilgrims were followed by a larger and more powerful group of Congregationalist Puritans of the non-Separating kind who were to form the Massachusetts Bay Colony.

If both groups were intent on returning Christianity to what they considered a more pristine—by which they meant more biblical—form of church organization, the theological project of each was to be affected not only by the extraordinary challenges of life in New England but also by political and religious developments in the Old England they had supposedly left behind. Until 1625, when Charles I came to the throne, the English or Anglican Church tolerated a certain latitude of belief that protected all but Separatists and other radical sectarians from religious censure and persecution. After 1630, however, this policy was to change dramatically with the appointment of William Laud as archbishop of Canterbury in 1633 and the enforcement, under his autocratic zealotry in matters of church polity and worship, of strict religious conformity. Archbishop Laud's "High Church" policies of intolerance were almost immediately to arouse opposition from Puritans and other religious dissidents that would in time boil over into the English Civil War from 1642 to 1651 during which Laud himself would be tried for treason and executed, King Charles I overthrown and similarly executed, his son Charles II exiled, and the English monarchy abolished and replaced by the Puritan Protectorate under the leadership of Oliver Cromwell.

This Puritan revolution in British rule could have been construed by those religious pilgrims who had been compelled to leave the Old World for the New as a confirmation of the principles for which they had emigrated. They had set out on what they conceived as a sacred errand to secure religious liberties both for themselves and for posterity. Their goal was not only to secure the freedom to worship God in their own way but also to establish a theocratic state at once civil and ecclesiastical, and organized according to scriptural precepts, that might serve as a model for the religious reformation of the rest of the fallen world. But the accelerating pace of these political and religious events must have also left them feeling bewildered and yet again betrayed. Within less than a decade, Cromwell had died of natural causes, the Protectorate had collapsed under the ineffectual leadership of his son, and the period known in British history as the Interregnum was over. James II was returned to the throne, and the Restoration of the Stuart line brought new waves of religious persecution that would end only with the Glorious Revolution of 1688, when James II was expelled and a year later the Act of Toleration was established. Thus while the American religious migrants found themselves with an opportunity to pursue and perfect their spiritual experiment in the New World, radical transformations of the English political and spiritual landscape dictated that they would have to pursue this spiritual experiment on their own, not only by themselves but essentially only for themselves.

Needless to say, that experiment in spiritual renewal was not, as John Cotton pledged in his 1630 sermon "God's Promise to His Plantations," or Thomas Shepherd repromised in his famous sermon twenty years later, "The Covenant of Grace," consistently triumphal and jubilant. From the point of view of Puritanism itself, it was closer in some respects to being dismaying, even deplorable, inasmuch as it resulted in a decline of piety that seemed to increase in direct proportion to the growing spiritual rigidity of its leaders and adherents. But before Puritanism's piety dissolved, and in some respects descended, into something else—over the next two centuries really into many other things—it lent itself to a variety of different literary uses. This was due in part to the underlying cohesiveness of the Puritan view of experience, but it also derived from the fact that the Puritan view of experience was intensely dramatic and, at the same time, adaptable to the circumstances of a people conceiving of themselves essentially as immigrants, as settlers in another country.

The Primacy of Experience in the Puritan Equation

The doctrines that the Puritans brought with them from the Old World to the New had been systematically formalized in Holland in 1619 at the Synod of Dort. Classically Calvinist, those doctrines were five in number. The first postulated that Adam and Eve's sin of disobedience in the Garden of Eden inaugurated the *total depravity* of humankind. The second affirmed that the stain of this corruption was capable of being removed only because God's sacrifice of his own son, Jesus Christ, had made available a *limited atonement*. The third insisted that God was prepared to offer those He deemed capable of accepting this limited atonement *unconditional election*. The fourth acknowledged that those fortunate enough to be predestined for election would be empowered to embrace it through God's *irresistible grace*. And the fifth emphasized that God's undeserved grace would override the effects of universal human iniquity and contribute to the *perseverance of the saints* in their growth toward sanctity.

As tenets of belief, such doctrines were abstract and difficult to grasp. The Puritans rendered these doctrines more sensible, if not intelligible, by interpreting them within what they described as a covenantal view of history. Carefully laid out in Thomas Shepherd's sermon in 1651 entitled "The Covenant of Grace," this view of history presupposed that if the Fall had all but destroyed the original bonds between God and his human creatures, he had not left human beings without evidence of his purpose. Evidence of that purpose was to be found in the two divine covenants He had made with his people. The first was the covenant God had forged with Adam, a covenant based on works whose requirements were defined in the body of the Law, and particularly the Law delivered to Moses known as the Ten Commandments. When Adam and his descendants demonstrated time and again, as recorded by the prophets, that they could not keep the Law, God had established a new covenant with Abraham and his seed based on the unmerited nature of divine grace and sealed by the Incarnation, Crucifixion, and Resurrection of Jesus Christ. This was the new covenant that promised the possibility, though not necessary the probability, of salvation to all who, with divine assistance, were able to accept the truth of God's redeeming love.

Such covenants nonetheless fail to capture fully the belief at the very heart of Puritan spirituality that God calls human beings not just to give up their old life but to embrace the possibility of a radically new life. All of Puritan theology thus turned on the experience of conversion, which not only separated the believer from the unbeliever but brought with it a conviction that the communicant had been reborn. Just as this new birth separated the Puritan from the rest of humankind, so it separated the world of nature from the world of grace. The Puritans referred to this revelatory experience of shattering force—in which the individual soul was confronted with the awful majesty of God's judging but salvific love and, in effect, compelled to turn itself inside out—as the experience of *regeneration*. But the decisiveness of this experience carried with it no assurance that it would last, much less that those who underwent it could count on being among the chosen. Hence the necessity for incessant scrutiny of one's life for signs of backsliding or corruption, the relentless discipline of self-accusation and renunciation, and the ceaseless pursuit through repentance of moral growth. Being a Puritan, in other words, was a lifetime project of self-study and personal reformation.

Such a personal spiritual project was not intended to immunize Puritans against every form of pleasure. They thought of alcohol when used in moderation, as—in the words of Increase Mather—"a good creature of God, and to be received with thankfulness." Food and sport yielded them other delights, as did the world of print, which they employed for more than the production and perusal of sermons. Even sexuality had its place in their spiritual economy, at least for purposes of procreation; and to ease the problem of sexual restraint during courtship, they devised the substitute known as "bundling," where, of a cold evening, couples could actually share a bed with one another so long as a wooden bar or sword was placed between them. Thus the Puritans were not indifferent to the demands of the flesh even when their attention was focused on less corporeal matters. Indeed, the bliss of the marriage bed was thought by some to offer a foretaste of that heavenly place where they looked for more permanent fulfillment.

Such a personal spiritual project also belonged, however, to a drama of much larger historical proportions. This was a drama positioned halfway between the personal story of individual regeneration and the cosmic story of covenantal history. It was a drama whose components were outlined almost at the very commencement of the Puritan errand, even before the first colonists to Massachusetts Bay had disembarked from their ship. This drama was to have literary reverberations throughout the entire period of Puritan hegemony, but it was to begin to founder almost from the very outset of its historical expression as religious dissent gave way to intimations of decline, and the prospect of decline in the face of the hardening of Puritan attitudes in a rapidly changing world was to open up an entirely different way of conceiving the religious thrust of American thought and destiny.

Dramas of Faith

The terms of the historical drama of faith in America are usually assumed to have been set by John Winthrop, the first governor of the settlement at Massachusetts Bay, in the famous sermon he delivered aboard the flagship *Arabella* titled "A Modell of Christian Charity." Seeing himself as a latter-day Moses leading his people to a New World Canaan, Winthrop defined the social and theological ideal that the Puritans were called to realize in the New World as an attempt to build a "City upon a Hill" which might serve as an example to the rest of Western Christendom. The "City" was to be organized as faithfully as possible according to biblical precept and supported by the covenant and was designed to serve as a beacon of hope and inspiration to a world still struggling to fulfill the injunctions of the Protestant Reformation. Not least among the distinctive features of this sermon was the claim Winthrop made for the importance of love in this experiment of community building. Winthrop argued that the only force that could knit the people of God together with one another and with their Lord in a community strong and vital enough to become a model for the rest of the world was the power of charity.

As a possible instrument of governance, the rule of charity had already been put to the test ten years earlier in the Plymouth Colony and had often come up wanting, but it would be submitted again and again to reassessment during the entire course of the Puritan experiment. Its Plymouth expression possessed an able chronicler in William Bradford, an undisputed leader of the colony during much of its early history and for thirty years its governor. Though Bradford did not actually begin his famous book *Of Plymouth Plantation* until ten years after the founding of the colony, it took him another twenty to finish it before it was then subsequently lost and only found again at the beginning of the nineteenth century.

Bradford intended his book to be a theological history of the first Puritan settlement in the New World that showed how its destiny was always guided by the hand of divine Providence. His object was to arouse in the minds and hearts of his readers the same sense of quiet but heroic aspiration and fidelity that defined the first generation of Plymouth pilgrims. Whether or not he actually succeeded in that task, he nonetheless managed with his plain style to leave his modern readers with a striking set of narrative images of the Puritans' initial suffering and continuing ordeal: the plight of the Pilgrims waiting in Holland for an opportunity to sail as their living circumstances became more and more difficult and time began to run out for the older members of the community; the mixture of hope and dread with which they faced a perilous crossing to an unknown land; the courageous realism they displayed in assessing their chances of survival and success; the unwelcoming prospect they faced when their ship missed the intended landfall for their new home in Virginia and deposited them on the rocky coast of Massachusetts; the heavy toll in suffering and death they endured during the earliest months after their arrival; the selfless heroism and devotion of the few Pilgrims not stricken with illness who nursed the colony through its first winter of sickness and despair; and the decency and cordiality, not to say helpfulness, of their first contacts with the indigenous population.

But Bradford's book also furnishes alternative images of Puritan consternation and intolerance, as in his response to the spectacle of wickedness and religious backsliding that had broken out both within and outside the colony after the first generation. Aside from various examples of communal and personal iniquity such as that associated most spectacularly with a hapless teenager found to have committed numerous acts of sodomy with barnyard animals, Bradford's chief source of torment, besides the non-Separatist colony at Massachusetts Bay, was Plymouth Plantation's sometime neighbor Thomas Morton, who had promoted a carnivalesque atmosphere of licentiousness and ribaldry in the nearby community of Merry Mount.

Morton was reputed to have been "pettifogger" or lawyer (though the record is unclear) and came to Massachusetts as a fur trader in 1622. Soon finding himself in conflict with the Separatist colony of Pilgrims at Plymouth, just a few miles south of his trading post on Quincy Bay, Morton increased the friction between the two communities by selling liquor and arms to the Indians. Yet hostilities would not have broken out with such virulence on the part of the Pilgrims if the Anglican Morton had not attracted a group of rowdies to his home at Merry Mount and then in 1627 decided to erect an eighty-foot maypole, topped with goat horns, around which he and his companions conducted their revels, drinking and dancing with Indian maidens and composing poems to Eros. Such practices outraged his Plymouth neighbors, who moved swiftly and severely against this self-styled "Lord of Misrule" by imprisoning him and in fact twice sending him back to England.

Morton, however, was undeterred by these developments and during one period of exile from America took revenge on his pious Plymouth rivals by setting down his own spiritedly unorthodox views of America and publishing them in 1637, long before Bradford's history was completed, in a book entitled *New England Canaan.* In addition to satirizing his Puritan opponents, Morton provided an interesting account of the Indians and a description of New England itself. However at variance his morals were with those of his Puritan-Separatist adversaries, his provocative behavior may have been motivated at least as strongly by religious and political concerns as by salacious or satirical ones. Writing at a time when the pro-Catholic Charles I was on the English throne, Morton hoped that he might help get the charter of the Massachusetts Bay Company revoked by portraying the Puritans as anti-Anglican.

With such enemies as these without, it was difficult to keep one's eyes fixed mainly within so that one might obtain what Thomas Hooker, one of Puritan's greatest preachers, later called "a true sight of sin." But the temptation to sin, along with the evidence of moral relapses, was all around, and the correction of it required as much circumspection as it did severity. One of the virtues of Bradford's book is that while such spectacles deeply angered and alarmed him, they also in the end sobered and, in various ways, humanized him, enabling him to harvest from his experience at Plymouth a deeper sense of the American project itself in images that have endured ever since: of America as itself a kind of last chance for humankind; of the American adventure as a voyage into the unknown and the untried; of the American people as a community knit together by suffering and upheld by a sense of hope tempered with an understanding of always threatening defeat; and of the American experience itself as a grappling with adversity and dissension.

What Bradford could not foresee is the toll that the history of the Plymouth Colony eventually took on relations with the native population. Initially saved from certain destruction by the Wampanoags and their chief, Massasoit, with whom the Pilgrims and their descendants lived in comparative peace for nearly fifty years, the colonists were eventually attacked by Massasoit's heir, King Philip, as he wanted to be known, and responded with murderous resistance that led within fourteen months to the slaughter of the entire tribe, ethnic cleansing, murderous wars, and the destruction of the environment.[1]

But Bradford was not the only writer who found it difficult to reconcile the exactions of faith with the hardships and disappointments so often en-

countered in the New World. A similar experience of disillusionment to the
one suffered by America's first historian was also fated to befall its first poet.
Anne Bradstreet, along with her husband and parents, also sailed aboard
the *Arabella* to Massachusetts Bay and undoubtedly heard Winthrop deliver
his famous sermon. But upon landing in New England, Bradstreet later reports in her revealing autobiographical "Letter to My Dear Children," her
heart rose up less to embrace Winthrop's call to construct a "City upon a
Hill" than against the conditions and manners of her new surroundings.
Having left behind in England a life of relative comfort and modest privilege, she found her circumstances in the New World far less accommodat-
ing or tolerable than she had first hoped, but she learned to accept them
only when, like Bradford, she became convinced that her transplantation
was part of a larger divine purpose.

While her earlier poetry concerned itself with formal, often classical,
subjects, such as the four elements or the cycles of history, her later poems
addressed more personal and domestic issues, such as her husband's frequent absences from home on the colony's business, or the death of one of
her grandchildren, or the burning of her house. Less learned or artistically
ambitious than her first poems—at the outset Bradstreet clearly wanted to
establish a place for herself in the ranks of English poetry—her later poems
express the conflict between her need to take the full emotional measure of
her experiences, many of them daunting, and her obligation to submit to
what she believed to be God's will for her life. This tension in her later verse
makes for poetry of unusual candor and immediacy as she struggles with
the difference between writing what, as a Puritan, she thought she ought to
feel and what, as a vulnerable human being, she knew she actually did feel.

This same tension was not unknown to Edward Taylor, a reclusive Puritan minister who immediately after graduation from Harvard was called
to a frontier parish in Western Massachusetts, where he served from 1671
to 1729. Although Taylor is usually associated with the tradition of English
metaphysical poets that included John Donne, George Herbert, Francis
Quarles, Henry Vaughan, and Richard Crashaw, his personal library is reputed to have included the work of no other poet but Anne Bradstreet. At
first glance, Taylor's richly symbolic, often densely realized, poems that rely
on elaborate poetic figures, wordplay, and wit could scarcely seem more
different from Bradford's more domestic, candid, vulnerable later verse, but
among his books was found a 400-page manuscript of spiritual exercises
(discovered for the first time in 1939 in the Yale University library) of an often curiously un-Puritan character designed to prepare him to deliver the

sacrament of Holy Communion to those members of his church who were willing to confess publicly to the presence of God's grace in their lives. Entitled *Preparatory Meditations,* they were apparently written in secret because of their somewhat unorthodox sentiments that reveal, as do Bradstreet's later poems, that art is not, as many Puritans insisted, inimical to faith, and that meditative poetry need not settle for simply reflecting faith but could in fact sometimes both deepen and complicate it by struggling with it.

Dissent and Disorder

While it has sometimes been maintained that Puritanism produced a rigid uniformity of belief and practice in seventeenth-century New England, the record shows that this was far from the truth. No matter how much scrutiny they gave to their own and others' beliefs, the Puritans were never completely consistent with themselves, and never constituted more than a minority, however influential, of the population of seventeenth-century New England society. Moreover, dissension within Puritan ranks was bound to spread as Puritan leaders struggled to retain their authority in the face of increasing religious diversity and indifference among the majority of the white population, mounting hostility from the indigenous population, and the general expansion and differentiation of the economy. Two of the most important early voices of dissent came from Anne Hutchinson and Roger Williams. While Hutchinson challenged theocratic authority by questioning the clergy's right to mediate the covenant of grace that God makes, or may make, with each individual soul, Williams called the church establishment to account both for its intolerance of variant interpretations of Christianity like Hutchinson's and for its intrusion into state affairs.

Hutchinson had emigrated to Massachusetts in 1634 and quickly came into conflict with the religious and political authorities of the new colony when she began holding weekly meetings at her home, mostly for women, to discuss and critique sermons heard the previous Sunday. Initially an ardent disciple of John Cotton's, the Massachusetts Bay Colony's foremost minister during the first generation, she shared his view that God's grace is wholly unmerited and that salvation is possible only because it is given freely and without conditions. But Hutchinson went further by insisting that if the "covenant of grace" represented an unmediated relationship with God that is based on an individual's direct intuition or apprehension of His will, then those clergy in the Massachusetts Bay Colony who, with the exception of Cotton, preached that "the covenant of grace" was somehow conditional upon an individual's response or effort were preaching what to all radical Protestants like her was the detested "covenant of works." Such views, especially when they challenged the positions and words of male members of the clerical establishment, were held to be Antinomian (literally, "against the law") and precipitated a crisis of gravest magnitude for the Massachusetts Bay community when Hutchinson was brought to trial for what they described as "traducing the ministers and their ministry."

During the trial, Hutchinson was as eloquent in her silences as in her speeches, and throughout the whole of the proceedings she maintained an extraordinary poise and clearheadedness. While fear of intimidation was no part of her makeup, a kind of grace under pressure became her legacy. Although John Cotton, her mentor, originally supported her ideas, he eventually yielded to pressure from his peers and joined the rest of the male court in condemning her. Governor Winthrop, author of the "City on a Hill" metaphor, presided over this sorry business and banished Hutchinson and her family to Rhode Island in 1638. By 1642 the Hutchinsons had moved on to New York, where all but one of them was killed a year later in an Indian raid. Puritanism had showed its doctrinaire hand in the treatment of one of its ardent and most courageous disciples, and a woman no less![2]

William's punishment for dissent led to consequences nowhere as tragic as Hutchinson's, but it included the same verdict of banishment by the religious establishment soon after his arrival in New England in 1631. From Massachusetts Bay Williams made his way to Rhode Island, where he established the first settlement at Providence and finally obtained a charter for the new colony in 1644. Justly famous for his work among the Indians, Williams published the first American book on their language in 1643 entitled *A Key into the Language of America,* and he continued to move leftward religiously from Separatist to Baptist and finally to "Seeker," repudiating all orthodox creeds without abandoning his basic allegiance as a Christian.

As a disturber of the religious peace, Williams was most effective in two books written before he had completed his spiritual odyssey. The first, *The Bloudy Tenent of Persecution,* published in 1644, took strong issue with the doctrinaire position that God demands total uniformity of belief and conduct by asserting that all religious groups and individuals are entitled to religious liberty as a natural right. In so arguing, Williams anticipated the position later taken by such Enlightenment thinkers as Benjamin Franklin and Thomas Jefferson that church and state must be kept separate in order to protect the right to religious freedom. Six years later, in *The Hireling Min-*

istry None of Christs, Williams went even further by contending that freedom of belief will in fact assist the spread of Christianity in America rather than impede it.[3]

Dissent of a different order, however, was also to erupt at the end of the seventeenth century, when the spread of interest in the occult and magic, together with the increase of heretical ideas among the faithful and the growing insecurity of the Puritan establishment, culminated in the reported outbreak in 1692 of witchcraft in Salem, Massachusetts. Before the witchcraft trials were completed, nineteen people would die by hanging and numbers of others would be defamed, humiliated, and sometimes mutilated in what the hanging judge at the trials, Samuel Sewall, later referred to, in his recantation of his actions, as a shameful and sinful business. The mass hysteria that led to the witchcraft trials was, of course, by no means confined to Salem or, for that matter, to colonial America—during three centuries of the early modern period in Europe, reaching their peak in the wars of religion between 1580 and 1630, somewhere between 40,000 to 60,000 people were executed—and was the result of a variety of factors ranging from religious sectarianism to social, cultural, and even economic phobias. But the suspicions aroused about people under the control of the Devil and engaging in sorcery, necromancy, and other acts of conjuring reflected widespread psychological panic that the religious world was now under the threat of demonic forces from within as well as without and in radical danger either of being seized by alien powers or of collapsing altogether.

It is somewhat ironic that Samuel Sewall played a major role in these dark and tragic affairs. Though a devout Puritan whose *Diary* attests to his zeal in monitoring his own spiritual experience, it also provides a surprisingly full record of colonial existence during a period of rapid but not unwelcome change, when coastal New England was being transformed from a backward, provincial, semireligious society into a more secular, even somewhat cosmopolitan world. That worldliness was reflected most dramatically in Sewell's own book entitled *The Selling of Joseph,* published in 1710, in which he delineates the many reasons why he was against the institution of slavery. But it was also exhibited in his public declaration of the shame he felt and the forgiveness he needed for his actions at the witchcraft trials.

Long before Puritanism went into sharp decline at the end of the seventeenth century, due in no small part to the witchcraft mania and the anxieties underlying it, protests naturally arose to try to halt it. Some of these protests took poetic forms, as in Michael Wigglesworth's *Day of Doom,* but many of them took a more discursive form, as in Samuel Danforth's Election Day sermon in 1671 entitled "A Brief Recognition of New England's Errand Into the Wilderness." Employing the formula that Nathaniel Hawthorne was later to adopt for the sermon Arthur Dimmesdale delivers, also on Election Day, at the end of *The Scarlet Letter*, these sermons known as jeremiads seek to use graphic images of the spectacle of what preachers called "declension" to rehearse for their communicants the covenantal obligations that their parishioners and community members have consistently betrayed. Thus as a literary form, the jeremiad possessed a double focus and achieved a contradictory effect. Laying out in extensive, vivid detail the record of the community's history of degeneracy, these sermons at the same time use these details to remind communicants of the covenantal mission they have forsaken. The effect is, or at least was intended to be, electric. The reader or listener is at once reviled, as in Michael Wigglesworth's 1662 poem entitled "God's Controversy with New England," by a catalogue of corruption, iniquity, and the misery to come, and at the same time exalted by a recollection of the glorious future that awaits New England's fulfillment of its religious calling. Used over and over again on public occasions like Election Days, the jeremiad was turned into a public instrument for reinforcing and reviving the myth of cultural consensus by cataloguing the details by which it has been violated.

As profoundly troubled as Puritans were by their own failures of faith and will, they were also deeply disturbed by religious groups outside their communities, which included Anabaptists, Anglicans, and especially Quakers. Like the Anabaptists, Quakers belonged to the radical left wing of the Puritan movement and advocated reliance on what Christians had traditionally meant by the Third Person of the Trinity, or Holy Spirit, which they called the "Inner Light." Believing in the possibility of direct illumination by God's truth, which was sometimes accompanied by trembling or quaking (hence the name) and implied little need for trained clergy or the orthodox regulation of belief, the Quakers almost immediately came into conflict with the more rigidly hierarchical and theologically strict Puritan establishment. Exacerbated by the Quakers' simplification, if not almost complete abandonment, of religious ritual and the variety of ways that at least some Quakers witnessed to their faith, the Puritans' reaction was predictable and severe. Many Quakers were imprisoned in New England, often after being whipped through the streets, and some were physically mutilated by having their ears cropped or their tongues severed. This represented a hostility, at times as much psychosocial as it was moral and religious, not unlike that directed at possible witches, though its virulence was no match for the treatment Puritans accorded Native Americans after the initial honeymoon of their early relations broke down.

Conflict between whites and native Americans was bound to follow from the encroachment of colonists and settlers on Indian lands, but it was seriously aggravated by the religious predilection of so many Puritans, especially when their safety was threatened, to see the "savage" as Satanic and to view the American wilderness as the domain of the demonic.[4] Fed by Indian raids like the one experienced by Mary Rowlandson, this predilection led her to describe her captors as "a company of hell-hounds, roaring, singing, ranting, and insulting, as if they would have torn our very hearts out."[5] Such sentiments were expressed in *A Narrative of the Captivity and Restauration of Mrs. Mary Rowlandson* and turned the account of her tribulations during the Narragansett Indian uprising known as King Philip's War—when Rowlandson's town was attacked and burned and, together with three of her children, she was taken captive—into one of the most widely read books in late seventeenth-century America.

The wife of a Congregational minister in Lancaster, Massachusetts, Rowlandson suffered an extraordinarily harrowing imprisonment before she and her two surviving children were ransomed and freed. Not only did she have to witness the death of one of her children; she was forced throughout her captivity to endure the hardships and hazards of numerous "removals," as she calls them, as well as the rigors of daily existence among a hostile people in the American wilderness. Rowlandson wrote her narrative in gratitude for her deliverance and in hopes that she might testify to the providential meaning of her trials. Confident that her sufferings possessed a divine purpose, she believed that she had survived them only because God intended for them to be instructive. But in providing one of the earliest detailed pictures of native American life, her narrative also suggests, somewhat unintentionally, what kinds of accommodations, spiritual as well as physical, she was obliged to make simply to survive the ordeal of Indian captivity.

Not unlike the jeremiad, then, Rowlandson's narrative intended to use the experience of suffering she had endured for initially taking her own faith for granted to bring her readers back to God, but she also managed in the process, and without quite realizing it, to formulate what later writers would turn into an archetypal pattern of American acculturation. The story she told, in other words, was not only a tale of deliverance and redemption by a benevolent God but also a tale about the archetypal confrontation in America between the Caucasian self and its moral and spiritual "other." This was a confrontation in which the Caucasian or Western self manages to survive less because of divine intent or intervention than by learning how take on some of the attributes of that "other" for oneself. To survive captivity, she reports, she had to become like her captors. Such were the religious hazards in a world where God's plan, always difficult to follow in any case if not simply to detect, here had to compete with the challenges of what she called the "wilderness-condition." The first requires a conversion, so to speak, of the self upward toward a system of theological commitment that transcends it; the second required a conversion of the self downward toward a spiritual "other" potentially within it.

The appeal of the "wilderness-condition" was not reserved alone for whites made captive of it and compelled to adapt for the sake of surviving but extended to a surprising number of others in seventeenth-century society who once liberated from Indian captivity sought to return to it or who elected to join Indian society on their own. If most of these whites were men, it is nonetheless telling that almost no native Americans attempted to join white society. Benjamin Franklin had noted these anomalies as early as 1753, but Hector St. John de Crèvecoeur, the French émigré and author of *Letters from an American Farmer*, of whom we will learn more in the next chapter, addressed the issue most squarely by noting that while there were thousands of Europeans who had become Indians, there was no record of any Indians choosing to become European. "There must be in their social bond," Crèvecoeur reasoned, "something singularly captivating and far superior to anything to be boasted of among us."[6]

In the public world, of course, that is, the world outside the self, the Lord's people, as Puritans typically thought of themselves, prevailed. And they prevailed not, as they frequently supposed, following Mrs. Rowlandson, because the Lord was on their side but because the Lord's people possessed superiority in arms, supplies, and support. In the Pequot War of 1637, the colonists were finally able to corner what remained of their foe in Mystic, Connecticut, where they burned the Pequots alive in their wigwams or shot those attempting to escape. But final removal of the Indian threat in New England did not occur until 1675–76, when during King Philip's War more than three thousand Indians were killed and King Philip himself was captured, drawn and quartered, and beheaded. Puritan tactics and weaponry rather than Puritan spirituality and righteousness had carried the day, but the integrity of Puritan faith had received another wound.

Change and Its Costs

The decline of Puritanism was finally most completely determined by the pace, heterogeneity, and complexity of the process of colonial settlement itself. After the first generation and certainly by the second, the ranks of new immigrants numbered fewer committed Christians seeking the New World's redemption and more social and economic hopefuls and opportunists seeking the New World's promise. The latter group looked for political liberty, commercial opportunity, physical adventure, the opportunity to work off one's indenture, forgetfulness, or any number of other things. The motives for migration were as mixed as the social habits of the immigrants, and this process of diversification only accelerated upon arrival as people were quickly caught up in an economic environment growing more variegated and secular by the day and concerned less with saving the soul than with building a new society.

Consider, for example, the spectacle perhaps best imagined by the historian Edmund S. Morgan of the bustling and bewildering activity that awaited the eye of the colonial Puritan farmer, now settled in rural New England, paying a visit to the town of Boston around 1640, just ten years after the founding of the Massachusetts Bay community:

> Swine roamed everywhere, feeding on the refuse; drovers herded sheep and cattle to the butchers. Elegant carriages rolled impatiently behind lumbering wagons as great packs of barking dogs worried the horses. Sailors reeled out of taverns, and over the roofs of house could be seen the swaying masts and spars of their ships. The farmer had been told that the city was a nursery of vice and prodigality. He now saw that it was so. Every shop had wares to catch his eye: exquisite fabrics, delicate chinaware, silver buckles, looking glasses, and other imported luxuries that never reached the crossroads store. Putting up at the tavern, he found himself drinking too much rum. And there were willing girls, he heard, who had lost their virtue and would be glad to help him lose his. Usually he returned to the farm to warn his children as he had been warned. He seldom understood that the vice of the city, if not its prodigality, was mainly for transients like himself. Permanent residents had work to do.[7]

That work was soon to proceed at an equally rapid pace beyond Massachusetts. With other colonies already established first in Jamestown in 1607 and then in 1638 in Williamsburg in Virginia—colonies that were very quickly to develop a distinctive and much different way of life built around the cultivation and sale of tobacco and the exploitation of Virginia's network of tidewater rivers facilitating the expansion of trade—additional colonies were to spring up all along the Eastern Seaboard. Maryland was carved out of northern Virginia and founded as a refuge for Catholics in 1634. New Netherland had been established by the Dutch some years earlier and was reclaimed by the English and named New York in 1664. That same year New Jersey came into being through a grant from the Duke of York, and less than twenty years later, William Penn, the man Cotton Mather wanted to seize and sell into slavery, was awarded the territory now known as Pennsylvania, in which he immediately created the most liberal and religiously tolerant form of government in North America.

Not least among the institutions that, along with the general expansion of commerce, were to erode the hold of Puritan ideas over the minds of New Englanders was the printing press, which made its first appearance in the colonies at Cambridge, Massachusetts, in 1639 and issued its first publication, *The Bay Psalm Book,* in 1640. A second institution whose development contributed over time to the weakening of Puritan ideas was education. Harvard College was founded in 1636, followed by the establishment of the College of William and Mary in 1693 and of Yale College in 1701. Though initially created for the purpose of supplying the Protestant churches with clergy, these institutions became in time centers of learning that not only introduced their students to different ideas but soon began actively to encourage new thinking. But the gathering and dissemination of information that would weaken the appeal of the New England theocracy was perhaps most dramatically abetted by the creation at the beginning of the eighteenth century of that still more public institution known as the newspaper, which was in time to shape so decisively the career of someone like Benjamin Franklin.

The weakening and ossification of Protestant religious authority could not continue for too many decades, however, without producing a spiritual reaction that took the form of what is now called the Great Awakening. Part of a large revival and revitalization movement that quickly swept through the American colonies and abroad, it was to leave an evangelical imprint on the shape of European and American Protestantism that it has never lost. The first Great Awakening of the mid-1730s and early 1740s— there was a second directed at the unchurched as opposed to the churched that broke out at the beginning of the 1800s—was fueled by the preaching of the English itinerant Methodist minister George Whitefield, whose voice, Benjamin Franklin estimated, could carry to a crowd of thirty thousand. Convulsing many of the churches from the New England colonies to the Carolinas and Georgia, it was a titanic eruption of pent-up religious feelings, originally aroused and nourished by Puritan conceptions, that in the first third of the eighteenth century no longer found any forms—ecclesiastical, ceremonial, discursive—capable of by turns containing or releasing them.

One of the early centers of this revival was the town of Northampton, Massachusetts, located in the Connecticut Valley some hundred miles distant from the more religiously traditional Boston, in the church of a pious as well as brilliant young pastor named Jonathan Edwards. Set aflame by sermons like his "Sinners in the Hands of an Angry God," Edwards's parish quickly became a flashpoint for the spreading conflagration. No one was more surprised by these developments than Edwards himself, even though he had found the perfect target in the cancerous growth of self-regard that lay beneath the religious platitudes and theological formulas by which men and women of his age justified themselves to their God. Edwards was less interested in exposing this cancer than in attempting to cure it, but he was convinced that the seeds of the cure were not to be found simply in a re-educated mind or a redirected will but only in a reformed heart. Edwards thus set for himself the monumental task of rethinking the whole edifice of Puritan, really Calvinist, spirituality by relocating the seat of religion not in the life of the intellect or of the soul but in the life of the feelings, or what he termed the affections.

While Edwards's life was comparatively short, his literary output was truly prodigious, especially in view of his active and frequently controversial ministry. That ministry in Northampton was brought to an end in 1750 when Edwards became embroiled in a bitter controversy over the standards for church membership and was sent packing into the wilderness to a tiny church in Western Massachusetts where he become a missionary to the Indians. It was there in the obscurity of Stockbridge, once the controversies surrounding the Great Awakening in which he played such an important role had begun to wear themselves out, that he wrote the great theological and philosophical works for which he is now known. His exile was finally ended only when his increasing fame as a theologian eventually won him appointment as president of the new collegiate institution in New Jersey that was eventually to become Princeton University. Yet this recognition of what is now widely conceded to have been his staggering intellectual achievement was tragically cut short only two months after assuming this office when, as a result of volunteering for a smallpox vaccination, he suddenly died.

During the whole of his life, from the publication of his first essay on spiders at the age of fourteen until his death, Edwards's pen was ceaselessly active, producing everything from spiritual biography to narratives of the new religious awakening; from treatises on morality and the nature of the will to his great works on original sin and the purpose of Creation; from miscellaneous journals and notebooks to sermons like "A Divine and Supernatural Light" and his more famous, if uncharacteristic, "Sinners in the Hands of an Angry God." Edwards was in some ways most himself in his autobiographical *Personal Narrative,* where he was forced to explain the whole process of overcoming his early resistance to the doctrine of God's sovereignty by recourse to the language of aesthetics and the sweet sense it gave him of God's ability to reconcile such opposites as might and meekness, majesty and grace; or in his *Treatise on the Religious Affections,* published in 1746, where he shows how one's knowledge of God is not directed or unmediated but rather originates, like all knowledge, from sense experience as it registers itself in the mind and thus become the mind's idea of it; or in his *Treatise on the Freedom of the Will,* published in 1754, where he argues that while human beings remain free to choose what stands in the mind as the best choice among several (because otherwise they could not be held responsible for making the wrong choice), human beings are not by that fact wholly and completely free, since the one thing they cannot choose is their choices; or in *The Nature of True Virtue,* which appeared in 1765, where he shifts the discussion of morality and ethics from the language of prudentiality or utilitarianism to the language of beauty or perfection so that he might redefine goodness or virtue as disinterested benevolence, or "the consent of being to Being."

Three-quarters of a century after the First Great Awakening had run itself into the ground, the same situation would repeat itself at the end of the eighteenth century and the beginning of the nineteenth when an even more explosive charge of religious energy burst through the rationalistic—and rationalizing—surface of American religious and cultural life to form the Second Great Awakening. It was already becoming clear after the First Great Awakening that Puritanism and its evangelical offshoots were not undergoing a religious revival so much as suffering a religious sea change, and nothing signaled this more dramatically than Edwards's own need to embrace much of the "new thinking" of John Locke, Isaac Newton, and Frances Hutchison simply to keep the old faith alive. In intellectual terms, Edwards was compelled to turn to the Enlightenment, or at least to certain selected strains within it, to bolster the faith of Puritanism.

It was Locke's epistemology that provided the hinge. If knowledge does not derive from innate ideas like the image of God already implanted in the human brain prior to its experience of them but only from sense impressions as they are communicated to the brain and are then converted into the mind's conception of it, then a new age was indeed dawning. God did not have to rend the fabric of creation through transcendental acts of divine revelation to make his will known to his creatures; he merely needed to reveal himself indirectly through the material elements of ordinary, everyday experience. But this, in turn, did something both to the notion of experience and to the understanding of how it was affected. Experience itself in all its messy concreteness and unpredictability became the medium through which truth, divine or otherwise, was to be discovered, and the truth in question was not to be found in rational forms such as fledgling ideas but in affective forms as subjective feelings capable of inclining the understanding in one direction instead of another. Hence the stage was set for the emergence of a world whose energies would become directed less at divining the will of God than at addressing the collective needs of human beings.

THREE

Enlightenment and a New Age Dawning

Worlds in Motion

Evidence of a new age dawning can be detected in numerous ways, from changes in the theory of the mind to reconceptions of what the mind, or, as the Puritans preferred to call it, the soul, should attend to. Was the mind, as Jonathan Edwards agreed with John Locke, a kind of tabula rasa or blank slate on which the world beyond it imprints itself through sense impressions that then generate the mind's idea of them, or was it already inscribed with certain innate concepts prior to its experience of them that represent what is left of the image of God after the Fall? Conversely, was the world itself nothing but a landscape of temptation and deceit to be wrestled with if the soul has any hope of finding the path to repentance and possible salvation, or was it instead a realm of concrete issues and problems of which we can become sensible as the mind constructs ideas that can then assist us in negotiating their challenges and opportunities? If the world is the former, then the future is already preordained, and the only way forward is through reliance on scripture and church tradition; if the latter, then the future is yet to be made, and the surest guide to the future is a reliance on reason tempered with a respect for history.

In simplest terms, this distinction presented itself as the difference between an orientation that was this-worldly and one that was other-worldly, and by the turn of the century there was no doubt which way the balance had begun to tilt. If religion had held center stage in the 1600s, commercial development, social growth, political agitation and conflict, technological innovation, and even scientific curiosity would begin to assume that place by the middle of the 1700s. Questions of theology, of church organization, of religious practice, of personal rebirth, would continue to remain critical for many individual Americans, but they would no longer dominate public discourse as they once did. Within less than a century, America would declare its independence from England, fight a war to secure that freedom, and draw up and ratify a constitution creating "the United States of America." Along the way, the economy would expand and diversify, religious life would become more pluralistic and contentious, political dissent would eventually give rise to revolutionary fervor, and new territories beyond the Eastern Seaboard would be opened up for exploration and additional settlement. Thus the world that the signers of the Constitution helped bring into being would operate according to very different assumptions and be held together by very different structures of governance and feeling than the world familiar to first- and second-generation colonists in Massachusetts or even Virginia. What had ultimately changed was that the Puritan project in spiritual regeneration had slowly given way to an Enlightened experiment in revolutionary state making.

Literary Stirrings and the New Natural Order

Early evidence of this profound shift of orientation can even be discerned in the changing uses that American writers began to make of the literary resources made available to them by the English tradition. At the time of initial New World settlement, English literature was in a position to supply American writers with a variety of mythic paradigms and archetypal structures to frame the meaning of their experience. One was the Arcadian myth of a lost world of primal innocence, the second the biblical myth of a fallen world alienated from the sources of its being and in need of redemption, and the third a utopian myth built around the possibility of the restoration of a new Eden founded principally on the light of reason. But American colonial writers during the seventeenth and early eighteenth centuries not only borrowed material from these English models of more ancient archetypes but also reshaped them with the literary forms they had at hand in ways that forecast the new world of ideas, mindsets, and sensibilities to come. Chief among those forms, obviously, was the sermon, followed closely in popularity by the theological manual, although Protestant poetics, drawing on the vast number of biblical genres and types, furnished American authors with an array of other literary models, from biblical epics and providential histories to spiritual and secular autobiography, martyrology and hagiography, occasional meditations, confessional lyrics, and, not incidentally, promotional tracts. This is the form to which Captain John Smith inevitably resorted when, at the end of his adventures, he returned to England from his second journey to America to record his exploits and promote further travel.

Explorer, mercenary, entrepreneur, geographer, and colonial promoter, Smith is best known in legend for his capture by Chesapeake Bay Indians during his participation in the 1607 expedition that founded the colony at Jamestown and his subsequent rescue from certain death at the hands of Chief Powhatan by his daughter Pocahantas. Whether fact or fiction (Smith suppressed this incident in his first account of the expedition, and Native American historians have subsequently questioned it, as well as the myth-ification of Pocahontas, whose given name was Matoaka), the histrionics of that Jamestown expedition, dramatic and daring as they were, should not be allowed to overshadow a fair estimate of Smith himself. Clearly represen-tative of a new breed of explorers and colonists who were as equally inter-ested in financial gain as in personal fame, Smith was a tough, disciplined, no doubt courageous man whose leadership of the Jamestown colony from September 1608 to August 1609 almost certainly saved the colonists from starvation, even as his policy of "he that will not work will not eat" earned him the hostility of many. Returning to England to recover from a wound caused by the accidental explosion of his gunpowder bag, Smith made a second visit to America in 1614, this time to New England, and became so entranced by the region that he devoted two of his next books, *A Description of New England* in 1616 and *Advertisements for the Unexperienced Planters of New England, or Anywhere* (actually addressed to the Massachusetts Bay colonists) in 1631, to encourage and promote colonization by celebrating the virtues of the landscape. And thus was born a new genre of nature writing that was to flourish a century later.

As different as Smith was from the kind of person typically honored by Puritans, they were not indifferent to the kinds of aesthetic appeals on which his promotional writing depended. Alexander Whitaker's *Good Newes from Virginia*, which appeared in 1613, three years before Smith's *A Description of New England*, also helped define the mold but simultaneously broke it. Originally prepared as a sermon composed in part to be read by an audi-ence back in England, *Good Newes* was designed to broaden support for the transatlantic passage by providing a highly favorable description of the country. Inaugurating what might be thought of as the "celebrationist tra-dition" in American writing, it nonetheless deviated from the conventional form, as well from later writing of the same kind, by displaying a view of native peoples that was far from hostile. While viewing them, like all other "sonnes of Adam," as "servants of sinne and slaves of the divell," their com-mon parentage with the rest of humankind made him reluctant to regard them simply as potential candidates for demonization or for proselytization.

Insisting that the miserable conditions in which they lived should inspire compassion rather than contempt, Whitaker found much to admire about native people, from their physical prowess, dexterity at arms, and inventiveness to their often enlightened form of government. Possessing "reasonable soules and intellectuall faculties as well as wee," he found that they bore abundant traces of the divine image in which all human beings are made and thus deemed them fully capable of receiving the gospel.[1]

It was almost inevitable that early promotional tracts like Whitaker's and Smith's extolling the beauties and wonders of America would soon to give way to other kinds of travel and nature writing that would begin to make America's newness seem still more exceptional and less unapproachable. In works like Samuel Sewall's tribute to Plum Island from his *Phaenomena quaedam Apocalyptica* (1697), Robert Beverley's *The History and Present State of Virginia* (1705), William Byrd's *The History of the Dividing Line* (1728), and William Bartram's *Travels Through North and South Carolina, Georgia, East and West Florida* (1791), a new genre was beginning to take shape that would soon flower into a flourishing industry.

Samuel Sewall, better known was the "hanging judge" at the Salem witchcraft trials, who not only possessed the courage to publicly repudiate his participation in that miserable affair but also expressed his opposition to the institution of slavery, offers a foretaste of this new genre in *Phaenomena quaedam Apocaliptica*. To him, Plum Island north of Cape Ann off the coast of Massachusetts is not simply a place of spiritual refuge or renewal but almost a source in itself of that regeneration or "Inheritance" that awaits what he calls "the saints in light." Acknowledging his debt to Captain John Smith's *A Description of New England*, Sewall manages to step out of the conventional stereotype of the faithful but repentant Puritan to express his surpassing love of the natural beauties, seasonal rhythms, and animal life that vivify this landscape and make of it not merely an emblem of paradise but almost its surety or guarantee.

Robert Beverley's *The History and Present State of Virginia* furnishes a different perspective on this budding genre because of its Virginia setting. Tradition has it that Beverley undertook his book to correct misinterpretations in another manuscript soon to be published in 1708 under the title *The British Empire in America*. Beverley's aim is to counter not only the impressions created by this book but also those that might be associated with New England. Here, again, the emphasis is not, as in more religious writing, on the beauties of nature as a foretaste of the glories of heaven, or any world beyond, but rather on the "Native Beauty, Riches, and Value" of the world before him as first described by one of his heroes, "the learned and valiant Sir Walter Raleigh," in his own "incomparable book" on "the history of the world."[2] Beverley's tone throughout his book is less idyllic than worldly and cultivated, his tone somewhat bemused by the spectacle of people gullible enough to believe that the country could have been founded by individuals whose motives were entirely unselfish.

William Byrd was another Virginia landowner of great wealth who as a youth was sent to England for fourteen years to be educated and "finished" before returning to America to take over the management of his family's immense landholdings (the city of Richmond was eventually laid out on some of his property). In addition to owning a library of some four thousand volumes that was reputed to be the largest in the colonies, Byrd became a member of the Royal Society of London and served on two separate occasions for periods of eight or more years as a colonial agent in England. But Byrd's literary reputation is based in part on the commission he received to survey the boundary between North Carolina and Virginia and on the resulting *History of the Dividing Line,* where he revealed that there is no contradiction between an interest in scientific inquiry and exactitude and an appreciation of natural wonders. Like Beverley, Byrd adopted the posture of an English country gentleman, though his interest in adopting the manners of a wealthy planter leisured and well born should not be allowed to overshadow his achievements in observation and description.

In his *Travels* William Bartram goes even further by combining the acute eye of a born naturalist with the spirituality of a Quaker intent on directing his attention less on internal feelings than on the variety and plentitude of the external natural world lying, so to speak, at his doorstep. Regarded by Samuel Taylor Coleridge as a work of "high merit," Bartram's book had an appeal to Romantic writers like Coleridge, Wordsworth, and Chateaubriand. But as moved as Bartram was by the beauty and majesty of God's handiwork, his chief interest lay in showing his countrymen how some of nature's most original natural productions might be put to use by society itself. Here, then, was a forerunner of the Enlightenment perspective: a writer who believed that the essence of the spiritual life is to turn the divine glories of nature itself to human purpose.

No one, of course, is better known for the exploitation of the relation between nature's wonders and spiritual regeneration than Thomas Jefferson in the book he published in 1785 entitled *Notes on the State of Virginia.* Written in answer to questions about American customs and conditions that were put to him by the secretary of the French delegation in Philadelphia, it is a marvel of close observation and vivid sociological as well as naturalist description, as comfortable and elegant in its answers to questions about mountains, cascades, and caverns as in its discussions of Amerindians and religion. Famously declaring that "those who labour in the earth are the chosen people of God," *Notes from Virginia* is the epitome of a genre that started out by celebrating the extraordinary wonders of the natural world but actually linked such spectacles not only to the well-being of the American soul but also to the promise of the new nation. Describing "the passage of the Potomac through the Blue Ridge [mountains]" as "one of the most stupendous scenes in nature,"[3] and Virginia's "Natural Bridge" as "the most sublime of nature's works," Jefferson was out to portray scenes of sublimity as both literally and figuratively salvific: "It is impossible for the emotions arising from the sublime to be felt beyond what they are; so beautiful an arch, so elevated, so light, and springing as it were up to heaven!"[4]

Jefferson was clearly aware that his version of a Virginian Arcadia was potentially disfigured by the spectacle of slavery. Condemning it as an institution, Jefferson argued for the emancipation of African Americans and their removal to another colony where they might become free and independent. While this did not mean that the owner of three hundred slaves himself believed in racial equality, he was enough of a realist to foresee that the systemic prejudices of whites and the sense of injustice experienced by blacks would prevent the two peoples from ever living together successfully. Indeed, Jefferson sensed that if slaves were not emancipated in the near future, the consequences for the new republic could be disastrous. Slaves were the victims, after all, of what Jefferson had earlier described, in words struck from the Declaration of Independence in order for it to win the support of all thirteen colonies, as a "cruel war against human nature itself." Yet it was difficult for him to make the connection between the Arcadian fantasy that the presence of the Virginia wilderness tended to foster and the "execrable commerce," as Jefferson called it in those pages removed from the draft of the Declaration, which had always blighted it.[5]

This connection was also for the most part lost on the author of the celebrated *Letters from an American Farmer* published in 1782, five years before Jefferson's *Notes*. Michel-Guillaume Jean de Crèvecoeur was a Frenchman and trained cartographer who emigrated to Canada, served under Montcalm in the last of the French and Indian Wars, and then explored the vast wilderness of the Great Lakes region before eventually settling in New York State. Becoming an American citizen in 1765 under the assumed name of

J. Hector St. John de Crèvecoeur, he took up farming and began writing his celebrated *Letters*. Despite their idealization of the self-reliant American husbandman, whom he pictured as continually regenerated by the land from which he wrests his living, Crèvecoeur found his loyalties divided on the eve of the American Revolution and was forced to return to France during the War of Independence. Upon his return to America at the war's end, he found his farm destroyed, his wife dead, and his children separated, but he slowly put the remaining pieces of his life together by composing his letters before his permanent return to France in 1790.

Crèvecoeur's *Letters* are best known for the question he poses in his third epistle: "What, then, is the American, this new man?"[6] His answer is that the American is one who derives his manners and morals, not to say his metaphysics, from the new agrarian mode of life and thought that he has been obliged to adopt in the New World. This new mode of life was superior to anything Europe could boast of or provide because, like the seasons, it is perpetually renewable; like the labor of those who work for themselves, it is genuinely egalitarian; and like the industry of those who are free, it is potentially redemptive.

Such sentiments as these have echoed down through the years, particularly among those who conceive of the American environment as somehow decisive for the development of the American character and consciousness. Yet this definition of the American was not only idealized but immensely selective inasmuch as it left out of account all those nonwhite people who were already settled on the land before Europeans arrived and the at least two and a half million others who were forcibly brought to the New World in chains and sold as slaves. Nonetheless, Crèvecoeur was honest enough to insert into his idyll the portrait of one among many of those less fortunate inhabitants of the New World who were excluded from his romanticized definition of the "American." This portrait, which Crèvecoeur came upon by accident on a walk through the woods outside Charles-town, features the "living spectre" of a black man suspended in a cage whose eyes have already been plucked out by birds and whose lacerated body is covered with swarms of insects, left to die in agony—an image from which, as Crèvecoeur remarks, humanity herself would recoil in horror. He is finally moved to offer the suffering man some water before continuing on to his destination, where he learns from his hosts that this is punishment for the murder of a plantation overseer and sanctioned not only by the laws of self-preservation but also by the doctrine of slavery itself. Crèvecoeur may have wished he could put this memory behind him, but the image of human wretchedness it evokes remains indelible, forever staining his representation of America as a pastoral utopia.

Crèvecoeur and Jefferson were not the only writers to note the dissonance between America's professions of belief in itself as, to quote Emerson, "Nature's nation" and its practice of trading and owning slaves, but no one was more effective in challenging this institution than the Quaker John Woolman in his 1773 essay titled "Some Considerations on the Keeping of Negroes." Although it is often overshadowed by the literary and religious reputation of some of his eighteenth-century religious contemporaries, such as Jonathan Edwards (an owner of slaves himself) and even Edwards's chief opponent, Boston's Charles Chauncey, the English writer Charles Lamb nevertheless confessed that Woolman's autobiographical *Journal* was the only American book he ever read twice, and Emerson declared that he found more wisdom in its pages than in "any other book written since the days of the apostles."[7] The reasons are not hard to find. Among the first of his countrymen to confront the issue of poverty in the United States and to point out its degrading effects upon rich and poor alike, Woolman also anticipated Henry David Thoreau by almost a century in using the nonpayment of taxes as a carefully considered act of civil disobedience. But it was in response to the slavery issue that Woolman made perhaps his greatest religious contribution.

"Some Considerations on the Keeping of Negroes" mounts one of the most powerful arguments ever made against the right to own slaves and struck Samuel Taylor Coleridge as a model of Christian charity. Woolman's essay deserves such a description because, like the famous sermon whose title it recalls, delivered aboard the flagship *Arabella* in Massachusetts Bay nearly a century and a half before by John Winthrop in which Winthrop defined the kind of ethics needed for the Puritan errand to succeed, its purpose is not to proscribe a form of behavior but to prescribe a way of understanding it. Setting aside all the reasons for condemning such a practice, Woolman turns the moral issues it raises back on his readers by inviting them to consider this practice from the perspective of those who are subjected to it. What would it feel like if the subject positions of black people and whites were reversed, he asked, if we were to be put in their position and they in ours? What, then, would we make of an institution that allows people of one color to enslave those of another? If whites were capable of seeing themselves as being owned and subjugated by others, they would then, Woolman reasons, finally understand the logic of the biblical injunction to do unto others as you would have others do unto you.

Woolman is under no illusion that slavery is anything other than an offense to the notion that all human beings are made in the image of God, but he also comprehends that the achievement of human equality demands far more than a recognition of our likeness to others and theirs to us. Such recognitions remain utterly hollow unless they contain within them the capacity to discern and feel what it would be like for us, and people like us, to suffer forms of oppression, persecution, humiliation, and torment similar to theirs.

Women's Writing as a Harbinger of Change

Such insights into the meaning of human equality and the need for empathetic understanding were relevant not only to the condition of black people in or out of slavery but also to women both white and black everywhere. As females living in a radically patriarchal society and spouses or potential spouses living in a strictly gendered one, women were becoming all too aware even before the eighteenth century of the restrictions, coercions, and tyrannies suffered by members of their sex and yearned to resist some of their constraints. One of the first was Sarah Kemble Knight, who between 1704 and 1710 published her famous *The Journal of Madame Knight*. Apparently employed in legal as well as business affairs, she records in her *Journal* a journey she undertook to settle an estate for a friend. Setting out from Boston to New Haven and eventually beyond to New York for a period of six months, Madame Knight's trip was hazardous and arduous by any standards, but particularly difficult for a woman. In addition to the physical difficulties she faced—rugged topography, inclement weather, unfamiliar forests, unpredictable rivers, inhospitable neighbors, crude lodgings, bad food—there were the problems of a woman traveling alone. But Madam Knight was not easily daunted by such challenges. She traveled for the most part by following the postal routes, and when the way proved dangerous, she hired male companions to accompany her. A sharp observer of local incongruities and banalities, she also brought to her journey an intrepid interest in the world around her and a strongly independent critical spirit. Unencumbered by feelings of sexual propriety or decorum, she insisted on making her way in this new yet strange world of America on the terms set for her not by tradition or convention but solely by the world itself.

A very different image of a woman seeking autonomy and independence in an era undergoing rapid change is provided by Elizabeth Ashbridge. An unusually spirited English girl who was raised as an Anglican, she eloped at the age of fourteen, was widowed by the time she was eighteen, emigrated to America as an indentured servant before she was twenty, and then married again to escape the religious hypocrisy of her cruel husband, a worldly schoolteacher named Sullivan who became enamored of her dancing. Attracted in time to the religion of the Quakers, Ashbridge soon found herself in conflict with her husband as she attempted to live out the requirements of her new faith in the face of his growing abuse. Her autobiography, entitled *Some Account of the Fore part of the Life of Elizabeth Ashbridge . . . Written by Her Own Hand,* published in 1774, provides a poignant record of her spiritual struggle with guilt and fear as she openly describes her religious and marital ordeals. Prepared for publication with the help of her third husband, Aaron Ashbridge, to whom she was happily married two years after the death of Sullivan, her autobiography provides not only another conversion narrative but an unusually candid picture of gender relations in eighteenth-century America.

A somewhat different image of a woman recounting her passage through the shifts and alterations of eighteenth-century life is provided by Judith Sergeant Murray. The wife of John Murray, an Englishman who emigrated to America in 1770 and began preaching the doctrine of Universalism, or the possible salvation of all people, Judith Sargent Murray was the author of two plays, a novel, and a variety of prose pieces and poems that were published in two series, The Repository and The Gleaner. It was in the second of these series, which ran in the *Massachusetts Magazine* from 1792 to 1794, that Murray began to take up and explore some of the more pressing issues of late eighteenth-century American life that caught her interest, from the domestic education of children to the creation of a national theater, federalism, and the Universalist gospel. However, what most differentiated Murray from many, though not all, of her female contemporaries was the seriousness with which she took the republican virtues of liberty, patriotism, and, above all, equality. Thus in the most famous of her essays, "On the Equality of the Sexes," published in 1790, she insisted that egalitarianism between the sexes was essential not only to the advancement of women but also to the development of the new republic.

In this conviction Murray had support most particularly from Abigail Adams, the wife of John Adams, who in her case used letters rather than autobiography to explore the meaning of her changing experience. Given Abigail Adams's centrality to the history of the republic, if not to its actual making—it is important to remember that she was the wife of the second president of the United States, the mother of the sixth, the grandmother of the United States minister to Great Britain appointed by Abraham Lincoln who helped prevent the British from siding with the Confederacy, and the great-grandmother of one of the nineteenth century's most distinguished autobiographers, historians, and novelists—Abigail Adams was also a woman of independent intelligence with a first-rate mind who carried on an extensive correspondence, particularly with her husband during the long absences enforced by his years of public service. Her letters, eventually published in two volumes by her grandson Charles Francis Adams, testify both to the loving and spirited relationship that she and her husband enjoyed together and to her deep and thoughtful involvement in the affairs of the emergent republic.

A strong advocate for the reform of consciousness during the Revolutionary era, she often pressed her case with levity and wit as well as determination. Her strongest cause was freedom and equality for women. Referring to the "Code of Laws," or as it has to come to be called, "The United States Constitution," that her husband was then involved in developing, she urged him somewhat whimsically to "Remember the Ladies, and be more generous and favourable to them than your ancestors." But this request carried with it a less than whimsical admonition: "Remember all Men would be tyrants if they could. (If particular care and attention is not paid to the Ladies we are determined to foment a Rebellion, and will not hold ourselves bound by any Laws in which we have no voice, or representation.)" As she pressed still more firmly:

> That your Sex are Naturally Tyrannical is a Truth so thoroughly established as to admit of no dispute, but such of you as wish to be happy willingly give up the harsh title of Master for the more tender and endearing one of Friend. Why then, not put it out of the power of the vicious and the Lawless to use us with cruelty and indignity with impunity. Men of Sense in all Ages abhor those customs which treat us only as the vassals of your Sex. Regard us then as Beings placed by providence under your protection and in imitation of the Supreem Being make use of that power only for our happiness.[8]

Abigail Adams may have thought she was cautioning as well as encouraging her husband, who would one day become the third president of the United States, but like most men of the eighteenth century or perhaps any, once forewarned he was also forearmed. Insisting that he and all husbands were masters in name only, John Adams lightly dismissed his wife's wise counsel with the claim that all husbands were subject "to the Despotism of the Petticoat."[9]

Two other women who found their way to authorship—and, in one case, to considerable literary fame—did so through the novel by trying to awaken what another of the best-selling writers of the period, William Hill Brown, termed in the title of his 1789 novel "the power of sympathy." Susanna Haswell Rowson was to become the more widely recognized of the two. Though born in England, Rowson was raised in America and then returned to England, where she published five novels, including her best-known *Charlotte Temple* in 1791, to little critical acclaim. It was only after she reemigrated to the United States in 1793 and arranged for *Charlotte Temple*'s publication there, that the book, like her career, took off.

Charlotte Temple was but one of ten novels that Rowson produced in a busy writing life—she also produced six theatrical works, two volumes of poetry, six textbooks for her "Young Ladies Academy" in Boston, and a host of songs—and it was phenomenally successful. Quickly becoming the largest-selling book in America before the publication in 1852 of Harriet Beecher Stowe's *Uncle Tom's Cabin, Charlotte Temple* had gone into more than two hundred editions by the twentieth century and still shows no signs of losing its interest. Setting itself the task, like other works in the tradition of sentimental fiction associated with Samuel Richardson's *Clarissa*, published in 1748, of warning its readers about the ways of the world and particularly the wiles of men, it helped create an immense and grateful audience composed primarily of women who discovered in the book's cautionary intent and sympathetic understanding some of the terms of a new and more enlightened sisterhood.

Those terms of sisterhood were if anything deepened by Rowson's compatriot Hannah Webster Foster, in *The Coquette; or, The Life and Letters of Eliza Wharton*, published in 1797. An immediate success, *The Coquette* used the epistolary method first developed by Richardson's earlier novel *Pamela* in 1740. Foster's novel of temptation, seduction, confusion, and death in childbirth was based on the tragedy of a woman from Hartford, Connecticut, named Elizabeth Whitman, a distant cousin of her husband's (a clergyman she was married to for forty-five years and with whom she had six children), whose sad story was well known by the time Foster published her novel. Unlike other sentimental novelists, however, Foster did not moralize her tale by furnishing her heroine with a suitable mate whom she would then reject for a rake. Since both of Eliza's marital choices were unsatisfactory, Foster lifted her story above the tale of a fallen woman who must be made to pay the price of her disgrace by focusing instead on the discovery made by so many women in the eighteenth and nineteenth centuries that, to echo Eliza's lament, "Marriage is the tomb of friendship. It appears to me a very selfish state. Why do people in general, as soon as they are married, centre all their cares, their concerns, and pleasures in their own families? Former acquaintances are neglected or forgotten; the tenderest ties between friends are weakened or dissolved; and benevolence itself moves in a very limited sphere."[10]

Such candor takes considerable courage to exhibit, but it could not have been expressed if there weren't a literary form, in this case the epistolary novel, in which to express it. In fact, literary forms themselves, whether novels, letters, journals, autobiographies, or lyrics, were not only symptoms and signals of a changing era but also its enablers. As imaginative expressions responding to the interests of new female publics while at the same time giving shape to the feelings and identity of those publics, they were themselves the signs of the new world of experience they were helping to create. What was changing in the transit from the seventeenth century to the eighteenth was more than a mood, a style, or an ideology; it was a whole reconfiguration of feeling and imagination that would in time provide the scaffolding for a different sense of self, an alternative way of being.

Altering the Sacred Canopy

Some of the most consequential alterations marking these developments in the realm of ideas had occurred far from America's shores and in most cases long before the beginning of European settlement. Nicolaus Copernicus had already overturned the Ptolemaic notions of the universe that Christopher Columbus had carried in his head to the New World—notions supporting the medieval Christian conviction that the earth and its human inhabitants are at the center of the cosmos—by showing that the earth revolved around the sun rather than the sun revolving around the earth. Galileo Galilei then supported Copernicus's heliocentric theory of the universe by means of his discoveries of the laws of motion and his theories about the need for careful experimentation that can in turn lead to the discovery of new principles. But it was left to Sir Isaac Newton to provide a physical explanation of the unity of Copernicus's heliocentric universe by formulating the universal law of gravitation, which showed that earthly objects and heavenly bodies obeyed the same principle. As Alexander Pope wrote, "Nature and Nature's laws lay hidden in night / God said, 'Let Newton be!' and all was light."

René Descartes had then reinforced these discoveries by maintaining that the one thing incapable of being doubted is the rational capacity of human beings themselves. John Locke had subsequently proposed that our ideas come not from the mind itself, which is supposedly implanted with an image of its Divine Maker, but rather from the impressions derived from the experience of our senses, and had later proceeded to show that this same freedom in the state of nature allows human beings to enter with one another into social contracts whose purpose is to protect such freedom. Adam Smith had already confirmed that, as free agents, individuals are capable of acting in their own self-interest, but added that such self-interest can also contribute to the public good. Baron de Montesquieu had then extended these notions about freedom, consent, and responsibility by explaining that from the point of view of the governed, the best government is one that separates its various powers through the establishment of a system of checks and balances that will serve as the best protection against their various possible abuses.

Ideas such as these helped create an altogether different climate of opinion and feeling in the eighteenth century, a climate of opinion that we have come to associate with the Enlightenment. As a general term, the Enlightenment refers to all those European and American figures in the eighteenth century who had been sufficiently influenced by the scientific and intellectual advances of the seventeenth century to share several general convictions about the nature of reason, the primacy of experience, and the possibility of human progress. The commitment to reason had less to do with a shift toward the rational and empirical—much less, as alleged by some of the Enlightenment's most powerful modern critics,[11] to a trust in instrumental thinking—than with the more general view that one should turn for one's beliefs not to revelation alone, or to religious tradition, or to ecclesiastical authorities, but rather to the human mind itself. The reliance on experience simply meant that if the ultimate source of knowledge could no longer be restricted to scripture, orthodoxy, or instituted authority, then the mind must refocus itself, as Francis Bacon had advised, on everything that lies within the realm of experience itself, from nature and the past to contemporary human experience. But this then transformed the belief in progress from an empty article of faith into a grounded conviction that the critical use of reason on the actual elements of experience can produce improvements, material and otherwise, not only to life itself but also to the conditions on which it depends.[12]

Those who shared these convictions never constituted more than a small minority of primarily learned men, but they were to have an enormous im-

pact both on the reconstitution of intellectual culture in the United States
and also on the shaping of its political, social, and religious institutions.
These individuals were by no means agreed on how to bring about such
changes, much less how respond to them, but they were generally of the
opinion that reflection did not need to abandon entirely the orbit of religious reflection to be answerable to them. For one thing, this was impossible; there was simply too wide a range of Christian practice as well as belief that simply remained untouched by the Enlightenment or would never
be eradicated by it. For another, there was just enough of the metaphysician
in most Enlightenment thinkers to convince them that the only way that
knowledge could contribute to the relief of the human estate was by figur-
ing out how it was related to, and fit together with, some larger coordinated
system of order and meaning. If the conception of such a system, much less
an understanding of it, was somehow beyond them, an imaginative appreciation of what the American poet A. R. Ammons once referred to as the
"Overall," which he thought of as beyond him and most fellow moderns—
"the sum of these events I cannot draw, the ledger I cannot keep, the accounting beyond the account"—was not.[13]

This trace of the metaphysical, or sense of the "Overall," has been wittily
referred to as a "monotheism of the First Person."[14] This monotheism was
premised on the existence of a Creator God who had left evidence of his
intentions in, if nowhere else, the orderly patterns of the book of Nature.
While this book was by no means easy to read, God had not left his creatures
without resources. By endowing them with the capacity to reason, he had
thereby provided them with the potential to discern his will. If no single individual was capable of fathoming the whole of that will, all individuals were
nonetheless in a better position to discern some aspects of it if opinions
concerning that will remained free to circulate in a true republic of ideas.

Little wonder, then, that one of the more interesting religious consequences of this many-sided movement known as the Enlightenment was
the development of a distinctive theological position called Deism. Deism
was less a doctrine or theological system than what Franklin described, for
himself at least, as a kind of creed, and its inner essence was nowhere more
succinctly expressed than in in his *Autobiography*. In delineating what he
deemed to be the essentials of every religion, and what he himself had never
doubted, Franklin confessed to his belief in "the existence of the Deity, that
he made the world and governed it by his providence, that the most acceptable service of God was the doing good to man, that our souls are immor-
tal, and that all crime will be punished, and virtue rewarded, either here or

hereafter."[15] Deism's God, like Franklin's, then, was essentially Newton's God, a divinity who had set in motion his creation but refused to intervene personally in its direction, leaving that to his creatures, who could best fulfill their moral obligation to their creator by their actions toward one another in the assurance that justice will ultimately prevail.

But Franklin went even further. The "doctrine," as he described it, at the heart of his so-called creed went far beyond the substitution of a moral and rational Deity for a righteous and omniscient one; it took morality out of the hands of divinity altogether and put it in the hands of human beings. Of this doctrine Franklin wrote: "Revelation had indeed no weight with me as such, but I entertain'd an Opinion, that tho' certain Actions might not be bad *because* they were forbidden by it, or good *because* it commanded them; yet probably those Actions might be forbidden because they were beneficial to us, in their own Natures, all the Circumstances of things considered."[16] And when Franklin abbreviated this doctrine to the maxim that "vicious actions are not hurtful because they are forbidden, but forbidden because they are hurtful,"[17] he completely distanced himself from the prescriptions of traditional Christianity by grounding such "opinions" on "all the Circumstances of things considered" rather than on scripture or tradition. We know what is morally prohibited or permitted, outlawed or approved, even salutary, not from being told that it is but from having learned from experience that it is, but this was to turn on its head not only the religion of most of the religious in Franklin's age but also of the faithful in the Puritan era.

As different a faith as Deism was at least potentially from both the severe dogmas of the Calvinists and the evangelical confessionalism of the popular revivalists, it suited the purposes of most of the framers of the Constitution. While it still reserved a place for Jesus of Nazareth as the author, or at least the representative, of the best system of morals the world had ever seen, it generally held that this system had suffered various corruptions due to his disciples and later adherents, and it played down the issue of Jesus's divinity. Jefferson actually went so far as to deny that divinity outright and proceeded to write his own version of the Bible—*The Life and Morals of Jesus of Nazareth*—which removed all references to Jesus's miracles and the Resurrection and thus omitted the issue of his deity.[18] Franklin, on the other hand, was more circumspect, arguing as a man of common sense and compromise that the real issue raised by these so-called tenets of belief was not what you meant by them but how you acted on them. Whatever the final truth about such matters as the divinity of Jesus, which Franklin suggested he would learn in due course without much difficulty, he saw no harm in believing such things, as he assured Ezra Styles, the president of Yale College, "if that Belief has the good consequences, as probably it has, of making his Doctrines more respected and better observed; especially as I do not perceive, that the Supreme takes it amiss, by distinguishing the Unbelievers in his Government of the World with any Marks of His Displeasure."[19]

Franklin's ability to set aside an issue as momentous as the divinity of Jesus on the grounds that God was not likely to take exception to those who like Franklin might have reasonable questions about the actual form of God's redemptive plan for the world suggests just how radical the difference potentially was between Deism and Christianity. The difference, however, was no less stylistic than it was theological. For the Puritan or orthodox Christian, the only thing that mattered was the form of the redemptive plan itself, the role that the divinity of Jesus played in making it possible, and how to prepare oneself to submit to its requirements in order to be reborn. For the Deist, on the other hand, the chief thing that mattered was determining which parts of that plan you could accept, how to sort out its useful elements from those less useful, and what to do to assist in its realization.

In this task, Deists and other Enlightenment figures were not without ethical resources, but those resources came from political history as much or more than from religion. Their origins lay in the classical age of the Roman Republic and the writings of Cicero, Tacitus, and Plutarch, who lived in the years of corruption and disorder following its decline. For them that decline could best be understood in contrast to an earlier world of rustic simplicity and pastoral virtue that represented for them an image of the good life, civic morality, and public well-being. Later reworked into a tradition of civic humanism by the Italian Renaissance philosopher Machiavelli, these ideals became a kind of template to define the ideal society and successful politics, both dependent on the independent citizen prepared to devote his service to his country in a disinterested manner. In England this classical republican tradition had been passed on by writers like John Milton and James Harrington who then had a decisive effect on Franklin and other Founders.[20]

What republicanism gave to Deism, and through Deism to the Enlightenment, was an understanding of how best to serve one's fellow man. If Deism was the religious faith that underpinned the broad spiritual mindset or imaginary known as the Enlightenment, republicanism served as its appropriate ethic or code of conduct. Republicanism supplemented the Enlightenment's reliance on critical reason for the relief of the human estate with the belief that the governance of the social and political order will be best served by independent individuals whose worth is based on merit rather than birth and who are willing to sacrifice their own interests for those of the common good. Basing public order not on religious establishments, hereditary privilege, or bureaucratic patronage but rather on the practice of civic virtue was not without obvious risks. Despite competing interests and factions at stake in the creation of a new government, the Founders hoped that republican ideals, along with Enlightened self-criticism and a healthy dose of skepticism about democratic politics, would help contain partisan interests and personal selfishness. While such hopes were eventually to collapse in the early years of the nineteenth century, when the politics of civic virtue gave way to the politics of a more predatory individualism, Franklin nonetheless kept those hopes alive as almost no one else within the revolutionary generation of leaders.

Enlightenment Profiles

Indeed, no figure from the eighteenth century seems quite so thoroughly American as Benjamin Franklin. An apostle of the Protestant work ethic and a precursor of Ralph Waldo Emerson's image of the self-reliant individual, Franklin stands in many ways as the epitome of the self-made man and thus one of the classic American types bequeathed to America by the Enlightenment. But this printer turned businessman, inventor, maxim maker, humorist, scientist, statesman, autobiographer, student of manners, nation builder, and philosopher, whose spectacular financial success permitted him to retire at the age of forty so that he could devote the rest of his life to public service and private intellectual pursuits, was far more various and complex than he is usually credited with being. Yankee entrepreneur, Puritan workaholic, free-thinking Deist, Enlightenment moralist, and experimental scientist—Franklin has been called all these things and much more, but may well have been most himself because of his capacity to elude any simple, or for that matter compound, definition but perhaps that of shapeshifter. In his novel *Israel Potter,* Herman Melville probably came closest to capturing something of the distinctiveness of Franklin by describing him simply as a "Jack of all trades, master of each and mastered by none—the type and genius of this land."

Nowhere was Franklin more himself than in the composite figure he created of himself in his *Autobiography* and in the plan he devised for attempting to arrive at moral perfection and eventually creating a national society for the spread of virtue. That plan itself was a response to a series of challenges he had faced from the age of twelve when he was indentured by his father to an older brother to prevent him from going to sea and then later set off to England to assert his freedom. Though he had already taken steps to improve his writing while he was learning the trade of printer and then of adopting a new mode of self-presentation as "the Humble Doubter and Enquirer," his treacherous treatment by family, friends, and supporters finally convinced him on his return from London of the necessity to devise "a regular plan and design" to regulate "his future Conduct in Life." This plan required him, first, to achieve social acceptance in Philadelphia society, second, to obtain financial independence at an early age so that he might devote the rest of his life to public service, and third, "to acquire the Habitude of all . . . Virtues" he considered essential to happiness. While this last part of Franklin's plan failed of success because of his inability to acquire the habit of the last of these virtues, namely, humility, it also produced other plans, the most important of which was the creation of book entitled "The Art of Virtue" that would help found and direct an international "party of virtue." But this plan, too, failed to be accomplished, forcing him to settle instead for a substitute, which turned out to be the completion of his *Autobiography,* written in four installments over thirty years.

But Franklin's greatest achievement may have been one that he hadn't planned for even if it was perfectly consistent with his character. It occurred at the Constitutional Convention in Philadelphia at the very close of debate on its final day. There was fear that some of the delegates who had proposed earlier measures and been defeated might refuse to sign the document and thus prevent it from being ratified by the states. At this point Franklin was asked to speak on behalf of unity and managed to secure the necessary support by appealing not to his confederates' principles as much as to their wisdom and common sense. Admitting his own disapproval of some of the Constitution's provisions, he nonetheless added that experience had taught him that one's opinions can sometimes be changed on the basis of new information, that it is impossible in any case to obtain complete agreement in the face of so many different opinions, that it was unlikely in the face of these differences to achieve complete unanimity of opinion, that the success of the document depended as much on its administration as on the consensus it reflected, and that thus it might and should be approved if any who still harbored objections would join with him in doubting at least a little the infallibility of their own judgment. His argument, in short, was in accordance with his own principles, and his own principles assured him that the

science of government, like the science of life, required a measure of compromise and the humility that had heretofore eluded him.

Such reasoning, pragmatic and principled at the same time, would have
been harder for Thomas Paine to accept. Another enormously important
but more fiery member of the revolutionary generation, Paine's emigration
from England to America in 1774 had occurred only because of Franklin's
assistance; he had become impressed by Paine's knowledge and interests
and believed that his pen could be useful to the struggle for independence.
A political pamphleteer best known for his broadsides against tyranny and
oppression—*Common Sense* sold almost a half million copies and encouraged American rebellion—Paine's argumentative style, together with his
outspoken social and religious views, frequently got him into trouble with
authorities in England and France as well as in America. Barely escaping
arrest for treason in England when the first part of his *The Rights of Man*
was published in 1790, he was eventually imprisoned in France and narrowly escaped execution by the guillotine before his release at the time of
Robespierre's fall. Returning to an America that by this time had grown far
more conservative after the Revolution and the constitutional crisis as it
attempted to consolidate the gains of independence, Paine quickly found
himself forsaken by most of his former friends and admirers and died in
poverty. While John Adams could remark of Paine in 1805 that "I know not
whether any man in the world has had more influence on its inhabitants or
affairs for the last thirty years than Tom Paine," he was regarded by many
of his contemporaries as, in the words of one of them, "a loathsome rep-
tile," and his reputation was to continue to suffer from the general opinion voiced a century later by Theodore Roosevelt that he was "a filthy little
atheist."

As it happens, nothing could have been further from the truth, or less
fair to the breadth of Paine's mind. As he stated in *The Age of Reason*, his
great work in defense of Deism in 1797, he found the most compelling argument for the existence of God "in the immensity of the creation" and "the
unchangeable order by which the incomprehensible whole is governed." As
he later added in *Of the Religion of Deism Compared with the Christian Religion, and the Superiority of the Former Over the Latter* in 1804, "Every person, of whatever religious denomination he may be, is a Deist in the first
article of his Creed. . . . Whenever we step aside of this article, by mixing
it with articles of human invention," Paine added in agreement with many
others of this persuasion, "we wander into a labyrinth of uncertainty and

fable, and become exposed to every kind of imposition by pretenders to revelation."[21]

Words such as these could have easily won assent from almost all of the Founding Fathers, though Paine was not averse to carrying his Deist critique much further still by denying as contrary to the laws of reason most of the major doctrines of the Christian faith, from the Virgin Birth and other miracles to the resurrection of Jesus and the notion of the Holy Trinity. Such views were to bound to arouse deep anger on the part of Americans who had not lost their Christian faith, but these were some of the same Americans who years earlier had been stirred so deeply when Paine concluded the introduction to *Common Sense* with words of defiance and solidarity:

> The cause of America is in great measure the cause of all mankind. Many circumstances have, and will arise, which are not local, but universal, and through which the principles of all lovers of mankind are affected, and in the event of which their affections are interested. The laying a country desolate with fire and sword, declaring war against the natural rights of all mankind, and extirpating the defenders thereof from the face of the earth, is the concern of every man to whom nature has given the power of feeling; of which class, regardless of party censure, is THE AUTHOR.[22]

They would have been even more offended with the sentiments expressed in Paine's equally courageous and outspoken "Occasional Letter on the Female Sex," published in 1775. Here, as in so much of his polemical and political writing, Paine was simply carrying forward his underlying conviction that while true emancipation must begin with liberation from repressive institutions, it can only be completed by liberation from repressive ideas.

Jefferson couldn't have agreed more and underlined his reasons why in "An Act for Establishing Religious Freedom in the State of Virginia" (1776), which he regarded as one of the three most important public acts he performed in his life (the other two being the drafting of the Declaration of Independence and the founding of the University of Virginia at Charlottesville). Believing that God had created the mind free and that all attempts to influence it by force tend to encourage hypocrisy and meanness, Jefferson was convinced that truth would prevail only if left to itself. But he was also persuaded that truth could do so only if it were not disarmed of the natural weapons of free inquiry and debate that provide it with the surest defense against error. Hence his plea that all men should be free to profess and maintain their own opinions in matters of opinion without risk to their civil rights.

Yet it was in his draft of the Declaration of Independence that Jefferson inscribed the Deist faith into the very body of American public culture and life. When he wrote of the truths that are self-evident—"that all men are created equal; that they are endowed by their Creator with certain [inherent and] inalienable rights; that among these are life, liberty, and the pursuit of happiness"[23]—he in effect made political Deists of all Americans. More to the point, he placed Deism in support of a revolutionary movement that would subsequently broaden the possibilities for literary as well as political expression in the republic soon to emerge, and eventually, but only after nearly a century and a half of political pressure and protest, begin more aggressively to open the world even more widely, to the thinking and writing of women and various minorities of other kinds.

Surely no document besides the Constitution of the United States and the attendant Bill of Rights has been more important in American history than the Declaration of Independence; nor has any set out more clearly and succinctly the social, ethical, and religious views of the Founding Fathers. In its defense of the Lockean idea that a sovereign people may overthrow any government that systematically deprives them of their inalienable rights as human beings, the Declaration bases its argument on an escalating series of offenses committed by the British Crown. The offenses culminate (at least in the original version authored by Jefferson and included in his *Autobiography*) with the outrage perpetrated against all humanity through the Crown's promotion of, and participation in, the traffic of slaves. If there is no small irony in the fact that the author of this clause was himself the owner of nearly three hundred slaves and the father of a number of slave children, there is also no little irony in the fact that this last and most serious charge brought against the English king, the indictment that seals the case for declaring independence, had to be removed from the document's final draft because of objections raised by the two southern colonies of South Carolina and Jefferson's own Virginia.

Toward the Republic and New Literary Spaces

The steps leading to the creation of the republic to which the Declaration pointed were manifold and diverse. They began with the collapse of the Albany Plan of Union drafted by Benjamin Franklin in 1754 and designed to give the various colonies representation in a union whose president was to be appointed by the Crown. They then led to the French and Indian War of 1755–63, which was fought for control of the American continent and resulted in England's acquisition of the whole of Canada and the upper Mississippi valley. They would then proceed to the Stamp Act Crisis of 1765, which, just as the Boston Tea Party in 1773 was precipitated by the taxation of tea, resulted from England's need for funds to support its enormous American empire. From there they would move to the call for the first Continental Congress in Philadelphia in 1774, which issued a Declaration of Rights and Grievances; then on to the outbreak of conflict between the British regiments and American irregulars on the green at Lexington, Massachusetts, in 1775; next to the second Continental Congress of 1776, where a draft of the Declaration of Independence was prepared and approved on July 4; and finally to the Revolutionary War itself, which lasted from 1776 to 1783. When the war concluded, there was still to be drafted a constitution to replace the loosely applied Articles of Confederation, which had held the country together since 1781; and once this was completed at the Philadelphia convention of 1787, then the debate over the Constitution could begin, with most of its important points being argued in the eighty-five papers of *The Federalist* (1787–88), authored by Alexander Hamilton, James Madison, and John Jay, which were first published as letters to the New York *Independent Journal, Packet, and Daily Advertiser.*

These three Federalists—Hamilton is known to have written fifty-one papers, Madison fifteen, and Jay at least five (the rest were written by Hamilton or Madison or the two together)—signed themselves as "Publius" and argued for the importance of a central government with checks and balances because they feared the possibilities of factionalism and demagoguery. They were opposed by Anti-Federalists like Patrick Henry and George Mason, who were convinced that a strong federal government with no limits on the reelectability of the president would threaten the powers and rights of individual states. Strong objection to the ratification of the Constitution was also registered by those concerned about the absence of a bill of rights guaranteeing specific freedoms of religion, of speech, of the press, of assembly, of trial by jury, and others. With the assistance of the lucid, powerful arguments of the eighty-five essays that make up the *Federalist Papers,* the required nine colonies approved the Constitution by June 1788, and most of the rest expressed a willingness to grant provisional approval if a bill of rights was adopted. The Bill of Rights was created as the first ten amendments to the Constitution and was accepted by the last colony of Rhode Island in 1791.

During this momentous period, almost all of the literature of the late eighteenth century was produced, and a considerable portion of it played a crucial role in forwarding its motion. But it would be a mistake to suppose that the literature specifically created in response to historical forces constituted the only significant writing in the era of the early Republic. In addition to writing that recorded or in some manner served these events, there was a large body of expression that either responded to various and sundry of their meanings or that moved into the new personal as well as public spaces cleared by them. Three writers who sought to stake out some of the new territories of the imagination to which the new republic promised to afford them access were Philip Freneau, Phillis Wheatley, and Olaudah Equiano. But Freneau, Wheatley, and Equiano were, in distinctive ways, each a special case. They were special cases both because they were transitional and also because they were symptomatic. They were transitional in the sense that they were caught in the coils of a new order now struggling to establish itself in service to a new republic that needed to become more receptive and responsive to the narratives of all its prospective citizens. But they were symptomatic of the difficulties that many of those prospective citizens would suffer because of what the rhetoric of the Enlightenment was still covering up, leaving out, or disguising.

Take, for example, Philip Freneau. In literary terms a precursor of the nineteenth-century Romantics as well as a skillful satirist of British folly; in political terms an ardent Anti-Federalist and Jeffersonian described by Yale's president Timothy Dwight as a "mere incendiary, or rather as a despicable tool of bigger incendiaries" and dismissed by George Washington simply as "that rascal Freneau," Freneau was in biographical terms an early version of Ralph Waldo Emerson's "American scholar seeking to find an appropriate intellectual vocation in an age moving too fast for him to quite manage to define himself. Starting out after college as a teacher; turning to poetry at the outbreak of the Revolution; quickly shifting to the role of personal secretary to a prominent planter in the West Indies after discovering that poetry did not pay; getting captured by the British, not once but twice, before being exchanged on the point of death as a prisoner of war; then taking to the sea for six years as master of a small brig; upon his return to America marrying and assuming the editorship of several short-lived magazines, during which time he also held a minor government appointment as a translating clerk in the State Department; subsequently being driven by poverty to return to sea as a master of coastal freighters, all the while writing no less than five volumes of poetry during his lifetime, Freneau was a writer whose large and varied talent, despite the attention it attracted in its time, always remained somehow homeless in his world. Frustrated at almost every turn in his career, Freneau found in poetry not only a kind of consolation for his troubles but also a place to wait out the death of one age and the beginning of another.

Wheatley's career was even more poignant. Brought to America as a slave at the age of seven and sold to a wealthy tailor from Boston named John Wheatley, her precocious intelligence was almost immediately recognized by Wheatley's wife, Susanna, who, in addition to encouraging Phillis's voracious appetite for education, began to treat her as a virtual member of the family. Under such circumstances, it took very little time for Wheatley's literary gifts to display themselves. Reading some of the most difficult passages of the Bible within sixteen months and English as well as ancient classics soon thereafter, she published her first poem by the time she was thirteen and became an author by the age of nineteen, when her *Poems on Various Subjects, Religious and Moral* appeared in London in 1773, attributed on the title page to "Phillis Wheatley, Negro Servant to Mr. John Wheatley." So remarkable an identification by an author of a book of poems written in the prevailing Augustan mode required, before it could be accepted for publication, the prefatory testimony of no less than eighteen distinguished white citizens, including the governor of Massachusetts and John Hancock, merely to certify that these poems in fact "were written by Phillis . . . who was but a few years since, brought an uncultivated barbarian from Africa."

Notwithstanding Thomas Jefferson's cruel dismissal of her verse, Phillis Wheatley's achievement was, and remains, no less than astonishing, inasmuch as we can still hear in the cadence of her lines, despite their stylistic idiom, what the modern African American novelist Richard Wright once described as "the hope of freedom in the New World."[24] But recognition of her achievement was sadly short-lived. Sent to England to meet her patron, the Countess of Huntingdon, and to receive the attentions of an extremely admiring and more enlightened literary public than the one in which she had so remarkably come of age, she was immediately called back to America to attend her dying mistress. And even though she received her freedom when the Wheatleys died and went on to marry a free black man named John Peters, two of her three children preceded her in death, her husband turned out to be a business failure, and her last years as America's first female African American poet were spent in poverty and complete obscurity.

America's first male African American writer of note emerged from almost more daunting experiences but eventually achieved greater literary recognition. Oloudah Equiano was a young African kidnapped into slavery at the age of eleven who, upon his arrival in the New World, was fortunate enough to be purchased by a British sea captain and placed in service at sea. Having survived all the horrors of the Atlantic slave trade, which included, as for virtually all its victims, violent capture in his native village and separation from his family, brutal removal from the interior of the continent to the coast to await transshipment across the Atlantic, and then the hellish sea voyage at the hands of vicious and indifferent whites whose skin color alone left him terrified, Equiano managed to escape some of the depredations that awaited all slaves destined for the plantations and, through his extensive subsequent travels, was able to acquire a sense of a wider world. Within ten years he was able in 1766 to earn enough money to purchase his freedom, but he decided to remain at sea for the next twenty years, where he eventually wound up assisting in the transport of slaves himself, for which he was later sharply criticized. In time, however, he was persuaded by abolitionist agitation in Parliament to join the antislavery cause and in partial contribution to it composed his two-volume autobiography, published in 1789, entitled *The Interesting Narrative of the Life of Olaudah Equiano, or Gustavus Vasa, the African, Written by Himself.*

Equiano's *Narrative* found an immediate and admiring audience that included among others John Wesley, the founder of Methodism, who asked that this book be read to him on his deathbed. A precursor of slave narratives of the nineteenth century like *The Narrative of the Life of Frederick Douglass*, published in 1845, which became, along with his other work and writings, a major influence in the abolitionist movement as well as the movement for women's rights, and Harriet Jacobs's later *Incidents in the Life of a Slave Girl, Written By Herself*, which appeared in 1861 and first brought the sexual abuse of slave women out into public view, Equiano's work also draws on the rich tradition of spiritual autobiography that descends from the Puritan era.

At the end of the eighteenth century, then, American literature is still far from having achieved, if it ever has except intermittently, a distinctive set of voices that were in various ways answerable to one another. But many of the notes of freedom, liberty, human dignity, and inalienable rights that would eventually give American writing wider and deeper resonance had already been struck. In the coming decades, what can already be heard in the pitch and tone of early American writing was to gravitate to an even richer, more rebarbative timbre—many of the basic patterns of assonance and dissonance, of leitmotif and counterpoint, were by now distinctly in evidence and impressively varied—but only as they undertook during the nineteenth century, and in the face of altogether different representational challenges, a pragmatist turn. What precipitated that turn, and what had to be overthrown as a consequence, was nothing short of a set of spiritual co-ordinates that had defined experience in America up to this point, and what had to be discovered was an altogether different set of intellectual and spiritual algorithms to make sense of it. Religious dogma had been compelled to give up some of the assurances of belief to the deliverances of reason, and the deliverances of reason, in turn, were about to be compelled to learn that they must be refashioned, adapted, and revised to adjust to the changing contours of the experience of, and not just in, America. How American writing negotiated this transition in the nineteenth century is the subject of the following chapter.

FOUR

The Pragmatist Refiguration
of American Narratives

Worlds Being Shattered

No one foresaw more clearly the way the coordinates of experience at the end of the eighteenth century were to be transformed by the beginning of the twentieth than the Enlightenment's last great representative in the nineteenth century. That figure was the author of *The Education of Henry Adams,* who, in the book he pointedly refused to refer to as his autobiography, forced his readers to contemplate something far more shattering than the discovery that an eighteenth-century education, however painstakingly acquired and brilliantly adapted, no longer prepared a person to live a life of useful and productive service at the end of the nineteenth century. What breaks Adams's historical neck at the Great Exposition of 1900 in Paris as he looks up at the forty-foot dynamos in the Gallery of Machines is the discovery of "an irruption of forces totally new" that plunges him into what one of his later chapters calls "an abyss of ignorance." What was once a carefully ordered universe has now become a haphazard and chaotic multiverse, and when Adams tries to imagine what kind of education would prepare one to negotiate with this New World, much less, like his Puritan and Enlightenment forebears, to reform or reconstruct it, he is confounded:

He found himself in a land where no one had ever penetrated before; where order was an accidental relation obnoxious to nature; artificial compulsion imposed on motion; against which every free energy of the universe revolted; and which, being merely occasional, resolved itself back into anarchy at last. He could not deny that the law of the new multiverse explained much that had been most obscure, especially the persistently fiendish treatment of man by man; the perpetual effort of society to establish law, and the perpetual revolt of society against the law it had established; the perpetual building up of authority by force, and the perpetual appeal to force to overthrow it; the perpetual symbolism of a higher law, and the perpetual relapse to a lower one; the perpetual victory of the principles of freedom, and their perpetual conversion into principles of power; but the staggering problem was the outlook ahead into the despotism of artificial order which nature abhorred. The physicists had a phrase for it, unintelligible to the vulgar: "All that we win is a battle—lost in advance—with the irreversible phenomena in the background of nature."[1]

The problem for Adams was not simply that the constellation of ideas had changed, or that a new grammar of motives for managing it had been introduced; the real rupture had occurred in the idiom of experience itself and the kinds of moral and spiritual calculus required to measure its consequences. In scientific parlance, this amounted to a paradigm change, in religious terms to a revolution in spiritual algorithms. For Adams, however, the question of what to call it was less disturbing than the issue of what to make of it. The only analogue he could imagine to the cataclysmic changes foreshadowed in 1900 was the year 310, when the emperor Constantine began to establish Christianity as the official religion of the Roman Empire. For Adams, then, all the former intellectual and ethical conceits about life's predictability and beneficence had been rendered impotent after 1900, and much of American writing since has been an attempt to register the experiential meanings of this change that Adams was the first to describe and to devise strategies for coming to terms with it.[2]

A world so completely organized around and dominated by force, power, and sheer potency is a world that is no longer susceptible to understanding in terms of such Enlightenment values as balance, reasonableness, adaptation, freedom, skepticism, happiness, autonomy, optimism, and modulation. It is a world comprehensible more frequently in terms of religious myths of catastrophe, of metaphysical narratives of rupture, division, disinheritance, and destruction. As a consequence, the Enlightenment would seem to have become by the nineteenth and twentieth centuries the absent, or at least the forgotten, integer in the American equation of the relationship between faith and knowledge. Even where American writers retained an interest in characters who seem to have their origination in the quest for what William Ellery Channing, the leader of American Unitarianism, referred to in his 1830 Election Day sermon as "spiritual freedom," they were inclined to treat this essentially Enlightenment ideal ironically.[3] Thus the characters who aspire to it but then experience the mind's inability to achieve it—the list begins with Cooper's Leatherstocking and passes on to Poe's Roderick Usher, Hawthorne's Robin Molineux, Melville's Ishmael, Mark Twain's Huckleberry Finn, Hemingway's Jake Barnes, Fitzgerald's Jay Gatsby, Faulkner's Quentin Compson III, and Robert Penn Warren's Jack Burden—all attest to the literary questioning of the Enlightenment paradigm.

The Unitarian Moment and Its Transcendentalist Challenge

That paradigm was still available religiously at the beginning of the nineteenth century in the creation of American Unitarianism. While Unitarianism itself was born several centuries earlier almost simultaneously in Poland and Transylvania, its American expression centered on Boston and grew out of an attempt toward the end of the eighteenth century to liberalize Congregational Christianity and at the same time create a spiritual home for people influenced by Deism. Premised on the assumption, as Channing stated in another of his sermons, "Unitarian Christianity," that the Bible is "a book written for men, in the language of men" whose "meaning is to be sought in the same manner as that of other books," Channing refused to privilege divine revelation over human rationality and repudiated—like those of the same persuasion before him, such as James Freeman, Joseph Stevens Buckminster, and the more impressive Henry Ware, who became Hollis Professor of Divinity at Harvard College in 1805—the Trinitarian notion that God had actually expressed himself in what was referred as three persons in the form of the Father, the Son, and the Holy Ghost. Basing itself exclusively on God's oneness or unity of identity, Unitarianism followed Deism by honoring the moral authority of Jesus without accepting his divinity and by insisting that if human nature is not inherently depraved, faith in God is not incompatible with the use of reason, the development of science, or the exploration of human rights.

Such beliefs were soon to be combined with a moderate dose of the new Romantic spirit that began making its way across the Atlantic after the turn of the century. This was a Romanticism inspired by feelings released by the French Revolution even more than the American and centered on the new visionary prospects it opened up for the progressive improvement of humankind. Such sentiments were in time to produce a new spiritual orthodoxy with literary as well as religious pretensions that would eventually prove determinative for poets of the early nineteenth century like Oliver Wendell Holmes, James Russell Lowell, and Henry Wadsworth Longfellow. But its synthesis of piety, reasonableness, and intuition, which allowed Unitarianism to function as a kind of middle way between the Enlightenment and Christian orthodoxy, was soon to be challenged by a religious movement associated with Concord rather than Boston. This was a religious movement that sought to replace Unitarianism's reliance on scripture, reason, and common sense as the guides to truth with a more Romantic conviction that human beings are capable of an unmediated relation with the Divine. The name of this new religious perspective was Transcendentalism, and by the mid-1830s its chief literary, if not religious, spokesman had become Ralph Waldo Emerson.

If Transcendentalism started out as a family quarrel within Unitarianism, it would quickly become in Emerson's hands something else that soon included Henry David Thoreau, Bronson Alcott, and, for a time, Margaret Fuller before eventually spreading out to influence a large number of other midcentury writers, from Nathaniel Hawthorne and Herman Melville to Walt Whitman and Emily Dickinson. Emerson set the tone for the new movement by declaring in his first book, entitled *Nature*, published in 1836, that there are no questions human beings can ask that are unanswerable, because the perfection of creation guarantees that any curiosity "the order of things has awakened in our minds, the order of things can satisfy." Therefore Emerson reasoned: "Every man's condition is a solution in hieroglyphic to those inquiries he would put."[4] This belief was confirmed for Emerson by the ecstasy he had experienced for himself when he opened himself up to Nature's influences. It was an experience of "the perpetual presence of the sublime" that he described in negative terms as the disappearance of "all mean egotism" and in positive terms as his transformation into a kind of "transparent eyeball" where he has become nothing but sees all—"the currents of Universal Being circulate through me; I am part and parcel of God."[5] Such "perfect exhilaration," as he called it, which left him feeling "that nothing can befall me in life—no disgrace, no calamity (leaving me my eyes) which Nature cannot repair"—would, in later years, have to be tempered, if not entirely abandoned, as less optimistic essays like "Experience" and "Fate" clearly attest, but Emerson's early conviction that if we are capable of fully opening ourselves to Nature, life stands ready to answer our demands on it, that the facts of existence shall justify our experience of existence, nonetheless fired the imagination of whole series of nineteenth- and twentieth-century authors who would follow him. Whether everything that exists, as Emerson had convinced himself early on, has its analogue in the mind, the mind in its creative form as the imagination, Emerson continued to believe, holds the key to understanding all that can be.

Thus when Emerson broke sharply with the Unitarians and the Deists in his Harvard "Divinity School Address" three years after the publication of *Nature,* it was not over the relative place of belief and reason in the definition of experience but rather over the place of experience as the abode of the spirit in the redefinition of reason and belief. Few of his religious or literary descendants would speak in his voice, but almost all would have to conjure with its echo as they worked out their own relation to faith, thought, and experience. Emerson's radicality lay not so much in his doctrines as in his outlook. Even as his assumptions about the congruence between the mind of human beings and the nature of Being were forced to change, Emerson never gave up his call, in terms reminiscent of Jonathan Edwards, for a new kind of consent to Being itself, one that ultimately trusts in nothing other than the revelations of experience alone when the Soul has become reunited with its spiritual source. But this would in time do something both to the understanding of experience itself and also to the issue about how its meanings might be rendered intelligible, legible, interpretable.

Thus when nineteenth-century American writing finally got around to framing a narrative about post-Enlightenment spiritual experience, the traditional way of telling the story was to leave the Enlightenment, whether conceived as a historical project or as a set of principles, pretty well out of it and to treat religion instead not as a constellation of ideas and practices but as an attribute of the imagination and an aspect of form. Religion thus becomes associated with a quality of mind obsessed with moral oppositions and suspicious of thematic closure, indeed, skeptical of all metanarratives— a mind that characteristically tends to explore extreme ranges of experience and to rest in dichotomous, often conflicting or contradictory, frames of thought. Far from seeking through Christian strategies of redemptive catharsis to reconcile division and dissonance, the American literary imagination, both male and female, so this narrative of post-Enlightenment literature goes, concentrated its most important energies on exploring the aesthetic and even religious possibility of forms of alienation and disorder, and often in morally equivocal ways.[6] Hence even in a standard work like *The Scarlet Letter,* where transgression and repentance, autonomy and submission, and freedom and servitude constitute the principal poles between which much of the action oscillates, the novel resists all impulses toward intellectual or spiritual resolution by terminating, finally, in an image of tragic separation. While Hester and Dimmesdale both remain true to one another, their fidelity merely succeeds in condemning them to opposite or, at the very least, apposite ways of being.

The Romantic Male Narrative of Liberal Self-Revisioning

The customary way of reading the religious meaning of nineteenth- and twentieth-century literature has consequently gone something like this. If the representative American literary imagination displays characteristics that are undeniably Manichaean, these internal divisions have resulted not from its absorption with the predicament of human iniquity and its transcendence, nor with the problem of sexual domination and its displacement. They have derived instead from writers' preoccupation with the problem of human freedom and the impediments to its realization. When this preoccupation has taken narrative form, it has typically produced narratives that diverge sharply from the traditional pattern of the Protestant story about repentance and possible regeneration through faith, even when they use many of its presiding symbols, for the sake of telling a different tale about the limitations of selfhood and their heuristic value. This is a narrative, then, that turns on a dialectic that makes only the faintest gesture backward in the direction of the Enlightenment's ideology of mediated freedom before attempting to reconcile a later Romantic or Transcendentalist quest for unmediated being with the residue of an earlier Puritan, or at any rate Protestant, sense of human iniquity and the need for self-abasement.

The religious essence of this story is predicated on "an abiding dream . . . that an unpatterned, unconditioned life is possible in which your moments of stillness, choices and repudiations are all your own."[7] This is what, for example, Henry James's Isabel Archer seems to express when, in *The Portrait of a Lady,* she confesses that "nothing that belongs to me is any measure of me, everything, on the contrary, is a limit and a perfectly arbitrary one."[8] It is the same conviction that in William Faulkner's *Absalom, Absalom!* solidifies Thomas Sutpen's desire to wrest a house and a dynasty from a hundred square miles of Mississippi wilderness, as though, like the central figures in F. Scott Fitzgerald's *The Great Gatsby* or Walt Whitman's "Song of Myself," he was born of some Platonic conception in his own mind. It is the dream of an individual who, like Herman Melville's Captain Ahab in *Moby-Dick,* would be "free as the air" but discovers that "he is down in all the world's books."[9]

The corollary to this Romantic dream amounts to a correspondent and not un-Calvinist dread "that someone else is patterning your life, that there are all sorts of invisible plots afoot to rob you of your autonomy of thought and action, that conditioning is ubiquitous."[10] Thus Hawthorne again, in Chillingworth's self-excusing confession to Hester: "My old faith, long forgotten, comes back to me, and explains all that we do and all that we suffer.

By thy first step awry, thou didst plant the germ of evil; but, since that moment, it has all been a dark necessity."[11] Or the narrator in Faulkner's *Light in August,* who tends to view Joe Christmas and Percy Grimm as pawns on a chessboard drawn ever closer to their fated confrontation with an invisible Player, and the chief moral difference between individuals revolves around who, like the character Byron Bunch, is willing to pay the bill when it comes around.

The traditional nineteenth-century strategy for dealing with this predicament and narratively encompassing it is to submit the dreamer to the dread in order to determine what, if anything, he or she can learn from the experience. But because this experiment in what might be called liberal self-revisioning typically takes place in idyllic natural surroundings not only set at some distance from the domestic world of women and children but also in the company of ideal "others" whose moral and spiritual attributes simply mirror values that their protagonists long to acquire even when such values can nowhere be socially applied, it has long been criticized as dangerously antinomian and imperialistic by some critics and as a "melodrama of beset manhood" by others.[12]

The Romantic Female Counter-Narrative of Domestic Soteriology

We now know, of course, that this way of constructing and reading the story of nineteenth-century American literature and its relation to religion, and particularly to Protestant Christianity, isn't quite accurate, or, at any rate, doesn't constitute the whole story. Owing largely to the work of numerous feminist critics from the 1980s to the present, we know, for example, that Protestant orthodoxy of a certain kind has played a much more active role in the formation of at least some post-Enlightenment literature than was formerly acknowledged, and that within this literature it has proved as vital a force for cultural criticism and social renewal as the revisionary liberalism associated with many of the writers of the male canon. Interestingly enough, the reinstatement of Protestant religious orthodoxy in this feminist counter-narrative to the more canonical male story has been secured chiefly at the expense of more or less completely discrediting the Enlightenment altogether.

The feminist counter-narrative construes the Enlightenment, and particularly its stereotypical attitudes toward reason, nature, gender, liberty, and the realm of the personal and the intimate, as expressions of a patriarchal structure characteristic of much revolutionary and postrevolutionary society that had to be challenged, and in considerable measure displaced, if women were to be sufficiently liberated, not to say empowered, to assume something like a position of equality within the economy of human affairs. The instrument of their empowerment in this counter-narrative turns out to be the religion of early nineteenth-century Protestantism once its redemptive energies were released in the evangelical enthusiasm of the Second Great Awakening. These energies helped legitimate a new sentimentalization of American piety that resituated the institutions of the family at the center of American society and redefined motherhood, and the rituals of child rearing and homemaking, as central elements in this new version of the American story.

This version finds abundant exemplification in the antebellum soteriology of sentimental novels ranging from Rowson's *Charlotte Temple* and Foster's *The Coquette,* as previously mentioned, to Catherine Sedgwick's *Hope Leslie* and Susan Warner's *The Wide, Wide World,* and it achieves a kind of consummation in Harriet Beecher Stowe's *Uncle Tom's Cabin.*[13] Here Christian self-sacrifice—Little Eva's no less than Uncle Tom's—performs, at least for women, an invaluable kind of cultural work whose subtly dialectical patterns of critique and recovery, of repudiation and resurrection, animate as well such later works as Elizabeth Stoddard's *The Morgesons,* Kate Chopin's *The Awakening,* and Sarah Orne Jewett's *The Country of the Pointed Firs.* This is a literature that explicitly in some cases, implicitly in others, questions the prevailing image of America as dominated by upper-class white males who use the instruments of rationality, freedom, autonomy, common sense, and civic responsibility to consolidate their power over women. Instead, this writing by women seeks to replace that image with a less patriarchal one that views society as a kind of family held together by the sacrificial action of women whose heroic submission to the procreative and nurturing responsibilities of the household can, and should be, interpreted as a symbol of strength rather than weakness—a symbol with the power to transform the family into a source of moral and spiritual rebirth for society as a whole.

According to some critics, however, this feminist counter-narrative never quite manages to escape the pull of the masculine, and thus of the Enlightenment, values that it would repudiate. Even if the piety of a Little Eva eludes the charge that Christianity in *Uncle Tom's Cabin,* like religion in the sentimental novel generally, runs the risk of functioning for its readers as "camp," as a form of narcissistic nostalgic,[14] the counter-narrative itself never quite succeeds in freeing women from the culture of men. By politicizing the culture of sentimentality, it merely reinscribes the values of white, male individuality, and the ideology of dominance it supports, in the religious sensibility of women.

This becomes clear when one compares the writings of women in the Northeast with those from the South. As it turns out, many female writers, both African American and white, were made as uncomfortable by prevailing models of womanhood—particularly if those models sought to resegregate women in a gendered ghetto of religious sensibility isolated from the world of men—as they were by the images that men were trying to impose on them. No less assiduous than their Northern counterparts in exploring their own identity and independence, these Southern writers nonetheless were just as emphatically opposed to "the northeastern model of individualism"—Augusta Jane Evans's spectacularly popular *Beulah* is a particularly good example of this—"and celebrated woman's acceptance of her proper role within marriage and, above all, her willing subordination to God who guaranteed any worthy social order."[15]

Thus if empowerment is what many southern women sought, they did not find it either by dissociating themselves from the world of men or by repudiating the dominant culture that men had created to maintain, through religious and secular values, their control over women. Rather, they achieved it primarily by using that cultural world for their own purposes:

> Women and African-Americans, including African-American women, have developed their own ways of criticizing the attitudes and institutions that hedged them in. Confronted with rigidly class-, race-, and gender-specific models of acceptability, they have manipulated the language to speak in a double tongue, simultaneously associating themselves with and distancing themselves from the dominant models of respectability. Their continuous negotiation with the possibilities that the culture has afforded them has had nothing to do with a mindless acceptance of themselves as lesser. It has had everything to do with their determination to translate the traditions and values of their own communities into a language that would make them visible to others—and with their own determination to participate in American culture.[16]

African American Slave Narratives and Double Standards: Frederick Douglass and Harriet Jacobs

In no midcentury literary texts was the "determination to translate the traditions and values of their own communities into a language that would make them visible to others" more critical, or the need to speak in a double tongue more necessary, than in African American slave narratives. A form of writing whose mere composition, let alone publication, often put its authors in grave danger even after they were freed, slave narratives demonstrated how easily the appeal to religion and reason could be used to mask or legitimate both racial and sexual exploitation. Drawing on elements from Christian as well as Enlightenment traditions, they revealed what such bigotry actually looked and felt like when mirrored in the experience of those victimized by it.

Among male slave narratives, none is more famous than the *Narrative of the Life of Frederick Douglass* because it established many of the terms of the entire genre. Born into slavery in Maryland around 1817, in 1838 Douglass escaped to Massachusetts, where he married almost immediately, took a new name, and eventually became a well-known lecturer for antislavery societies. Yet during the early years of his escape from slavery to Massachusetts, he was in constant fear of recapture because of the Dred Scott Decision (in which the U.S. Supreme Court decided that no people of African ancestry, whether slave or free, could become citizens of the United States or sue in federal court), and was eventually forced to flee to England and then Ireland before being able to return to the United States to purchase his freedom. Once emancipated, Douglass established his antislavery newspaper, the *North Star,* which played an important role in the Abolitionist movement, lent his support to the parallel creation of the American women's movement, organized two regiments of black soldiers during the Civil War, and then served in a variety of political capacities that eventually led to his appointment as minister to Haiti from 1889 to 1891.

Such public achievements were, and remain, nothing short of astonishing, particularly when set against the background of the experience that, according to the *Narrative,* defined his youth. This was the trauma as a small child of witnessing his Aunt Hester being flogged. Interpreting this later as the experience that initiated him into the living hell of slavery, it also served as the gateway into Douglass's understanding of the depravity of those who justified such actions in the name both of religion and of reason. While he was able to escape this hell temporarily at the age of eight, when he was sent to live with what appeared to be a less racist couple, he was soon plunged back into it when his mistress's attempts to teach him to read and write were summarily terminated because of her husband's fear of creating a literate slave.

During the middle chapters of the *Narrative,* Douglass discovers the hypocrisy of his Christian slaveholders, who disguise their cruelty and debauchery with professions of piety. But this period of darkness in his life gets still worse when his new owner decides to rent him out for a year to another farmer, named Edward Covey, who was notorious for breaking young slaves. Douglass is then subjected to repeated beatings whose intention is nothing short of completely and utterly dehumanizing him, of rendering him an animal: "Mr. Covey succeeded in breaking me. I was broken in body, soul, and spirit. My natural elasticity was crushed, my intellect languished, the disposition to read departed, the cheerful spark before that lingered about my eye died; the dark night of slavery closed in upon me; and behold a man transformed into a brute." Realizing somewhere within himself that he will die if he does not try, even at the risk of his life, to resist this bestialization which constitutes the very essence of slavery, Douglass finally summons the will to fight back against his oppressor and undergoes, as he recalls it, an experience of religious deliverance. "It was a glorious resurrection," he writes, "from the tomb of slavery, to the heaven of freedom."[17] No longer a slave in fact even if he remained a slave in form, Douglass not only succeeds in stopping the violence—Edward Covey never again attacks him, even though Douglass admits to continually attempting to provoke him— but feels himself reborn. Soon thereafter he turns his sights on freedom by starting a Sabbath school to teach other slaves about freedom and then planning his own escape. Though his first attempt is a failure, his second, six months later, succeeds and eventually sets Douglass on the path to becoming a liberator of his people. Providence has been at work throughout his trials, and the rest of his life can be turned into an acknowledgment of its grace.

One of the more interesting features of Douglass's *Narrative* is that its shaping suggests several significant parallels with Franklin's *Autobiography*. For one thing, the text is constructed as a story not only of self-recreation but of self-authoring that enables it to enact what it seeks to represent; the *Narrative* represents the quest for freedom itself. From another, it is built, like Franklin's text, around its author's plan to rescue himself—in Franklin's case from indenture, in Douglass's from enslavement—and the methodological steps he took to reach his goal. From still another, both texts are fashioned as American success stories that are simultaneously designed as how-to manuals to show others how they might achieve a similar outcome. From yet another, they both recall the jeremiads of the seventeenth century insofar as they seek to remind a fallen people of the covenant they have betrayed but must now fulfill. Therefore each uses the form of a spiritual autobiography to diagnose the profound religious and moral lapses of the nation while at the same time finding, in terms associated with the Enlightenment project, the language to reaffirm the endangered national mission of freedom and liberty for all.

Harriet Jacobs's *Incidents in the Life of a Slave Girl* is a slave narrative similarly forced to employ a double tongue but for a distinctly different reason. Jacob's victimization is due not only to being an African American woman in slavery but also to the fact that as a slave woman she is held to a different standard of morality from white females. Her use of a double tongue thus results from her need to tell not one story but two. The first story has to do with her struggle to escape the repeated sexual advances of her master and protect her children from his control, which compels her to make the agonizing decision to hide out from him for seven years in the attic of her aunt's house while she watches her children develop under her aunt's protection. "When he told me that I was made for his use[,] . . . [t]hat I was nothing but a slave whose will must and should surrender to his, never before had my puny arm felt half so strong. . . . My master had power and law on his side; I had a determined will. There is might in each."[18] The second story shifts focus from the spectacle of a wronged woman heroically exiling herself from her children in order to protect them from her white male assailant to the sexual compromises she is forced make in an ultimately futile attempt to contain his sexual depredations. If the first story can elicit sympathy from all her potential readers, both white and free black women, the second exposes her to censure by those same readers, who are likely to judge her sexual compromises as sinful. Her conduct thus stands doubly condemned by her own conscience as well as by a set of moral norms, both religious and Enlightened, that fail to comprehend the moral as well as physical and sexual vulnerability of all women in slavery.

This double plot makes Jacob's autobiography different not only from male slave narratives but also from the narratives of free white women. Douglass's liberation from slavery allowed him to refashion himself as a new man in any one of several forms associated with religion and the Enlightenment, but Jacobs's liberation denies her such supports because the religious and Enlightenment models of regeneration and freedom available to sexually abused slave women contain a double standard. Thus her heroism consists not only in her struggle to escape the shackles of slavery but also in her courage to confront the duplicity of the religious and Enlightenment norms that still condemn her as a fallen and corrupt rather than liberated and free human being.

Reinscribing Aspects of the Enlightenment

In these revisionist slave narratives, which are in truth less interested in countering contemporary white narratives than in correcting and thus complementing them, the Enlightenment, or at least certain of its characteristic emphases, is accorded an importance, and exhibits an influence, rather different from those associated with conventional interpretations. Conventional interpretations generally assume that the Enlightenment's largest impact on the formation of post-Enlightenment literary and intellectual culture in the United States derived from those traditions that emphasized reason, moderation, balance, order, compromise, progress, materialism, and common sense, what is often called the rational and didactic Enlightenments, and exercised the least authority through those traditions that were either utopian, radical, and prophetic or critical, agnostic, iconoclastic, and pragmatic, namely the revolutionary and especially the skeptical Enlightenments.

Henry F. May, the historian who first delineated these four American Enlightenments, was convinced that the tradition of the village atheist that descends from Voltaire and Diderot, and runs in America from Abner Kneeland to Clarence Darrow, has never led more than a minority and distinctly paradoxical existence in this country, because religious skepticism here has rarely amounted to a questioning of all moral values, and the deeper skepticism associated with David Hume that is prepared to doubt the operations of all minds "and the validity of all general principles" has, at least until very recently, found no fertile soil in America.[19]

In the narratives by Douglass and Jacobs, as well as in the more traditional narratives of so many other American writers, the relative contribution of these several strains needs to be reversed almost exactly. The Enlightenments that seem to have played a more decisive role in shaping American literature in the modern age were, in Douglass's, the revolutionary Enlightenment and, in Jacobs's, the skeptical, and they did so often by combining forces to challenge, and eventually to undermine, many of the foundations of Protestant thinking in much nineteenth-century literature. Thus skepticism of the Humean variety, which casts suspicion on all mental operations, erupted intermittently but recurrently throughout nineteenth- and twentieth-century American writing and can be found in works ranging from "The Narrative of Arthur Gordon Pym" and *Pierre* to Quentin Compson's anguished meditations in *Absalom, Absalom!* and the torments

of many of John Berryman's Henry poems. The trope of the village atheist was given a new cynical twist in the nineteenth century with the emergence of the figure of the confidence man, a figure first anticipated by some
of the stratagems Benjamin Franklin reports adopting as a young man in
his *Autobiography;* then memorialized in Melville's novel by that title; later
given feminist expression in some of Emily Dickinson's poems on God's
duplicity; carried forward in that admonitory strain of Robert Frost's poetry
that includes "Design," "Fire and Ice," and "Provide, Provide"; subsequently
rendered comical, corrosive, or both in Wallace Stevens's "The Emperor of
Ice-Cream" and "A High-Toned Old Christian Woman"; eventually pushed
to brilliant extreme in Ralph Ellison's portrait of Rinehart the Runner in
Invisible Man; and given searing expression in the unillusioned candor of
Adrienne Rich's *An Atlas of the Difficult World* and Sharon Olds's *Stag's
Leap.* Furthermore, these currents of religious skepticism have always been
fed by a vast underground literature that is by turns witty, derisive, caustic,
freethinking, subversive, and parodistic.[20]

Another way of saying this would be to suggest that some of the most
important work of the skeptical or critical Enlightenment in France and England, if not the revolutionary Enlightenment as well, was not accomplished
in the eighteenth century but rather in the nineteenth, and not on European
side of the Atlantic but on the American.[21] That work proceeded, at least
from a literary perspective, toward the dismantling of virtually all of the religious assumptions on which American literary culture was then based. At
the beginning of the century it was assumed that the chief representational
function of literary art was to legitimate a world centered on God and illus-
trative of his purposes, particularly as they were revealed in the orderly processes of Nature and as they worked themselves out in the unfolding salvific
pattern of history. This theory of representation is perfectly exemplified in
the "prospect" or "rising glory" poems of the misnamed "Connecticut Wits,"
where, in texts like *The Rising Glory of America, The Conquest of Canaan,
Greenfield Hill,* and *The Columbiad,* poets such as Philip Freneau, Timothy
Dwight, and Joel Barlow envisaged a redemptive future for the United States
whose symbolic outlines were to become even more familiar much later in
such concepts as the Monroe Doctrine and Manifest Destiny.[22] By the end
of the century, it would be fair to say that in critical terms the only element
left of this theory was a belief in the importance of representation itself and
in the perceptual instrumentalities that made it possible. Those instrumentalities amounted to what was variously meant by the term *consciousness,*
now understood not as an entity or set of contents so much as a function or

kind of operation, and in turn held to be accountable for representing little more than the processes and perspectives that made it up.

Foreshadowing the Pragmatist Turn

What enabled this extraordinary transition, at least religiously and philosophically, is what I have called the pragmatist turn. This turn refers to a refiguration of some of the more characteristic conceptual and affective elements of seventeenth-century religion and the eighteenth-century Enlightenment as spiritual imaginaries or forms of *mentalité,* refigurations that made them more available to literary appropriation. That figurative appropriation was nowhere foreshadowed more dramatically than in the writing of two of the most important writers of the American midcentury, Herman Melville and Emily Dickinson. What both were to discover is that living in a world experienced as in some sense de-divinized, a world in which if God is not dead, he is no longer felt except as form of absence or Unconcern, does not necessarily condemn one to living in a world that has been completely desacralized. Loss of the sense of transcendence, of that which stands above and beyond and over against the self, as in most Christian thinking, does not necessarily deprive one of the experience of the presence or accessibility of that which is sensed to be radically set apart from and fundamentally different or "other" than the self. This was Melville's great discovery in *Moby-Dick,* which recounts his struggle, played out in the whole sweep of his career, to explore what spiritual possibilities remain after the event of deicide. It was also Dickinson's discovery when she realized that the only way to survive the spiritual divisions that Christianity and Transcendentalism had left her with was to colonize the realm of "internal difference/ Where the Meanings, are."

Herman Melville

Melville's career as a writer spanned nearly half a century. Beginning well before the outbreak of the Civil War in 1861 with the publication in 1846 of a narrative based on his own South Sea adventures in the Marquesas Islands entitled *Typee: A Peep at Polynesian Life,* and not concluding until his death in 1893, when he left unfinished in manuscript the short novella *Billy Budd, Sailor,* which was only published posthumously in 1924, Melville's writing straddles an era of extraordinary, almost cataclysmic, historical change in America. Not only did the United States undergo during this period the greatest threat to its existence since the American Revolution in the War between the States; it also transformed itself within forty years from a society that was predominantly rural and agrarian into one that had become industrialized and increasingly urban. Add to this the occurrence of three other social, cultural, and political transformations of historical proportions during this same period, and one begins to comprehend the momentous times in which Melville wrote. The first was a result of America's attempt after the Civil War to bury its problem with race by permitting the South to work out its own brutal accommodation with the former victims of slavery during Reconstruction, an accommodation that quickly led to the institution of Jim Crow laws, the spreading practice of lynching, the establishment of segregation, and the continuation of a regime of inequality that the United States is still struggling and failing to overcome. The second occurred more specifically in the North and is associated with what Henry James was to call "the great grope of wealth" that led to the financial excesses and indulgences of what Mark Twain aptly described, in the title of one of his books, as "the Gilded Age." The third occurred abroad and is associated with the expansionist politics that precipitated the Spanish-American War and established America as a colonial power in the Pacific.

All this and more is reflected in Melville's fiction and poetry. *Typee* and its sequel, *Omoo: A Narrative of Adventures in the South Seas* (1847), detail, among other things, the potentially genocidal effects of the West's attempt to discipline native ways of life by bringing them under the tutelage of "civilization." *Mardi, and a Voyage Thither* (1949) started out as a South Seas adventure story in response to critical attacks on the veracity of *Typee* and *Omoo* but then turned into a kind of romance before becoming, finally, a rambling philosophical narrative in search of spiritual truth. *Redburn: His First Voyage* (1849), the novel influenced by Melville's memory of his father's bankruptcy and built around Melville's first journey abroad to Liverpool returns from the realm of fantasy and speculation to the spectacle of economic misery that was already emblematic of injustices produced by the emerging industrial and commercial order of ante- and postbellum America. *White Jacket; or, The World in a Man-of-War* (1850), the novel Melville published immediately after *Redburn* ("two jobs . . . done for money"), reveals, amid the social and political inequities of life aboard a naval warship, a betrayal of the democratic ideal that Melville had himself found so handsomely honored among the gallant foretop men he worked with and idealized during his own years before the mast. *Moby-Dick,* completed a year later, and building on lessons Melville had learned in the composition of all his earlier books, returns to some of the larger and more unwieldy metaphysical speculations that he had begun in *Mardi* but now brilliantly reframed in a quest narrative that permitted him, at one and the same time, to expose many of the myths that were soon to fuel America's imperial ambitions abroad while questioning the understructure of those beliefs and ethical values, loosely Christian and Enlightenment, that so often and so paradoxically supported and reinforced them. Melville's next book, *Pierre; or, The Ambiguities* (1852), shifted ground abruptly by turning away from the ever more perplexing and infinitely elaborated cosmic world without to investigate the duplicities and contradictions of the modern self within, discovering in the interior corridors that wind down into the center of human willing and striving forces so dark as to leave all attempts at human fulfillment, much less ethical defiance, seriously crippled.

Pierre was eventually to be followed by *Israel Potter: His Fifty Years of Exile* (1855), another novel that broadened his canvas by showing how common people are viciously exploited by the twin demons of war and deprivation, but its weakened literary intensity signaled that Melville's literary agenda had somewhat shifted in the interim. During the years between the publication of *Pierre* and *Israel Potter,* Melville had in fact turned his attention, at least temporarily, toward a different reading audience by producing a number of brilliant shorter works for literary magazines. Though these texts were more restricted in length and less indifferent to the conventions of the medium, they were no less original, daring, and masterful than some of his earlier, lengthier books. The story "Bartleby, the Scrivener," the novella *Benito Cereno,* and the tales collected in *The Encantadas* all bear out Melville's continuing capacity to depict the human condition in all its diverse postures of puzzlement, resistance, indifference, stupidity, heroism, meanness, and suffering. But before concluding this phase of his career, which was eventually to be followed by a second achieved almost completely in the face of public obscurity, Melville decided to have one last go at a longer narrative that might sum up his disillusionment with the world, his public, and himself. The result was *The Confidence-Man: His Masquerade* (1857), a book that launches an assault on the very grounds of truth itself. Yet despite the cynicism it expresses about all human motives, *The Confidence-Man* also reveals an exquisitely shrewd social, political, and moral grasp of the myriad ways that nineteenth-century American idealism, like romantic utopianism everywhere, could be employed for purposes of deceit, manipulation, and corruption.

Melville's later career displays no less concentrated an absorption with the chief issues and preoccupations of his times when adventurism in America was propelling it outward in ever more global spirals. While Melville's preferred literary medium during this later phase of his writing life now became verse rather than fiction—the exception being his posthumously published *Billy Budd*—his engagements with his age and its centrifugal forces remained in their way no less insistent, complex, or passionate than before. There was, apparently, a first volume of poems that was produced in 1860, some of whose texts appeared in his later *Timoleon* (1891) and the posthumous *Weeds and Wildings Chiefly: With a Rose or Two* (1924), but the first manuscript that was to appear in this later period of Melville's career was *Battle-Pieces and Aspects of the War* (1866), a collection that grapples with a world torn asunder by violence and seeks to find in writing itself the power to envision the partial reknitting, if not reuniting, of the national ethos. *Clarel,* the poetic masterpiece that in many ways matches his epic masterwork *Moby-Dick,* uses Melville's own seven-month journey in 1856 to the Holy Land and Europe to stage a remarkable "conflict of convictions," as the title of one of Melville's later poems depicts it, among a group of latter-day spiritual pilgrims. Their discussions about all the great issues of faith and doubt, of hope and despair, of charity and venality, that vexed the latter half of the nineteenth century in America and England, tear at the fabric of the Victorian mindset, while permitting the poem to display how an entire age lent itself body and expression by, so to speak, recognizing itself in its own intellectual and spiritual fractures.

Clarel was not followed by another volume for twenty years, until Melville published *John Marr and Other Sailors* (1888), where he could finally declare of his spiritual struggle with his times, though not without an element of self-doubt, "Healed of my hurt, I laud the inhuman Sea." Nonetheless, there remained, along with various miscellaneous poems, the extraordinary manuscript Melville left lying unfinished on his desk that was initially inspired by another poem of his called "Billy in the Darbies." That poem was the basis of the novella *Billy Budd* in which Melville returned to a world at war to revisit those ancient questions that had always engaged his deepest curiosity, questions about innocence, goodness, malevolence, truth, treachery, monomania, and moral compromise. In a world where, as the text's Captain Vere remarks at the drumhead court he has summoned to try Billy Budd for murdering the master-at-arms, Mr. Claggart, "forms, measured forms are everything," Melville found himself asking whether there is any place left for what is called, after the name of the ship from which Billy was impressed to serve on, the H.M.S. *Indomitable*, the "Rights-of-Man."

Melville's final question attests the global reach of his vision. His writing encompassed all five continents, examining cultural practices, prejudices, preoccupations, and perversities from all quarters of the globe. An "Anacharsis Clootz deputation from all the isles of the sea" is what Melville christened his motley gathering of "meanest mariners, renegades, and castaways" in *Moby-Dick,* and the phrase suffices to suggest the catholicity and internationalism of his characters as well as his canvases. They are drawn, like the "congress" of foreigners for whom they are named—and which the Prussian nobleman Baron Jean Baptiste de Clootz presented to the first French Assembly after the French Revolution—as representatives of the entire human race, and they mark Melville's texts as in certain respects more cosmopolitan than anything produced in American writing either before or since.

But nothing in the Melvillean canon so completely foreshadows the pragmatist turn as *Moby-Dick.* Often read religiously as an attack on the whole Christian system, *Moby-Dick* has been interpreted too rarely as also a prefiguration of the kind of pragmatic consciousness that was, in the late nineteenth and twentieth century, to take its place. Moreover, *Moby-Dick* is a work whose rootage, through much of the text devoted to Ahab's concerns, in the theological world of seventeenth-century Puritan metaphysics is nicely balanced by its structural reliance, during many of the stretches when Ishmael's voice becomes more dominant, on the literary form known as the anatomy that was so often reappropriated in the intellectualized, ironic, satiric world of the eighteenth century.[23]

From a pragmatist point of view, the problems that afflict Ahab are those of a latter-day Puritan who, on the one hand, inherits a system of belief that can no longer answer or evade the questions he puts to it but who, on the other hand, cannot escape from the tyrannous coils of the system itself. Ahab is the last, fullest, and most perverse flowering of the high Calvinist tradition in America, a tradition that here, in its death throes and in the name of Christian values that Ahab himself constantly transgresses, turns against itself by calling God himself to account. When God fails to listen, or, from the text's perspective, seems indifferent, the tradition then destroys itself in a maddened, if not fiendish, act of self-immolation.

This is not, of course, how Ahab experiences his predicament. Ahab's experience is defined by his desire to determine what lies behind the pasteboard mask of appearance that has been shoved so brutally in his face. This desire is endlessly frustrated, for the mask turns out to be impenetrable, and its nearness only compounds the outrage. "That inscrutable thing is chiefly what I hate," says Ahab, thus referring to "the ambiguity of the meanings that lure him on and the resistance that objects present to the inquiring mind."[24] The only way Ahab can end this torture is by terminating his voyage in quest of truth, and the only way he can accomplish this is by settling for only one definition, or set of definitions, of the pasteboard mask and then hurling himself, all mutilated and mutilating, against it.

Ishmael's predicament seems to be the very opposite of Ahab's, or eventually becomes so. Initially daunted by the indefiniteness of the novel's quest for the mystery that lies behind the pasteboard mask—an indefiniteness Ishmael recurrently experiences in earlier parts of the book as the ultimate horror of a world that constantly blurs all distinctions in an insubstantial medium that seems, as he notes in "The Whiteness of the Whale," purposefully deceptive—Ishmael gradually becomes himself the vehicle through which we discover a world whose insubstantiality is but the reverse side of its fluidity and diversity and even procreativity. Such a world can be comprehended only by a frame of mind that is the very opposite of Ahab's. If Ahab's mind, outraged by a world that defies his quest for certainty, traffics in signs, equivalences, and linked analogies that are supposed to represent the things that they are, Ishmael's mind, undismayed as it finally becomes by the multitudinous expressivity of the world's plurality, trades in images, metaphors, and symbols that acknowledge the surplus of meanings that language carries within itself when it is used tropologically rather than allegorically.

The book's major movement is the transition from Ahab's mind to Ishmael's, from the "old consciousness," in D. H. Lawrence's terminology, that Ishmael initially shares with Ahab and that must be sloughed off, to the "new consciousness" that is forming underneath.[25] The outmoded consciousness that we identify with Ahab, and that Ishmael shares with him at the beginning, is a theocentric, monologistic, moralistic consciousness that is predicated on the possibility of reducing reality to opposing elements of the divine and the demonic, the sacred and the profane, good and evil, love and hate, life and death, male and female. The new consciousness that begins to emerge underneath in the polymorphous, polyphonous discourse of Ishmael's narrative is one that views such traditional binaries as "interweavingly" intermixed in experience, and responds by adopting an attitude that is tentative, experimental, provisional, improvisatory, eclectic, changeable, and even contradictory.

This consciousness is in many parts of the book no more than a matter of style, of an idiom as various and fluid as the circumstances of experience itself, but it is not too much to say that its creation and elaboration becomes the book's real spiritual destination.[26] This consciousness is identical with the style of Ishmael's buoyant, metaphoric voice as he records his "doubts of all things earthly" and his "intuitions of some things heavenly" while, at the same time, "knowing this combination makes neither believer nor infidel" but a person "who regards them both with equal eye."[27] This is the idiom of a consciousness that is far less interested in vindicating a grievance or developing a philosophy than in exploring another way to be.

Thus if there is a god in *Moby-Dick,* a Presence that exists behind the pasteboard mask of all appearances, that god is not to be identified with Moby-Dick himself, or with any of the other anthropomorphic deities that human beings create in their own image—Father Mapple's Old Testament Jehovah, Captain Bildad's Quaker Taskmaster and Warrior, Gabriel's Shaker God Incarnate, Pip's Divine Inert, Starbuck's reasonable Pantokrator of the Quotidian, Queen Maachah of Judea's "grandissimus," Bulkington's "Great God Absolute, the Center and Circumference of our Democracy," Queequeg's Yojo, or even Ahab's fatherless Spirit of Defiant Darkness—any more than Moby-Dick can be identified with any one of the partial interpretations he elicits. This is not a god to whom one can pray nor from whom one can receive vindication, even less a god on whom one can rely or because of whom one can hope. Immanent in Nature but in no sense identical with it, this divine Power that threads life with death in some larger pattern that is beyond human understanding and seemingly indifferent to human desire is, like Moby-Dick himself, infinitely more than the sum of his realizations.

This is the oceanic, in truth potentially cosmic, vision afforded from the perspective of what Melville calls the "mysterious, divine Pacific" that "zones the world's whole bulk about; makes all coasts one bay to it; seems the tide-beating heart of earth."[28] It is a perspective that completely reverses our territorial, land-based perspective by inviting us to reposition ourselves in the unshored landlessness that surrounds it. From such an epistemological position, all possibility of finding, much less securing, coordinates of spiritual placement or orientation give way to the open-ended, ever-ambiguous, always incomplete quest for them.

Emily Dickinson

Emily Dickinson's spiritual quest, however various, was nothing quite this fluid or indefinite but remained even more unresolved. Hers is dramatized as a process of continuous crisis of incomplete and fragmentary conversion that is undertaken in the context of two somewhat different religious environments. The first is distinctly Christian and evangelical but is constantly being challenged by the anti-Christian thought of so much eighteenth- and nineteenth-century intellectual culture: "The Bible is an antique volume / Written by faded men / At the suggestion of Holy Spectres" (#1545); "'Faith' is a fine invention / When Gentlemen can *see*- / But Microscopes are prudent / In an Emergency" (#185). "I know that He Exists. / Somewhere—in Silence," she writes somewhat mockingly in another poem, but from the perspective of "Death's—stiff—stare," it all begins to appear like no more than "an instant's play" or "fond Ambush—" that forces one to ask: "Would not the fun / Look too expensive! / Would not the jest— / Have crawled too far" (#338).[29]

The second of the environments in which she seeks conversion is Transcendentalist, but the Emersonian moment of rapture, ecstasy, transformation is often subverted, turned upside down. Where Emerson saw Nature not only as intentional but also benevolent, Dickinson discerns the intentionality but more often than not finds it treacherous and inscrutable. "The Bat is dun, with wrinkled wings," she writes in #1575; "Empowered with what Malignity / Auspiciously withheld—." To be sure, Nature is capable of conferring moments of intense elation and bliss, of sublime transfiguration, but such moments are often fleeting and can lure one into a false sense of security where Nature, it feels, often takes a kind of revenge.

Or, again, Dickinson agrees with Emerson that Nature is redolent of meaning, but often discovers it to be a meaning that must be read in terms of its disappearance, emptiness, blankness. "Infinitude," she asks in "My period had come for prayer" (#564), "Had'st thou no Face that I could look on thee?" But "Infinitude" neither answers nor provides any evidence of its former residence: "His house was not—no sign had He— / By chimney— nor by Door." All the speaker can detect as she looks out are "Vast prairies of Air / Unbroken by a Settler—." After putting her question, it is as though the Silence condescends to stop creation, leaving the speaker to confess, in words that recall the Puritan pilgrimage to the wilderness, "Awed beyond my errand— / I worshipped—but did not pray—."

Part of the reason for the inverted or aborted conclusion to these spiritual journeys in whichever direction is due to another failure her poems record. This is the failure of the speaker to relinquish herself, to renunciate the will, to reject the world. Rather, the speaker of these poems suggests, or in any case implies, that she can almost compensate for this loss herself by measuring with such exactitude the spiritual price that must be paid for these thwarted quests. Hence the real terror her poems risk is not hellfire and brimstone at the hands of a judgmental or angry god, nor even death as a kind of termination or extinction, so much as oblivion, or the agony of not knowing, or both. If this be death at all, then, it is not just any kind of death but the death that is most terrifying to an artist who is also a woman. It is a death of the senses, the cessation of feeling, which she imagines occurring in any number of ways, from freezing or suffocating or being made immobile to being deprived of conclusion, of suffering a kind of eternal free fall, or experiencing a stopless life. Hence the recurrent fantasies of dying, often staged as spiritual exercises within a Christian or Transcendentalist framework, that fail to yield the intended result. Instead of serving as the propaedeutic for the reconciliation and redemptive reunion of human beings with a transcendent Father in the Christian dispensation, or as overcoming the opposition between ego and non-ego or subject and object in the Romantic-Transcendental one, death simply gives way to the abyss or nonbeing.

This spiritual predicament is beautifully portrayed in #465, her great poem about the fly buzzing in the room in which, figuratively speaking, the speaker has died already. But this poem is not a dramatization of the speaker's own death so much as an ironic, shrewdly theatrical, reversal of the conventional religious expectations, whether Christian or Transcendentalist, about the event of dying itself. Everything is supposed to be gathering toward that instant when the King, or rather God, is witnessed in the room, that is, when mourners are afforded the opportunity to see the soul of the deceased give itself up to its Creator. Dickinson plays this religious expectation fairly straight up to the moment when the fly intervenes, but then something happens that is not a religious revelation at all but more like the parody of one. The King witnessed is not God but a messenger of death, and instead of vouchsafing to the speaker any final vision of what lies beyond this world, this world simply fades from the speaker's eyes: the light in the window fades and then the speaker cannot see to see, and in that moment loses faith as well as sight. The onset of blankness is relieved only by the "Blue—uncertain stumbling Buzz" of the fly which has now taken the place of the King or God at the beginning of the poem and interposed itself "Between the light—and me," thus constituting all the mystery or, as the poem calls it, "the stillness between the heaves of storm," that the speaker will experience as she expires.

The most interesting aspect of the poem, however, is not the conclusion it portrays but the strange form of pride it discloses. Even though the speaker is reporting the moment of her own death, when the self is supposed to lose

its autonomy, to submit to what is no more, this self holds on to that autonomy as long as humanly possible. Rather than depicting the yielding or
succumbing, much less submitting, to the disintegration of the self in dying,
or to its slow transformation as it prepares religiously to pass beyond death,
the poem represents the inextinguishable hubris of a self that can use even
the imagination of her death itself to assert her queenly rights.

In this light, a poem like #985, "The Missing All," also reflects a pride of
Dickinson's particular kind. Having lost the possibility of salvation, she is
not about to be disturbed by other losses—of a world's departure from a
hinge or the sun's extinction. Neither of these things is felt by the poet to be
large enough to arouse her curiosity or to cause her to lift her head from her
work. Her work instead is noting the difference that is made by "the Missing
All," and the sheer bravado entailed in risking such metaphysically desperate measurements is nothing short of spectacular.

While the same sense of spiritual audacity can be found in "The Soul
Selects Her Own Society" (#303) or "Publication—is the Auction / Of the
Mind of Man" (#709), Dickinson often strikes another note when making
such measurements. Her more characteristic note is struck in #258, where
she speaks of "a certain Slant of Light, / Winter Afternoons" that can oppress
like the weight of cathedral music. This is an anti-Transcendentalist poem
that purposely inverts the Emersonian, not to say Edwardsean, expectation.
Nature may be suffused with agency, with intention, but it is directed not
on behalf of the self but rather against it. Its oppression is like the weight of
religion itself that we must wrestle with to lift lest we be crushed. Its weight,
however, is not substantial or material so much as phenomenal or ephemeral, and the pain it causes leaves no mark or scar but rather spiritual emptiness where significance should be:

> Heavenly Hurt, it gives us—
> We can find no scar,
> But internal difference,
> Where the meanings, are—

This, it seems to me, is the realm of her major poetry, the record of her
experience in a post-Puritan world: the interior history of her attempt to
retain a measure of individual sovereignty, even the sovereignty of loss, in a
world of power. Sometimes the power is personal, sometimes supernal, but
always it is masculine and almost always it is indifferent. And though this
power does not prevent her from experiencing less desperate, less cruel, less

hopeless feelings, it colors the whole of it. At one extreme, there is a spiritual fervor where feeling exceeds belief:

> I dwell in Possibility—
> A Fairer House than Prose—
> More numerous of Windows—
> Superior—for Doors—
> . . . .
> Of Visitors—the fairest—
> For Occupation—This—
> The spreading wide my narrow Hands
> To gather Paradise. (#657)

At the other extreme, there is only the bitterness, the mystery, the abandonment of loss:

> Those—dying then
> Knew where they went—
> They went to God's Right Hand—
> That Hand is amputated now
> And god cannot be found—

As a consequence, as she says in the next stanza, we must learn what to make of what Robert Frost once called "a diminished thing":

> The abdication of belief
> Makes the behavior small.
> Better an ignis fatuus
> Than no illumine at all. (#1551)

This recognition of the ubiquity and ignominy of loss is then summarized in the poem that goes:

> Finding is the first Act
> The second—loss—
> Third—Expedition for
> the "Golden Fleece"
> Fourth, no Discovery—
> Fifth, no Crew—
> Finally, no Golden Fleece—
> Jason—sham—too. (#870)

What Dickinson does is to move back and forth within this structure of desire and despair, from experiences of potential deliverance and re-birth that are never quite consummated to imagined confrontations with the prospect of her own death and dissolution. At one point the world will hint of an eternal bliss that remains for the most part always out of reach. At another it will confront the obstacles that stand in her way and block her attempts for release or knowledge. But such movements as these are almost never completed in either direction.

At their best they present her with images of beauty or perfection that become perceptible, as in her great poem on the hummingbird, in their vanishing:

> A Route of Evanescence
> With a revolving Wheel—
> A resonance of Emerald—
> A Rush of Cochineal—
> And every Blossom on the bush
> Adjusts its tumbled Head—-
> The mail from Tunis probably,
> An easy Morning's Ride—(#1463)

From an image of trajectory ("Route") in the first line, to one of motion ("re-volving") in the second, to one of sound ("resonance") in the third, to one of color ("Cochineal") in the fourth, we move in the fifth and sixth to the effects of this miraculous passage on the ordinary natural world it leaves behind ("Blossom," "bush," "tumbled Head") and in the seventh and eighth to a gen-tly ironic rendering of the mystery of this magical vanishing. "All we secure of Beauty is its Evanescences," Dickinson had written in one of her letters, and this poem captures the marvel and poignancy of that felt realization.

At their worst, on the other hand, they leave her feeling abandoned, deso-lated, cast out in the wilderness of despair:

> The Auctioneer of Parting
> His "Going, going, gone"
> Shouts even from the Crucifix,
> And brings his Hammer down—
> He only sells the Wilderness,
> The prices of Despair
> Range from a single human Heart
> To Two—not any more—(#1612)

This poem adds a new dimension to the idea of the disappearance of God. Here it is not that God is no longer present, has merely absented himself from his creation; it is rather that God is represented as selling to the highest bidder another kind of separation or vanishing that might be called "gone-ness."[30] He is therefore depicted as the agent shouting from the cross and offering his clients not death, which his "Hammer" ends, terminates, but rather the "Wilderness" of "Despair." Death would have brought an end to suffering, but gone-ness, the infinity of absence, makes it endless. In another poem despair is described as "that White Sustenance," Dickinson's image of spiritual desolation.

But the image of "that White Sustenance—Despair" is perhaps most brilliantly evoked in the final stanza of her anti-Emersonian, anti-Transcendentalist poem already discussed, #258, in which she describes it as "An imperial affliction / Sent us of the Air." When despair arrives, it intensifies our experience of reality itself—"The Landscape listens / Shadows—hold their breath"; when it departs, or at least the consciousness of despair departs, the landscape disappears, the world is extinguished, and we are left with nothing but "the Distance / on the look of Death—," an image of utter emptiness, of the void.

Dickinson is thus divided within herself and is unable bridge the chasm. All she can do is endlessly explore that chasm, that spiritual fissure, itself, which becomes the true sign or signature of her special control, her self-mastery of consciousness:

> I felt a Cleaving in my Mind—
> As if my Brain had split—
> I tried to match it—Seam by Seam—
> But could not make them fit.
> The thought behind, I strove to join
> Unto the thought before—
> But Sequence ravelled out of Sound
> Like Balls—upon a Floor. (#937)

The Pragmatist Regrafting of Relations between Religion and the Enlightenment

So defined, consciousness in its late nineteenth-century variants was either what the Enlightenment had omitted from the conception of the mind altogether or had too often truncated in it; consciousness was also what a certain group of American philosophers and other intellectuals could not resist transforming into a new subject of intellectual and aesthetic investigation.[31] With help from useful adversaries like Josiah Royce and important precursors such as Charles Sanders Peirce, William James, along with other pragmatic-minded thinkers like Charles Horton Cooley and George Herbert Mead, was able to show how the Enlightenment's confidence in the work of the mind might yet yield additional discoveries into what had once been thought to be the sole property of American religion. It all depended on developing a method of intellectual inquiry that would permit consciousness to explore what still remained ineffable and undecidable but also irrepressible on its own borders. James spoke of this as "the reinstatement of the vague to its proper place in our mental life."[32] What he referred to by the term "vague" was that whole mysterious shadow world of feeling, intuition, relations, and transitions that undergirds cognition and motivates action but that continues to remain invisible or discredited in so many late nineteenth- and twentieth-century versions of experience.

"Everything," as Emerson had noted in his *Journals* for June 1847, "teaches transition, transference, metamorphosis: therein is human power, in transference, not in creation & therein is human destiny, not in longevity but in removal. We dive & reappear in new places."[33] This was the kernel of the perspective that James was to convert into his own theory of consciousness, a theory that now supposed that the reality in need of representation was not simply "substantive" but also "transitive." What awaited full exploration and expression was the whole realm of affect that the Enlightenment, with its more restricted understanding of mentality, had tended to discount, and that religion, with its more urgent requirements for reassurance, often tended to displace. Nor was pragmatism's affinity with both religion and the Enlightenment in this case any accident. For if some of the roots of the pragmatist impulse lay in the strongly experiential tenor of seventeenth- and eighteenth-century American religion, no less than the anti-Calvinistic metaphysics of William James's father, Henry James Sr., much of its intellectual effectuality derived from a concentration on the practical, the observable, and the empirical that goes back directly to the antimetaphysical bias of some of the most radical Enlightenment philosophes.[34]

But what was there about James's thinking and feeling, indeed of his view of thought as a certain kind of feeling and of feeling as a certain kind of thought, that made his philosophy so amenable to literary use even by writers who never read him? To answer such questions, we will need to examine what might be thought of as the many William Jameses who emerged from the different ways he could be appropriated in different eras from the Victorian to the late or postmodern. We will also need to see how he turned the pragmatic method of inquiry into the key to the meaning of truth. Viewing the operations of truth, or, rather truth-making, more like a credit system than a bank depository or lending library, we will then be in a position to understand how for him truth could become, as it also became for so many modern writers in America and elsewhere, a form of consciousness that makes itself known less as convictions to which we give assent or as concepts for which we seek credibility than as aspects of temperament, to use James's phrase, or, as Gilbert Ryle later put it, dispositional modes best conceived in terms of a set of capacities, propensities, tendencies, proclivities, and even habits. In this pragmatic sense, consciousness is represented not by its contents so much as by its actions, processes, inclinations, and because these actions, processes, or inclinations have to be sensitive to what James called the "transitive" as well as the "substantive" dimensions of experience, the only method of knowing that would work would have to be as agile in following the traceries of feeling as the promptings of thought. No other method would do in a world like the modern and eventually the postmodern so broadly in flux and so perennially in crisis.

FIVE

The Jamesian Component

The Many Uses of William James

William James is a thinker whose charm as well as importance derives at least in part from his ability to appeal to different readers in different eras and for different reasons. This remarkable availability for repossession by such varied readers in so many eras would be less likely, perhaps, if James were not so protean a thinker. Indeed, to call him a "philosopher" in the traditional sense is to risk doing him an injustice. While he eventually made it his business to address many of the questions around which philosophy defined itself in his age, such as epistemology, metaphysics, ethics, and the theory of truth, he received his degree in anatomy, wrote his first, and many believe his greatest, book (in two volumes) on "the principles of psychology," and was constantly turning philosophy itself into a more accessible form of public discourse capable of reflecting on such philosophically nontraditional subjects as the stream of consciousness, religious experience, educational theory, social thought, politics, culture, and contemporary morals and manners.

Yet what sets all of James's writing apart, rendering it simultaneously so attractive and so accessible, were his immense and varied gifts not only as a thinker but also as a writer. James was brilliantly adept at producing an American middle style that makes up in suppleness, wit, grace, and fluidity for what it sometimes lacks, at least for certain kinds of readers, in rigor and internal consistency. James writes always out of the decencies, fundamentals, and reasonableness of ordinary human experience, which he welcomes into his thinking not only as an old and trusted, if also frequently amusing, friend but also as an ever-renewing and renewable source for reflection and inspiration. Thought should never rise so far above the plane of common life, James seems to say, that it forgets where it came from and to what it must finally be accountable.

There is, moreover, a relaxed cordiality as well as conversational informality to his prose that functions to draw his readers in rather than hold them off. James clearly wanted to communicate as well as convince, but he also hoped to invite his readers into the processes and play of his own reflections. The mind is not a passive receptor of information that it then simply translates into another medium, James believed; it is rather a creative, inventive, imaginative instrument that responds to previous descriptions of reality not as existing simply for themselves but as stimulants to further thought. "We *add*," James wrote in one of his most famous formulations, "both to the subject and to the predicate part of reality. The world stands really malleable, waiting to receive its final touches at our hands. Like the kingdom of heaven, it suffers human violence willingly."[1]

This is what James wanted his readers to experience in his own prose: not just the inventiveness or perceptiveness of his own reflections but the stimulation of their own minds in response, along with the accompanying sense that such stimulations actually "enhance the universe's total value."[2] In this he was assisted by a gift for idiomatic expression and the rhythms of everyday speech that was as "game-flavored," to quote another of his famous figures of speech, "as a hawk's wing."[3] James's colleague at Harvard and sometime fellow pragmatist, the philosopher George Santayana, got it just about right when he described him as "an impulsive poet: a master in the art of recording or divining the lyric quality of experience as it actually came to him or to me."[4]

Beyond that, however, there was the sheer vitality, brilliance, edginess, unconventionality, and disarming candor of the man. To his students, James was ready for almost anything and hated any system that closed off further possibilities for thought. "We must never set up boundaries that exclude romantic surprises," Santayana again remarked. "He retained the primitive feeling that death *might* open new worlds to us . . . ; also the primitive feeling that invisible spirits *might* be floating about among us, and might suddenly do something to hurt or to help us."[5]

Little wonder, then, that just as James's own contemporaries turned again and again to him for illumination of their own quandaries, so subsequent generations of readers have inevitably brought to him their own very different questions and concerns. James's earliest readers sought him out either as one of the first—and still one of the greatest—psychologists of the inner life, or as a moral thinker who could adumbrate the experiential grounds of reasonable belief, or as an anatomist of religious feeling. Later admirers during the middle part of the twentieth century valued him instead for developing a simpler calculus for weighing the merits of ideas, or as the proponent of a worldview that was radical in the seriousness with which it took the relational character of existence, or as an advocate of the social theory known as democratic pluralism. Now, at the beginning of the twenty-first century, we find still other things to value in James, whether it be his conviction that most of our certainties (even about matters of fact) are susceptible to correction in the light of future experience, or his emphasis on contingency, chance, and novelty, or his sensitivity to what he calls, in the title of one of his most famous essays, "a certain blindness in human beings." But this only confirms what James would have anticipated himself. If philosophy is, as his fellow pragmatist John Dewey later contended, merely the history of its own time in thought (the idea was first introduced into philosophy by the nineteenth-century German philosopher G. W. F. Hegel), then it should surprise no one to discover that different historical eras put very different queries to themselves, or at least find themselves confronted by very different challenges and conundrums.

Placing James Historically

James was living at a moment when the spirit of the "modern" was beginning to break free of the ethos of the "Victorian." The Victorian era had been marked by a strong belief in the permanence and validity of certain moral values associated with words like "duty," "selflessness," "decency," and "truth." It also assumed that such values are inscribed nowhere more deeply than in the texts and practices associated with high culture, and that as long as such values are permitted to influence the course of the present, then human history will continue to display a record of steady progress.[6] The modern era, on the other hand, and particularly modernism of the sort that James helped stimulate in America, assumed that values are, like life itself, more unstable, provisional, and circumstantial; that people are confronted with a world whose intellectual and symbolic constructs no longer house or nourish their deepest feeling; and that history presents itself less like a story of steady but uneven advancement and progress than a tale told by an idiot full of sound and fury. T. S. Eliot captured this benighted side of James's modernism perfectly when he remarked that in the struggle for cultural and spiritual values, we fight to keep something alive rather than in the belief that anything is certain to prevail. Or, as James put it for himself at the end of his essay "Is Life Worth Living?," what matters is not having won but having tried.

But there was a good deal more than this—and a good deal that was more radical—to James's American modernism, much of which is indicated in the great early essay he wrote on the nature of human consciousness entitled "The Stream of Thought." I refer not simply to his view that life confronts us with a series of obstacles to be overcome, of problems to be addressed, but to his belief that consciousness comes before sensation, that thinking can be likened to the behavior of a stream, that thought can therefore be differentiated into moments that are stable and moments that are not, that the relations between such moments are as much a part of experience as the moments they connect, that we can have feelings about those moments as well as about the things conjoined by them, that thought is therefore a kind of algebra that does not need to translate all its operations into ideas in order to perform its work, and that, as a result, consciousness should be reconceived as a process and not a substance. I also mean that "The Stream of Thought" gives early expression to James's belief that modern philosophy needs to redirect its efforts toward the reinstatement not of the elements of the obvious or the unquestioned in our mental life but of the indefinite and the ambiguous; that it foreshadows his later opinion that philosophical history is to a large extent a conflict of different dispositions rather than merely of different opinions; and, finally, that it reveals his lifelong penchant for meliorism, for exploring the middle ground between oppositions and contradictions. In all these ways—and one could name others—James was already in possession of some of the most radical elements of his own modernism, to say nothing of many of his most recurrent themes, by the time he had published his first major work, which was not a work of philosophy but a work of psychology!

James has now of course been rediscovered in a historical and cultural moment that is somewhat different from the one he first helped to energize. This is the moment we have come to call late, or post-, modern, if only because it seems to exist both in continuity with, but also in disjunction from, the cultural moment just preceding it. By "cultural moment" I simply mean a time whose general intellectual framework and emotional tone possess a distinctive and discriminable ethos for those who live in it. While such structures of feeling may be difficult to define, precisely because they are composed of nothing more palpable than patterns of impulse, restraint, aspiration, foreboding, confidence, or distress, they nonetheless lend an unmistakable sense and character, even attitude, whether conscious or subconscious, to one's subjective experience of the social world. Viewed in these terms, the contrast between James's so-called modernist moment and our so-called late or postmodernist one might be reconceived as the difference between an era in which belief in life's fundamental unity and coherence had been seriously eroded, or at least fundamentally questioned, without loss of the nostalgic desire for its recovery, and an era that, in its bleaker versions, acknowledges that life seems to lack any sense of underlying unity or purpose at all beyond, perhaps, the pursuit of pleasure and the creation of a therapeutic culture to sustain it, but that, in its more robust moods, insists that bricolage, parody, irony, playfulness, anarchy, and jouissance may provide new avenues to the sublime.

The American poet Wallace Stevens can help us sharpen one side of this distinction, just as the French philosopher Jean-François Lyotard can assist us in honing the other. Stevens associates modernism with an age of disbelief in which people who have experienced the disappearance of many, if not most, of the gods are forced to look elsewhere for the consolations once provided by religious faith. Such consolations, which included above all the mediation of a reality not their own, a "something 'wholly other,'" as Stevens refers to it in *Opus Posthumous,* "by which the inexpressive loneliness of thinking [and feeling] is broken and enriched,"[7] must now be sought in more secular, profane forms such as literature, painting, dance, and philosophy itself. Here spiritual survival depends on what, in "Of Modern Poetry," Stevens describes as "the finding of a satisfaction, and may / Be of a man skating, a woman dancing, a woman / Combing."[8]

Lyotard, on the other hand, finds such spiritual substitutes ineffective at best, self-deceiving at worst. The great metanarratives of the past, which once taught us, if not exactly what the world is really like, then at least in what direction to think about that world and how to care for it, have essentially collapsed, or at any rate have been outgrown, and there is little to console the self but the endless recirculation, often narcissistic, of outmoded images of such things. This means that all storytelling, all narrativizing, is plural, provisional, sentimental, and, above all, genealogical: an attempt out of the various, fragmentary plots at hand to rewrite the story of the past in light of the outcome we would like it to have. In such a cultural climate, James's pragmatism presents itself less as a simple philosophical and moral alternative to postmodernism than as an intellectual correction and deepening of some of postmodernism's own preoccupations with the fluidity, open-endedness, belatedness, randomness, and undecidability of experience.

Such terms as these, which have come to be regarded almost as hallmarks of the postmodern, should serve to remind us that pragmatism has never been an exclusively American phenomenon or movement. Long before

James had settled on the vocation of philosopher, much less developed any sense of the pragmatist project, he had undergone, while reading the French philosopher Charles Renouvier's writings on the will, a kind of "conversion" that would stay with him throughout much of his life; and once James's range of intellectual interests acquired sharper philosophical focus, he was to find himself in extended conversation with two other pragmatist philosophers from abroad, F. C. S. Schiller in England and Luigi Papini in Italy. But almost as soon as James's ideas began to circulate beyond the shores of the Atlantic, following the publication of *The Principles of Psychology* and particularly *The Will to Believe,* people were detecting European precedents for his thinking in the work of everyone from Fichte, Nietzsche, and Schelling in Germany to Bergson in France (who denied a connection), and were moreover claiming that it communicates in interesting and important ways with the writings of Georg Simmel, Edmund Husserl, Hans Vaihinger, and even members of the Vienna Circle, such as Ernst Mach and Ludwig Wittgenstein.

At the time of his death in 1917, for example, the great French sociologist Émile Durkheim was preparing to deliver a major series of lectures on pragmatism, and soon thereafter pragmatism began to attract a good deal of attention, almost all of it negative, in Germany. But if German philosophers like Martin Heidegger, Max Scheler, Theodor Adorno, and Max Horkheimer (Simmel, the father of German sociology, being a notable exception) assumed before midcentury that pragmatism represented technological reason at its worst, Jürgen Habermas, Germany's greatest philosopher after midcentury, found in pragmatism the key to his reconstruction of reason as a mode of communicative action. Habermas, however, is only one of a number European and world philosophers who have more recently discovered themselves in dialogue with ideas that were first developed by James. Others would include, in France, Pierre Bourdieu, Michel Foucault, and Julia Kristeva; in Germany, Hans-Otto Appel and Hans Joas; in Greece, Cornelius Castoriadis; in Brazil, Roberto Unger; and in Belgium, now Paris, Luce Irigaray.

The Pragmatic Rule and the Conflict of Temperaments

James first employed the term *pragmatism* in a lecture entitled "Philosophical Conceptions and Practical Results," delivered before the Philosophical Union at the University of California at Berkeley in August 1898. He was borrowing the term from his friend and sometime colleague Charles Sanders Peirce, who had first developed it in an essay that appeared in *Popular Science Monthly* in 1878 entitled "How to Make Our Ideas Clear." Peirce had in turn reported discovering the term in Kant's *Metaphysic of Morals* where, interestingly enough, it is contrasted with the term "practical"—Kant associates the "practical" with a priori moral laws, the "pragmatic" with rules of art and technique derived from experience—but for both Peirce and James pragmatism was essentially a new name for some older ways of thinking that could be found in everyone from Socrates and Aristotle to Spinoza, Locke, Berkeley, Hume, Kant, and Mill.

But the genealogical impulse can also be carried too far. When the pragmatic becomes merely another name for the practicable, its origins can be pushed back to the beginnings of primitive magic and early religion, from which it can then be said to have moved into ancient Greek literature, eventually becoming associated with certain Hellenistic schools of salvation; it was subsequently discovered by early Christianity, was later picked up and reexpressed during the Middle Ages by the Franciscans, eventually found its way into definitions of the "new knowledge" propounded by modern science, and was ultimately retrieved by American colonists who threaded it through Puritanism, the American Enlightenment, the opening of the West, and a host of other "American" moments since. If the contexts differ, the effect is the same. Linking knowledge with results, thought with power, ideas with action, may produce little that is new but also yields little that is distinctive: "the dictum holds for any interpretation of practical uses, sacred or profane, whether it be taken as recommending the subservience of all things to a moral aim or to material gain."[9]

Peirce's interests centered more narrowly than Dewey's or, for that matter, than James's on the problem of meaning: the pragmatic method, which he was at one point tempted to call "practicalism" and at another "pragmaticism," the latter, he hoped, being an ugly enough term to prevent it from being stolen by James and his followers, addressed this problem by proposing that all distinctions of thought can ultimately be reduced to differences in practice. Assuming further that our conceptions of things are no more than our idea of their sensible effects, Peirce devised the following pragmatic rule: "Consider what effects, that might conceivably have practical bearings, we conceive the object of our conception to have. Then, our conception of these effects is our whole conception of the object."[10]

What Peirce wanted was a procedure for determining the rational meaning of a word or concept, which for him lay "exclusively in its conceivable bearing upon the conduct of experience." Hence the "rational meaning of every proposition," Peirce asserted, "lies in the future," its meaning being "that form in which the proposition becomes applicable to human conduct, not in these or those special circumstances, nor when one entertains this or that special design, but in that form which is most directly applicable to self-control under every situation, and to every purpose."[11]

This was Peirce speaking like a scientist intent on establishing a rule for intellectual clarity that was sufficiently rigorous to stand up to laboratory conditions of exactitude, consistency, and logical coherence. Ideally, Peirce felt, scientific investigation should operate like a force of destiny, carrying the most radically antagonistic minds toward the same inevitable conclusion. "No modification of the point of view taken, no selection of other facts for study, no natural bent of mind even, can enable a man to escape the predestinate opinion." Truth is no more than "the opinion which is fated to be ultimately agreed to by all who investigate," Peirce maintained, "and the object represented in this opinion is the real."[12] That, and that alone, is what we should mean by reality.

By contrast, James was convinced from very early on that reality definitely exceeds the conclusions on which reasonable people can logically agree. Reality constantly overflows our intellectual formulas and findings and may be, as James observed only much later in "A Pluralistic Universe," "if not irrational then at least non-rational in its constitution."[13] James therefore wanted a less scientifically scrupulous or psychologically sanitized method for clarifying the meaning of principles, ideas, and language. After all, even scientists possessed needs, desires, biases, and preferences, and however laudable and necessary it was to submit those to scrutiny and possible modification and improvement through scientific investigation, one could not do away with them entirely. One's subject position, as we would now call it, is not irrelevant to one's investigative presuppositions and techniques.

More to the point, most of James's potential readers were not scientists, and the issues and concerns with which they were confronted did not, for the most part, lend themselves to scientific analysis. What they wanted were answers to larger, more unwieldy and amorphous questions, such as why to go on living, what constitutes the moral life, how to reconcile the many with the one, why truth matters, and what makes one view of the world better or truer than another. Consequently, philosophy needed to stop focusing all of its attention on its own problems and begin asking itself, as James put it in *Pragmatism,* "what definite difference it will make to you and me, at definite instants of our life, if this world-formula or that world-formula be the true one."[14]

Thus when James decided, in his lecture to the Philosophical Union at Berkeley in 1898, to borrow the pragmatic method from Peirce (he had actually heard Peirce invoke it in the early 1870s and had himself employed less-developed versions of it in his earlier writing), he sought to give it much more general application. While remaining in complete agreement with Peirce that beliefs are guides for action and that truth must be measured by the consequences to which it leads, James nonetheless felt that the pragmatic principle should be opened up. If the ultimate test of any truth is the conduct it produces, James reasoned in "Philosophical Conceptions and Practical Results," then one must grant that it produces or inspires this conduct only because it initially "foretells some particular turn to our experience which shall call for just that conduct from us." James was thus prepared to revise Peirce's principle to say that "the effective meaning of any philosophic proposition can always be brought down to some particular consequence, in our future practical experience, whether active or passive; the point lying rather in the fact that the experience must be particular, than in the fact that it must be active."[15]

The upshot of this expansion of Peirce's original definition is, first, that it permitted James to apply the method to a vastly broader terrain of experience than Peirce had considered. James was not interested in a method that works only under the controlled conditions afforded by laboratory apparatus or the classroom. He wanted a method that could be employed across the board, in all concrete cases. Second, it enabled James to turn pragmatic reasoning into an exercise that was less severely rational or deductive and more loosely interpretive and conjectural, one involving a good deal of mental guesswork as well as more stringent intellectual calibrations. To attain intellectual clarity, then, as James paraphrased Peirce both in his University of California address and, as here, in his chapter from *Pragmatism* entitled "What Pragmatism Means," "we need only consider what conceivable effects of a practical kind the object may involve—what sensations we are to expect from it, and what reactions we must prepare. Our conception of these effects, whether immediate or remote, is then for us the whole of our conception of the object, so far as that conception has positive significance at all."[16] *In Some Problems of Philosophy,* James simplified the method still further:

> The pragmatic rule is that the meaning of a concept may always be found, if not in some sensible particular which it directly designates, then in some particular difference in the course of human experience which its being true

will make. Test every concept by the question "What sensible difference to anybody will its truth make?" and you are in the best possible position for understanding what it means and for discussing its importance.[17]

James's definition of the pragmatic method clearly opened up Peirce's formulation to more comprehensive use while at the same time rendering it, much to Peirce's displeasure, a good deal less precise. The new imprecision of James's description of the method derived partly from some of the phrases it left open for further elucidation—"conceivable effects," "practical kind," "may involve," "sensations . . . to expect," "reactions . . . may prepare," or, in the phrasing from *Some Problems of Philosophy*, "sensible difference" and "course of human experience"—but it also stemmed from the way James put imagination back into the operations of rationality. To determine "some particular difference in the course of human experience which [a concept's] being true will make," as in the latter definition, or, to calculate, as in the former, "what sensations we are to expect from [the object], and what reactions we must prepare," was to put much greater reliance on the inferential and the projective capacities of the mind than Peirce had done. "Pragmatism unstiffens all our theories," James proclaimed, "limbers them up and sets each one at work,"[18] and the work our theories do is suppositional, hypothetical, and presumptive as well as analytic. Assessing notions in terms of their practical consequences often entailed reflection on matters that had not taken place yet, that could only be surmised rather than substantiated, imagined rather than corroborated. Where theories and beliefs had been for Peirce merely precepts, templates for action, for James they became instruments for imaginative speculation as well as catalysts for change.

Pragmatism could thus be said to coincide with, and reinforce, many philosophical orientations. "It agrees with nominalism, for instance, in always appealing to particulars; with utilitarianism in emphasizing practical aspects; with positivism in its disdain for verbal solutions, useless questions, and metaphysical abstractions" (28). It could also be seen as continuous with the practice of everyone from Socrates to Hume. But all of these forerunners had practiced it piecemeal. James was recommending that pragmatism be applied more universally and in a form that was intellectually more supple, accessible, and predictive. Even if it seemed to lack any presuppositions of its own and stood for no particular results, the pragmatic method could nonetheless serve as the solvent of all other philosophical theories, as the medium in which they conducted their investigations. Giovanni Papini, the Italian pragmatist, had caught exactly this dimension of the prag-

matic method when, in a particularly apt metaphor, he likened its operations among all theories to the way a corridor functions in a hotel. While
innumerable philosophical chambers open off of and onto this corridor,
each housing a particular way of thinking, and all of them have rights to it,
the corridor itself is philosophically neutral. It merely serves as the conduit
that all schools of thought must use if they are to exit their rooms, much less
circulate among one another.

If this was to say that the pragmatic method lacks an intellectual agenda,
it did not mean that it is bereft of any philosophical presuppositions or, more
to the point, that its adoption was without consequences. James, in fact, was
convinced that its broad-scale employment would spell the end of many
of the practices to which philosophers had become habituated over the
centuries. More specifically, it meant "*looking away from first things, principles, categories, supposed necessities,*" and "*towards last things, fruits, consequences, facts*" (29, italics James's). More generally, it meant "the open air and
possibilities of nature, as against dogma, artificiality, and the pretense of fi-
nality in truth" (27). If pragmatism was a method only, then it was a method
with, as we now say, an "attitude." James considered the implementation
of the pragmatic method nothing short of revolutionary and for a time
even imagined that he might be launching a new Protestant Reformation.

It should come as little surprise that, with ambitions such as these, James
shared with the British writer G. K. Chesterton the belief that the most important and practical thing one can know about individuals is their philosophy or worldview. By philosophy or worldview, however, James did not intend refer to anything derived chiefly from books but rather to one's "more
or less dumb sense of what life honestly and deeply means." Something acquired from the whole course of one's experience, one's philosophy is in this
sense simply "our individual way of just seeing and feeling the total push
and pressure of the cosmos" (7). James was prepared to concede that most
of us have no very clear idea of such matters; indeed, he was persuaded that
on large issues the great majority of us rarely know our own minds at all. But
he was also of the opinion that no individuals, professional philosophers
included, are indifferent to their "*Binnenleben,*" as he called it in "Is Life
Worth Living?," that mute "region of the heart in which we dwell alone with
our willingnesses and unwillingnesses, our faiths and fears" (240). "The history of philosophy," he therefore boldly proclaimed, "is to a great extent that
of a certain clash of human temperaments" (8).

That philosophical divisions can to a large degree be reduced to no more
than a difference in temperament is a claim that philosophers were no more

prepared to hear then than they are now. Violating all their preconceptions of and pretensions about their work as reasonable, objective, and disinterested, it provoked, not surprisingly, a torrent of criticism. But if philosophers remained for the most part adamant in defending themselves against such a charge, James was no less adamant in pressing it. Temperament might well be the last thing that philosophers wanted to admit into their practices, much less admit about them, but it was the first thing they trusted, James was certain, when it came to reaching their conclusions. Temperament "loads the evidence . . . just as this fact or that principle would" (9). The philosopher wants a universe that matches his or her temperament and rejects those that don't. The philosopher "feels men of opposite temper," James argues, "to be out of key with the world's character, and in his heart considers them incompetent and 'not in it,' in the philosophic business, even though they may far excel him in dialectical ability" (9). In *A Pluralistic Universe*, he went even further:

> If we take the whole history of philosophy, the systems reduce themselves to a few main types which, under all the technical verbiage in which the ingenious intellect of man envelops them, are just so many visions, modes of feeling the whole push, and seeing the whole drift of life, forced on one by one's total character and experience, and on the whole *preferred*--there is no other truthful word—as one's best working attitude.[19]

The conflict of temperament that marked his own period, James believed, set rationalists, as he called them, against empiricists. Rationalists were committed to abstract or timeless principles and tended to be intellectualistic, idealistic, optimistic, religious, monistic, and dogmatic. Empiricists, on the other hand, were committed to facts and thus tended to be materialistic, sensationalistic, positivist, pessimistic, fatalistic, pluralistic, and skeptical. While neither type was pure—traces of these differences can be found in some mixture in most of us—the clash between them could be discerned throughout literature, government, art, religion, social thought, and contemporary manners, as well as philosophy, and seemed to be reducible to a basic distinction between two types of personality. On the one side are the "tender-minded," who cling to the belief that facts should be related to values and values should be seen as predominant; on the other are the "tough-minded," who want facts to be dissociated from values and left to themselves. Just as the "tough-minded" find such things as idealism and intellectualism laid too heavily over the path of life, so the "tender-minded" complain that the path of life is choked with the weeds of positivism, relativism, utilitarianism, and naturalistic determinism. The "tender-minded" find the "tough-minded" callous and unfeeling, the "tough-minded" charge the "tender-minded" with sentimentality and fuzzy thinking. This clash has produced what James describes as "the dilemma in philosophy," a dilemma that has left thoughtful people who seek a philosophy for the whole person suspended between two seemingly irreconcilable and equally unattractive alternatives: either an empirical philosophy that leaves too little room for values and principles, or a rationalistic or intellectualistic philosophy that has lost touch with the concrete facts of human experience.

James offered pragmatism as a solution to this dilemma. Pragmatism could reconcile the ideal with the material, the rational with the concrete, because in addition to being a theory of meaning, pragmatism was also a theory of truth. As a theory of truth, James argued, pragmatism holds that ideas are not only abstractions from experience and generalizations about it but also aspects or components of it. Ideas, that is, do not simply comment on experience but actually constitute important elements of it. For example, ideas are the forms that life takes for us when we are living under the sway of ideologies or experience a feeling of solidarity with others who belong to those "imagined communities" called nationalities, religions, ethnicities, and so forth. More than that, ideas are what, for us, experience consists of when, even temporarily, our sensibilities undergo the reshapings of art and serious thought. Were this better understood, James assumed (and Dewey never tired of remarking), the importance of education, and the directions it should take, would be much more apparent to most people than they currently are.

Making Truth or Finding It

But if ideas are in fact aspects of experience and not simply interpretations of it, then ideas become true, James reasoned, or at any rate become true instrumentally, just insofar as they help place us in more constructive, more effectual, more valuable relations with other parts of our experience—just to the extent that they exhibit what James termed, borrowing an unfortunate metaphor from business, "cash-value." James's use of such commercial metaphors was not intended to imply, as he has been crudely misinterpreted to mean, that the truth of ideas or concepts is determined solely by, or reducible to, what they are good for in the intellectual or cultural or any other marketplace. He was merely restating and reaffirming what he thought Dewey and other members of the Chicago school had established, and what other disciplines as various as geology, biology, and philology now routinely accepted: that truth is not an inherent property of ideas as such but rather a property of their working connection with other things that already belong to the assemblage of the true.

James was here drawing from a familiar theory of how individuals typically acquire new opinions and establish their veracity. Truth normally lives on what James elsewhere refers to as a "credit system": "Our thoughts and beliefs 'pass' so long as nothing challenges them, just as bank-notes pass so long as nobody refuses them" (91). When some new experience emerges that unsettles the stock of already accepted opinions and thereby creates discomfort, the mind seeks to escape from this discomfort by attempting initially to modify the mass of already accepted opinion as much as possible. If this doesn't relieve the sense of inward unease, then one must await the discovery of some new idea that can be grafted onto the stock of older opinions with a minimum of difficulty, "some idea that mediates between the stock and the new experience and runs them into one another most felicitously and expediently." New truth functions as a kind of "go-between, a smoother-over of transitions. It marries old opinion to new fact so as ever to show a minimum of jolt, a maximum of continuity" (31).

One of James's chief interests in this subject is the part played by older truths in the acquisition of new truths. Even as knowledge grows, it only grows in spots and leaves most of what is already known completely intact. The greatest enemy of a new truth is thus likely to be the rest of our other truths. And even when a new truth can get itself grafted onto the stock of the old, it almost always comes "cooked" rather than "raw": "New truths . . . are resultants of new experiences and of old truths combined and mutually modifying one another" (75–76). In this connection, James's most startling assertion is that the body of truth that strikes most of us as no more than ordinary common sense may actually represent the distilled wisdom of some ancient genius whose discoveries have survived the long night of history to form a kind of "stage of equilibrium in the human mind's development" (76), a level that later stages of knowledge supplement without ever completely replacing. Thus, even if common sense does not represent the most complex or advanced stage of human understanding—James reserves this for science and critical philosophy—it shows us how knowledge increases and why truth is always relational. Truth is relational because it is never encountered alone or in isolation; it always emerges in association with its antecedents and allies, its previous models and affiliated figurations.

James deduced from this that truth is not so much found as made, and made in part out of former truths constantly being remade because they prove useful both as material for such remaking and as beliefs that do something for us.

> We plunge forward into the field of fresh experience with the beliefs our ancestors and we have made already; these determine what we notice; what we notice determines what we do; what we do again determines what we experience; so from one thing to another, altho the stubborn fact remains that there *is* a sensible flux, what is *true of it* seems from first to last to be largely a matter of our own creation. (255)

Truth therefore ceases to be a category distinct unto itself and becomes for James a species of the good. *"The true is the name of whatever proves itself to be good in the way of belief, and good, too, for definite, assignable reasons"* (38, italics James's). In purely functional terms, truth is, whatever else it is, what we say about it; "the reasons why we call things true is the reason why they *are* true, for 'to be true' *means* only to perform this marriage-function" (64). We accept things as true, then, not because of what, in and of themselves, they say about the real but rather because of what saying this about the real does to and for our relations with it.

Such views were, of course, bound to arouse a storm wind of disapproval, since they put James on a collision course with all those philosophers and laypeople who maintained instead that truth represents a correspondence with reality. In this more conventional notion of truth—which, as it happens, is the same notion that common sense holds, even if common sense portrays truth as something else—truth is a reflection of what is already there in existence prior to our perception of it. And what is already there in experience prior to our perception of it is simply the realm of the real that our ideas are supposed to copy. Empiricists in James's time, no less than in our own, supposed that the realm of the real is composed essentially of material facts or hard data. The rationalists and idealists who opposed them in James's time insisted instead that the real also includes our perception of purely mental notions like goodness and beauty and the relations between them. In James's estimation, however, both overlooked the fact that the real is also composed, as James had shown in his discussions of common sense, of the whole funded tradition of experience already accepted as true.

If this latter claim, even if not original with him, was one of the distinctive contributions of James's theory of truth, it immediately created problems for any who wanted to champion the view that truth is simply a matter of correspondence. The problem was how to square the idea of truth as correspondence or agreement with this threefold conception of the real as relating to facts, to ideas, and to history. James's answer was simple. Inasmuch as the idea of copying never worked in the first place for many of the things we already take for reality—James's examples include such things as "power," "spontaneity," and "time past"—he concluded that truth as "agreement" between an idea of something and the thing itself could only in the widest sense mean "*to be guided either straight up to it or into its surroundings, or to be put into such working touch with it as to handle either it or something connected with it better than if we disagreed*" (93, italics James's).

James's phrasing here is very important. Without disputing the fact that some ideas do indeed copy the reality they name, and thus coincide with reality more or less perfectly, he wishes to indicate that "agreement" in this literal sense is far from essential to what is most salient in our working notion of truth. For many purposes of truth—and particularly those we can never corroborate, so to speak, face-to-face—it is sufficient for ideas to lead us in the direction of reality and to aid us in our dealings with it. James speaks of this process of worthwhile leading as one by which an idea's truth is verified. Truth is not, in other words, ingredient in ideas from the outset but is acquired by them. Truth is what happens to an idea when it is put into the relations that confirm it. More than a description of the agreement that obtains between an idea and its referent, then, truth is an action, an event, a process, by which an idea's "agreement" or "correspondence," in only this widest sense James is talking about, is verified, validated. An idea's verity, however, is not to be confused with the process of its, as James called it, "veri-*fication*" (88). Truths are verified only retrospectively, and are always subject to further revision by later experience.

James was willing to admit that others might find this way of talking about "agreement" confusing, if not disturbing, but it was necessary if "agreement" was to apply to "any process of conduction" by which a present idea moves constructively or, to use James's term, "profitably" to a future conclusion. In any case, what all truths have in common, James was convinced, is "that they *pay*. They pay by guiding us into or towards some part of a system that dips at numerous points into sense-percepts, which we may copy mentally or not, but with which at any rate we are now in the kind of commerce vaguely designated as verification. Truth for us is simply a collective name for verification-processes" (96).

Describing truth as but another name for verification-processes was scarcely likely to silence James's critics, because verification-processes so often occur only at second- or thirdhand. Their belated nature derives from the fact that thinking is so wholly "discursified," as James put it, anticipating the insights of philosophers from our own time such as Jacques Derrida and Michel Foucault. By "discursified," James means that thinking is thoroughly mediated through interlinked systems of communication and exchange. Thus, as truth "gets verbally built out, stored up, and made available for every one," and verifications are lent and borrowed through "social intercourse," fewer and fewer of these ideas receive direct verification but are instead confirmed or disconfirmed by their relations with other discourses and discursive regimes (94).

James's notion of truth thus contains several elements that must be kept in view if one is not to be misled by its somewhat informal and digressive articulation. Predicating his argument on the assumption that truth involves agreement with reality only in the most general sense, James is careful to resist any imputation that "agreement" involves "one and the same relation in all cases" or that "agreement" is ultimately achievable only in some infinite mind that transcends the limitations of all human points of view.[20] Moreover, while truth involves for him something that works, that has practical effects, that is conducive to change, James's theory also owes something to Peirce's association of truth with reasoned consensus.

James may have come as close to sorting out these various elements as clearly as anywhere else in an interview he gave to the *New York Times* the same year that *Pragmatism* was published. Countering the charges that pragmatism denies any possibility of a theoretical knowledge of reality or truth, and that it functions for too many people as a practical substitute for philosophy itself, he insists, a bit defensively, that pragmatism has "proved so over-subtle that even academic critics have failed to catch its question, to say nothing of their misunderstanding of its answer":

> Whatever propositions or beliefs may, in point of fact, prove true, it says, the truth of them consists in certain definable *relations between them and the reality* of which they make report. . . . Philosophers have generally been satisfied with the word "agreement" here, but pragmatists have seen that this word covers many different concrete possibilities. . . . Thus the vague notion of "agreement" with reality becomes specified into that of innumerable ways in which our thoughts may *fit* reality, ways in which the mind's activities cooperate on equal terms with the reality producing the fit resultant truth.[21]

Statements such as this—or his more famous claim that "'[t]he true' . . . is only the expedient in the way of our thinking, just as 'the right' is only the expedient in the way of our behaving" (97–98)—have always furnished James's opponents with an excuse to brand him as an irresponsible subjectivist, and little he said later in *The Meaning of Truth,* where he attempted to address the strongest arguments of his best critics, has fully silenced his detractors. Indeed, when James tries to explain, as in the chapter "Humanism and Truth" from *The Meaning of Truth,* some of the implications of his theory by describing truth as "a relation, not of our ideas to non-human realities, but of conceptual parts of our experience to sensational parts," he only aroused them the more by maintaining that the "truth-relation," as he terms it, describes something that works, whether physically or intellectually, actually or merely possibly, in establishing relations within concrete experience (159).

Critics have taken this as further evidence that James denied the existence of real objects outside of or independent of the mind. James considered this charge malicious nonsense. Neither he nor any other pragmatist (he was thinking of Schiller and Dewey) had ever denied that the object in a truth-relation, if it be experienceable at all, is transcendent to the subject. How otherwise, he asked, to explain Dewey's insistence, with which he himself emphatically concurred, that the whole purpose of thinking is to intervene in and attempt to change the world *outside* the mind? "[Dewey's] account of knowledge is not only absurd, but meaningless, unless independent existences be there of which our ideas take account, and for the transformation of which they work. But because he and Schiller refuse to discuss objects and relations 'transcendent' in the sense of being *altogether transexperiential,* their critics pounce on sentences in their writings to that effect to show that they deny the existence *within the realm of experience* of objects external to the ideas that declare their presence there" (140).

While it seemed incredible to James that his most intelligent critics could have gotten him so far wrong, some of their misunderstanding was at least moderately intelligible. Part of the problem was that he was not writing primarily for professional philosophers but for members of an educated public that was more in need of intellectual encouragement and moral support than of precise definitions and logical arguments. In addition to being a source of irritation for some, this was also a source of bewilderment to others. A second factor was James's talent for vivid expression. If this produced a continuously conversational, sometimes even colloquial, prose style that was rich in figurative maneuvers and surprises, it frequently yielded metaphorical analogies that left much room for alternative and sometimes discrepant interpretations. Still a third reason for his problems with critics had to do with some of his formulations themselves. Many of his essays were written to meet publisher's deadlines, before he had time to think through all the implications of their arguments, and others were constructed with an eye to reconciling his theory of truth with his slowly evolving metaphysics.

Meaning and Beyond

James had been interested in what holds experience together since his ruminations on "the stream of thought" in *The Principles of Psychology*, and he had returned to this theme in various essays on the same subject that he had published in the first decade of the new century. In the essay "Does Consciousness Exist?," for example, he had continued to challenge dualistic thinkers who severed the mind from the body and viewed consciousness as an entity rather than a function. Insisting that consciousness refers to an "external relation" rather than "a special stuff or way of being," James had asserted that *the peculiarity of our experiences, that they not only are, but are known, which their conscious quality is invoked to explain, is better explained by their relations—these relations themselves being experiences—to one another.*[22]

But it was in the preface to *The Meaning of Truth* that James gave to this relational view of reality the name "radical empiricism" because it starts with parts rather than with wholes, with particulars rather than with unities, and then goes on to explain how the relations between parts relate to the parts themselves. Expanding on this series of assumptions, James said that radical empiricism consists of a postulate, a statement of fact, and a generalized conclusion. Its postulate is that philosophers can find the terms necessary to define all the things worthy of debate within experience itself. Its statement is that the relations between things are just as capable of being directly experienced as the things themselves. And its generalization is that the parts of experience are held together by relations that are no less elements of experience than the parts themselves. From this James concluded that the universe as we know it needs "no extraneous trans-empirical connective support, but possesses in its own right a concatenated or continuous structure" (138).

James's commitment to radical empiricism did not deter him from believing that this self-contained relational system of experience can still yield a sense of a "More" continuous with it but not confined by it, and in a late essay entitled "The Continuity of Experience" he came closest to explaining how this sense relates to his theory of consciousness. Even for a radical empiricist who believes "that the parts of experience are held together by relations that are no less elements of experience than the parts themselves," there was no contradiction in arguing that our consciousness of those relations also possesses a margin or horizon that surrounds its center but "shades insensibly into a subconscious more. . . . What we conceptually identify ourselves with," James continued, "and say we are thinking of at any given time is the centre; but our *full* self is the whole field, with all those indefinitely radiating subconscious possibilities of increase that we can only feel without conceiving, and can hardly begin to analyze."[23]

James was careful here not to step outside of experience to find the terms to describe something he sensed as capable of extending beyond its conceptual boundaries, and thus he was convinced, even if he was never able before he died to work out its full metaphysical implications, that radical empiricism was in no sense inconsistent with the essential pragmatist project. His aim all along, after all, had been to return philosophy to its earliest roots in the power of the imagination, where the meaning of ideas can only be determined by outcomes unable to be verified in advance but merely inferred or projected, consequences never absolutely assured but only anticipated or presumed, and in so doing he made philosophy uniquely available to literary uses.

The Pragmatist Disposition

No one made more of those uses than William's brother Henry. Though William and Henry James have come in for their fair share of comparison, such comparisons have paid surprisingly little attention to the specific philosophical and methodological connections between William's pragmatism and Henry's critical theory and literary practice.[24] There are no doubt various explanations for this, ranging from the tendency still prevalent in some circles to see Henry and William as intellectual as well as temperamental opposites to the belief that pragmatism has always remained too crude a philosophical instrument to be entertained by a mind as aesthetically refined as Henry's. Such prejudices can be maintained, however, only at the expense of suppressing the admission, wrung from a surprised but elated Henry upon the completion of William's book on pragmatism, that he was "lost in wonder of the extent to which all my life I have (like M. Jourdain) unconsciously pragmatised."[25] And upon finishing William's *The Meaning of Truth,* Henry was even more effusive and confessional:

You surely make philosophy more interesting and living than anyone has made it before, and by a real creative and undemolishable making; whereby all you write plays into poor "creative" consciousness and artistic vision and pretension with the most extraordinary suggestiveness and force of application and inspiration. Thank the powers—that is thank *yours*—for a relevant and assimilable and *referable* philosophy, which is related to the rest of one's intellectual life otherwise and more conveniently than a fowl is related to a fish. In short, dearest William, the effect of these collected papers of your present volume . . . seems to me exquisitely and adorably cumulative and, so to speak, consecrating; so that I, for my part feel Pragmatic invulnerability constituted.[26]

Such confessions might count for less if there was not such an abundance of textual evidence to support them. Much of the mystery surrounding a complicated literary text like Henry's masterpiece *The Turn of the Screw* would be dispelled if critics were more sensitive to these remarks. As in so much of his later fiction, Henry is investigating the experience of things that exist, as William would have said, on the very edge of consciousness and that, from a pragmatist perspective, challenge the kind of hysterical religious and moralistic intelligence that is tempted not merely to essentialize the presumed sources of those experiences but to demonize them. On this reading, it matters far less to the outcome of the story whether the ghosts are actually real or the children corrupted by merely thinking they are. What matters is that their governess is compelled by motives that are at once psychosexual and religiously superstitious to imagine that the children can be nothing else but demonic and is thereby transformed herself by the end of the story into a kind of monster from hell.

In similar fashion, Henry explores in *The Beast in the Jungle* the moral failure of a character who refuses, in effect, to become a radical empiricist. John Marcher's sin can be summarized as the continuous rejection of numerous opportunities to follow the pointings, as it were, of his own experience with May Bartram, to connect, if we can think of this in a broad sense, the subjects of his sentences with the predicates they imply. While none of this is expressed discursively, James renders it dramatically by, to give pragmatism another name, the "ambulatory" method he shared with William.

Ambulation is the intellectual method that enables us, as William stated, to move toward a knowable object by means of the impulse, and not the content, which the idea of it communicates to us. A trenchant description of the method of what Henry perfected in his later writing, pragmatic ambulation is premised epistemologically on the belief that the greatest threat to the inquiring mind is the temptation to interrupt the process of its continuous construction and reconstruction by arresting and isolating some moment from the ongoing process and taking it for an image of the whole. Seeking instead what Wallace Stevens was later to call the "ghostlier demarcations" and "keener sounds" of consciousness in motion, the later fiction of Henry James was an attempt to render life not only as process but as passage from one state of mind to another, from one set of feelings to another.

Much of the deep affinity between William's later philosophical method and Henry's literary one derives from the suspicion with which both regarded the self-possessive individualism and obsession with cultural authority that marked the traditional Victorian conception of identity at the end of the nineteenth century. Both were drawn to a more relaxed, fluid, spontaneous, and pluralistic sense of self that was bent on dissolving the genteel boundaries between subject and object, detachment and commitment, self and other. If this modernist project in pragmatic self-refashioning sounds a good deal more like the William of *Pragmatism, The Meaning of Truth,* and *A Pluralistic Universe* than the Henry of *The Lesson of the Master, The Sacred Fount,* or the critical essays, it was nonetheless Henry as much as William who, as a literary pragmatist, cultivated an intellectual disposition and style intended to loosen the intellectual, emotional, aesthetic, and other restraints placed on consciousness by Victorian, bourgeois culture and to replace it with a more relaxed curiosity and receptivity desirous of encompassing the shifting, contradictory, enigmatic, and continuously disruptive contours of experience itself. Indeed, by emphasizing the historicity and provisionality of such categories as individualism, consciousness, and identity in all the writings of his "second major phase," Henry was committed as strongly as his brother William, as we shall see in the next chapter, to the development of social institutions and practices in America capable of dissolving the artificial and brittle distinctions of the present in favor of new forms of agency, empowerment, and value that might be enabled to take their place.[27]

SIX

Religion and the Enlightenment under the Sign of the Modern and Beyond

Style and the Modern

When American philosophical pragmatism began to be worked out in modern literary terms, it took the form of a theory of representation that attempted to reconcile what was still epistemologically viable about the Enlightenment's quest for a sense of reality that was tangible, empirical, rational, substantive, and scientifically accessible with what was still culturally exigent about American religion's imagination of a kind of otherness that cannot simply be put by, cannot be glossed or disregarded. As a theory of representation, then, American pragmatism presupposed a theory of the real. It was a theory that proposed that if the real lies neither wholly beyond the self, in some hypostatizable world set over against it, nor wholly within the self, in some spiritual core or biological deposit that exists independent of its actualizations, then the real is to be found in the experience of those events, processes, and actions through which the self interacts with whatever is felt to be external to it. In other words, the real, or rather our notion of it, is no mere object or entity that exists outside of, and prior to, our perception or consciousness of it, and our perception or consciousness of it does not exist independent of the whole funded system of past experience that has furnished us with the repository of concepts, ideas, notions, and images to make cognitive and emotional sense of it. What we make of the real is as much a function of imagination as of mind, and how we relate to it as much an expression of style as of automatic reflex.

Style in this sense is the very opposite of an instinctive, or casual, or even idiosyncratic response to something or mode of treating it. It is part of a larger system of behavior that is, perhaps, best understood in relation to Pierre Bourdieu's notion of *habitus*. *Habitus* refers to the social process by which past experience is transmuted into a kind of embodied knowledge that takes the form of lasting dispositions that organize and structure the specific ways that people come to think, feel, and act in relation to recurrent situations and problems.[1] While these ways are in some sense learned, that learning is more tacit than explicit, because it is based not on mastering a set of rules but on absorbing patterns of potential responses to, and representations of, specific conditions. Such dispositional patterns and propensities are not fixed but generative. Themselves the product of improvisations, extemporizations, and experiments, they generate new improvisational possibilities that permit these same dispositional patterns and propensities to be transferrable over time both from one situation to another and from one context to another. Style in this broad Bourdieuian sense, then, is no mere expression of individual taste affecting the manner by which some particular object or phenomenon is presented but a distinctive form of expressive inventiveness that is produced when the symbolic capital represented by one kind of embodied knowledge is converted and reproduced, or, as I put it, pragmatically refigured, across the symbolic field of another. In such terms as these, styles of representational improvisation are social forms that are just as capable of characterizing the literature of an entire era as they are of explaining how the ideational forms created in one era can survive as spiritual imaginaries in another.

According to popular belief, no event had a more decisive impact on the creation of the modern style than the Great War, as it is still referred to, in the second decade of the twentieth century. The first international conflict in which hostilities were no longer confined to the battlefield, World War I wound up engulfing the citizens of all the nations involved and in the end destroyed no less than seven empires. By comparison with its staggering consequences, its principal new weapons of destruction—the machine gun, barbed wire, and trench warfare—were comparatively few, but in three and a half years the double line of trenches separating the combatants, which eventually extended from the Swiss border to the North Sea—the Allied Powers of France, Russia, Serbia, the United Kingdom, Italy, Belgium, and eventually the United States on one side, the Central Powers of Austria-Hungary, Germany, and Bulgaria on the other—never moved more than ten miles in either direction but produced 37 million victims (16 million dead, 21 million wounded).

Yet the enormity of the loss could not be calculated solely in terms of the number of casualties: "Not only did the young suffer in the war," as John Peale Bishop wrote, "but every abstraction that would have sustained and given dignity to their suffering."[2] No one captured this aspect of the loss, or stylistically inscribed its horror more effectively, than Ernest Hemingway in the words he gave to his protagonist in *Farewell to Arms*, Lieutenant Frederic Henry:

> I was always embarrassed by the words sacred, glorious, and sacrifice.... I had seen nothing sacred, and the things that were glorious had no glory and the sacrifices were like the stockyards at Chicago if nothing was done with the meat but to bury it. There were many words that you could not stand to hear and finally only the names of places had dignity.[3]

Hemingway's bitterness, obvious as it is, might well have been lost on his readers if he had not found a suitable technique for expressing it. The technique he devised was the method of irony, which enabled him to employ the comparison between the slaughter on the battlefield and the slaughter in the stockyards of Chicago to dramatize the gross disparity between the rhetoric used to justify and legitimate the war and the meaninglessness of the terrible sacrifices the war entailed. Hemingway could have settled for sarcasm and disgust, but the understatement of irony was more appropriate for rendering the monstrous disproportion between ends and means. Not only was irony more suitable for identifying, drawing forth, and finally shaping "into significance an event or a moment which otherwise would merge without meaning into the general undifferentiated stream,"[4] it was also the only tropological form capable of registering at the same time the innocence that had been shattered in the process.

As the Danish philosopher Søren Kierkegaard once noted, historical recollection is never confined to the simple repetition of a previous experience but is coupled with the re-creation of it in memory, which in turn awakens that memory to new life. This new life is not the original experience simply recalled and reframed but rather that former life actively reborn and thus made available for reexperiencing under different conditions that can trigger it. From this perspective, the sense of irony originally aroused by the terrible discrepancy between aims and results in World War I could be, and so often was, later re-aroused and extended not only by World War II but also, as can be seen in American war fiction from Norman Mailer's *The Naked and the Dead*, James Jones's *From Here to Eternity*, Joseph Heller's *Catch-22*, Kurt Vonnegut's *Slaughterhouse Five*, and Tim O'Brien's *The Things They Carried* to Siobhan Fallon's *You Know When the Men Are Gone*, David Abrams's *Fobbit*, and Jesse Goolsby's *I'd Walk with My Friends If I Could Find Them*, by all the American wars that have succeeded it.

This perception that what we actually confront in life is not the absolutely original and unprecedented so much as the past reawakened into a new form reinforces the humanistic idea—Freud proposed it in a different way—that the past constitutes much of what we face in life: "it may be shadowy," as the Canadian literary critic and theorist Northrop Frye once observed, "but it is all that is there."[5] Frye turned this observation back on Plato's famous Allegory of the Cave in which human beings gain access to the objective world only indirectly through the shapes that flicker against the walls around them from the light outside the cave cast by reality's so-called True Forms. But if Plato's theory of True Forms is rejected, this analogy breaks down, Frye believed, and turns the shapes dancing on the walls into images of the past, and the light we see them by as illumination coming from within ourselves. In this case, Fry asserted, the past is converted into something more than "the memory of mankind"; it is rather a reflection of our own buried life whose study leads to recognition scenes in which we see not simply that part of our lives lost to the past "but the total cultural form of our present life."[6] Thus without accepting Fry's revision of Plato, it is not too difficult to understand how the radical disproportion between ends and means, as represented by total war in the twentieth century, could become the modern recognition scene par excellence and irony the stylistic mode of its representation.

Pragmatism and Modernist Representation

At the risk of oversimplification, I would suggest that this is the theory of the real variously put to the test in that kind of twentieth-century American literature we traditionally refer to as modern. The test itself assumed that there is no other light by which to illumine life but that which comes from ourselves, and particularly from our own hidden past. It also assumed that this past is not something that belongs to us individually but instead to the entire cultural collective to which we belong. The critical task for the writer is not, however, to reproduce that collective memory in its entirety but rather to find events, situations, stories, images, processes, that might serve as something like what T. S. Eliot meant by the term "objective correlative"—"a set of objects, a situation, a chain of events which shall be the formula of that particular emotion; such that when the external facts, which must terminate in sensory experience, are given, the emotion is immediately evoked."[7] Eliot employed this term somewhat crudely to refer to the mechanism by which emotion is evoked in a reader, but when applied more broadly to culture as a whole, it is suggestive of the way Frye's "total cultural form of our present life" might find embodiment in particular representations and stylistic instances.

This was a challenge that was obviously to take a variety of forms, ranging from Hemingway's belief that "the greatest difficulty, aside from knowing truly what you really felt, rather than what you were supposed to feel, was to put down what really happened in action; what the actual things were which produced the emotion you experienced"[8] to Faulkner's efforts to recover the "presentness of the past" in fictions whose elaborate methods of technique—unreliable narration, stream-of-consciousness writing, mythic parallels, chronological disorientation, historical flashbacks, montage effects, philosophical brooding, and structures of detection—were intended to historicize his readers' sense of the present. In some cases, that test involved parsing something as indefinable as what Stevens meant by his reference in "The Snow Man" to "Nothing that is not there and the nothingness that is."[9] In others, "'making it new,' to employ Ezra Pound's motto for modernism, entailed embrace of the claim that 'poetry is a sort of inspired mathematics, which gives us equations, not for abstract figures, triangles, squares, and the like, but for the human emotions.'"[10] The challenge, whether in Marianne Moore's poetic experiments in exacting attention or Katherine Anne Porter's fictional reproductions of the technology of memory, William Carlos William's epistemological inquiries into how much "depends upon / a red wheel barrow / glistened with rain water / beside the white chickens," or Langston Hughes's ruminations on the sources, both ancient and contemporary, of African American experience, was to represent life stylistically, as it were, *in actu.*

As a theory of representation, then, this pragmatist belief about the real, which was in truth a theory of consciousness, or, rather, a theory of the consciousness of consciousness, could still survive the tests put to it by modern circumstances—even in such desperate gestures of self-definition as Adrienne Rich's "Diving into the Wreck" or such self-doubting acts of social investigation as James Agee's *Let Us Now Praise Famous Men*—so long as the spirit of an increasing late modernist skepticism could be prevented from rebelling against consciousness itself by calling into question its belief that imagination and style represent not, as Robert Frost put it in "The Most of It," one's "own love back in copy speech, / But counter-love, original response."[11] Yet when the spirit of a more radicalized criticism began to invade the precincts of consciousness itself, its contents no less than its creations could be quickly reduced, as in the stories of a Donald Barthelme, to a series of clichés, what he calls the "dreck" of contemporary society, or to mere critical and aesthetic "junk," what John Barth portrays in *The Sot-Weed Factor* as the "refuse" of literary history or what William Gibson evokes in *Neuromancer* of the digital replicability of cyberspace.

Texts such as these tend to presume that consciousness is little more than a construct made up of "used" components that, like the cigarette butts, old Kleenex tissues, and discarded food wrappers left behind in second-hand cars when they are traded in, symbolize only the pathos of their own disposability or, in a more digitalized world, their interchangeability. In a world composed of little more than trash, or what Pynchon wittily referred to as early as the 1960s in *The Crying of Lot 49* as "W.A.S.T.E.," the contents that consciousness was once held to represent—feelings, relations, aspirations, intuitions, passages, interruptions, detours, aporias—dissolve into thin air and are replaced by gestures, signs, and marks as innocently empty of significance and as infinitely replicable as the mind of Chance the gardener in Jerzy Kosiński's *Being There,* whom the television producers rename "Chauncey Gardener," or as indeterminate and sometimes unreadable as the "art of distilling / Weird fragrances out of nothing" that constitutes the subject of John Ashbery's *Self-Portrait in a Convex Mirror and Other Poems.*

Style and the Postmodern

Do deconstructive texts of such comparative depthlessness and de-realization, of such pastiche and parody, point to anything beyond themselves, or are they, from a pragmatist perspective, the template of new modes of diffidence, perhaps different kinds of irony? Literary criticism since the Romantic period has often been haunted by the prospect of irony threatening to open up in the direction of "infinite absolute negativities,"[12] but it may simply be a case of "the song of the prisoner," as David Foster Wallace once noted, "who's come to love his cage."[13] Either way, there is no doubt that contemporary reality has itself taken on forms that defy many efforts of literary representation. As long ago as the early 1960s, Philip Roth complained about how American reality had already become "a kind of embarrassment" to the writer's imagination: "The actuality is continually outdoing our talents, and the culture tosses up figures almost daily that are the envy of any novelist."[14] But now the embarrassment has turned into a significant dilemma as fiction has been replaced by reality TV, reality TV by twenty-four-hour news cycles, perpetual news cycles by social media, and social media now by digital surveillance and the obliteration of privacy.

American modernism counted on a sense of privacy to give irony a space in which to work its pragmatic refigurations of the contrast between ends and means, expectations and outcomes. The object of such exercises was not the achievement of a new sense of the sublime or the beautiful, as the French poet Charles Baudelaire hoped, but a new sense of the authentic, the genuine, or the real. But American postmodernism, if it actually constitutes a new period style as opposed to a mere assemblage of tastes and preferences for discontinuity, incongruity, indeterminacy, and the superficial, uses irony, if at all, to remind us that authenticity is itself the true fiction and that the only way of getting over it is by accepting the fact that reality is no more than a house of mirrors.[15] Where modernism seeks to negotiate a kind of ironic transcendence downward through the mud and slush of opinion, commercial kitsch, and bad faith that covers the globe, to adapt an image from Henry David Thoreau's *Walden,* until we come to something that feels unadulterated, spontaneous, and true, such as William Butler Yeats's "foul rag and bone shop of the heart, where all the ladders start,"[16] postmodernism finds that its own efforts at downward transcendence merely disclose something like a set of Russian nesting dolls, or matryoshka as they are called, where each figure contains within itself a smaller copy or resemblance of itself, thus suggesting that reality is made up of nothing more than identical reproductions arranged in a diminishing order of size and significance. Where modernism is absorbed with depths, intensities, complexities, and subtleties, postmodernism prefers surfaces, exteriors, facades, reflections, and reminders. While modernism seeks the image below which one cannot descend, postmodernism fastens on the image of other images that go as far down as one can see.

The question is whether a period style and cultural sensibility like the postmodern can tolerate, much less accommodate, what I have been describing as the pragmatist cultural project in America—the project of re-grafting those parts of the critical, self-reflexive heritage that survived the seductions of Enlightenment essentializations of rationality, materialism, progress, and didacticism to those elements of the seventeenth-century religious heritage that resisted the soporifics of certainty and self-righteousness. The answer seems to depend on which Enlightenment we are talking about and what kind of religion survived those soporifics. While postmodernism may well represent a cultural mindset in America that is deeply alienated from the religious and other enthusiasms that surround it, it is quite possible that postmodernism has not seen the last of some of the mindfulness originally associated with the Enlightenment. In late modernist and post-modernist American literature, the critical or skeptical Enlightenment is, in one of its forms, clearly in the process of seeking to avenge itself against one of its own principal earlier achievements. That achievement, according to Michel Foucault, was the creation of the philosophical subject known as "Man" that in former epochs underwrote such important projects as democratic governance, Freudian psychology, and the humanistic tradition, but that in ours tends to be viewed as just another discredited technique by which human beings reinvent themselves as privileged objects of their own study.[17]

This act of critical self-consumption has, to be sure, cleared the intellectual and cultural field of much of the metaphysical and moral debris that had accumulated there over the last several centuries, but at the same time it has left the field morally and spiritually eviscerated. To some observers, this may merely signify America's return to the state of moral and spiritual poverty that, on their reading, has always been its natural condition, or at least has always been the condition most propitious for its creative development. The philosopher Stanley Cavell, along with the literary and cultural critic Richard Poirier, has turned this double conviction into what is probably the most powerful defense ever mounted of an American literary and philosophical tradition that originates with Emerson and was expanded by Thoreau, a tradition that defines the philosopher or thinker as a kind of artist, explorer, surveyor, voyager, or, in Thoreau's coinage "saunterer," in search of what, echoing Emerson, Cavell calls, in the title of one of his later books, "this new yet unapproachable America."[18]

America's New Unapproachability

Cavell's image of the thinker or philosopher in America as ever in motion and discovering all acts of founding, as Emerson put it, in the experience of finding "could not have presented itself as a stable philosophical proposal before the configuration of philosophy established by the work of the later Heidegger and the later Wittgenstein."[19] Cavell describes this reconfiguration, or, better, refiguration, of philosophy as "the establishing of thinking as knowing how to go on, being on the way, onward and onward." If explanations come to an end at each step or level," Cavell continues, "there is no level to which all explanations come, at which all end."[20] Thus when Emerson famously opened his essay "Experience" by posing the question about where we find ourselves, his answer was that we find ourselves "in a series of which we do not know the extremes," on a stair whose step may be the only destination we reach because the true destination is in the stepping and not

the arrival. This renders Cavell's philosopher, like James's ambulatory pragmatist, both products of what Emerson called "the Fall of Man," the "very
unhappy, but too late to be helped, discovery that we exist."[21] No longer anticipating the possibility of a reunification with Nature, as the Romantics
hoped, or a reconciliation with Being Itself, as the Puritans hoped, they are
all spiritual exiles searching to find and "be born again into," as Emerson described it for himself, "this new yet unapproachable America in the West."[22]

But what now, if not then, makes the America that Emerson "found
in the West" both new and unapproachable? Cavell posits that it is unapproachable because in a negative sense its culture is conformist, which is
the same thing as saying that for Emerson it is unoriginal. Being unoriginal,
American culture does not know, at least in its "official" versions of itself,
what it might or could originate, does not even have a language to speak of
or think such things, except in the realm of technology. In a more positive
sense, America is "unapproachable" because it is undiscussable, and it is
undiscussable because it offers no terms of approach to what it has not yet
begun to be—to the experience, as Cavell goes on to say, that it has not had
of what it has yet to experience.

This may be as simple as saying that America has—or, at least until Emerson's time, had—no language of its own, but Cavell questions whether
this can be supported. Cavell's way out of this dilemma is to turn back to
the project of Emerson himself for what amounts to a description of his
own philosophical practice in America's continuing economy of cultural
scarcity:

> The classical British Empiricists had interpreted what we call experience as
> made up of impressions and the ideas derived from impressions. What Em-
> erson wishes to show, in these terms, is that, for all our empiricism, nothing
> (now) makes an impression on us, that we accordingly have no experience
> (of our own), that we are inexperienced. Hence Emerson's writing is meant
> as the provision of experience for these shores, of our trials, perils, essays.[23]

If Emerson was correct in arguing that America's unapproachability derives from its own lack of experience, Cavell is correct that Emerson sought
to address this lacuna by turning his own writing into the instrument by
means of which to reverse it. The question is what reversing it would mean
if the problem wasn't simply America's unapproachability as such but rather
why that unapproachability was not approachable to itself. Was there something about America's lack of experience that prevented it from recognizing,
much less coming to terms with, its own unapproachability, and could that

be fixed, as Emerson believed, by the substitution of one kind of language, one way of speaking and thus seeing, for another?

Between Emerson's time and ours "the theatre has changed," as Wallace Stevens said of modernism, and with it the kind of play that can be staged there. The play may still remain a drama about America being "new yet unapproachable"—a drama where religion and the Enlightenment, belief and reason, continue to struggle for control of the definition of experience—but the setting has been transformed and with it the stakes involved. Not only have the coordinates of experience been altered, as Henry Adams noted in his *Education,* putting power and force in the place of faith or reason, but so have the optics by which to bring them into focus. The issue for twentieth-century America was not only how to comprehend a world reorganized around the coordinates of energy, process, mutability, force, and power but how to cope with such a world if the two great spiritual imaginaries once used to illumine it, much less cope with its alterations, have had to be significantly refigured in a less essentialist and more pragmatist direction.

Henry James and *The American Scene* Pragmatized

No one at the beginning of the twentieth century perceived this crisis more clearly or diagnosed its symptoms more shrewdly than William James's brother Henry. But when Henry James looked at his country pragmatically through the eyes of its own religious and Enlightened sense of itself, what he saw was not a blank check on the future that the United States might write to relegitimate its present, but rather a bill of indebtedness that the United States had already accumulated on its religious and Enlightened past. This bill of arrears revealed the inconsistencies, lapses, and contradictions inherent from the beginning within America's own spiritual imagination of itself, and it encouraged James to believe that this debt could not, and would not, be settled without a full accounting of its costs to the treasury of national values and a full assessment of its consequences for a redefinition of national purpose.

James's *The American Scene* presents itself as a travel narrative based on impressions that James obtained during a lengthy trip from England to America at the beginning of the twentieth century, a trip that took him from New England into the Deep South and eventually out to the Far West. During this extended journey, he was struck again and again by how difficult it was to make out the meaning of his materials. The difficulty was not that they resisted being read but that there was nothing behind or underneath them to read them by. In other words, their meaning, once James had devised a method for interrogating them, was somehow related to their unapproachability, and their unapproachability ultimately lay not in what America had done but rather in what it had left undone.

The difference between the two was crucial. What America had done, because of its appetite for the infinite material expansion and "perpetual increase of everything," had only contributed to what he called "the triumph of the superficial and the apotheosis of the raw."[24] What it had left undone, because of obligations it continuously deferred and possibilities it recurrently postponed, was the realization of those dreams on which this "growth of the immeasurable muchness," as he called it, was presumably based—greater spiritual well-being for the many along with social justice, human rights, and democratic governance for all. In short, what it had all too readily managed to accomplish was a betrayal of the ethical requirements of America's religious and Enlightenment heritages. America's "pretended message of civilization" had thus been transformed from what he had initially judged simply to be a history of "ravage" into what he now felt was "a colossal recipe for the *creation* of arrears, and of such as can but remain forever out of hand" [465].

But why should these arrears remain forever out of hand? What kept these debts not simply from being paid but even from being acknowledged? The answer was to be found in what James called the "American postulate" that enabled the more fortunate citizens of the United States to consistently defend themselves against such recognitions by seeking "to make so much money that you won't, that you don't, 'mind' anything" (237). There was thus in the America of James's time, as there is in ours, "such a thing . . . as freedom to grow up blighted," and this freedom might still remain, as James ruefully but prophetically added, "the only freedom in store for the smaller fry of future generations?" (136–37).

This shift in the basis of his assessment of the American experiment involved a fairly tricky moral calculation. By training a product of the Victorian era who based his judgments on the criterion of perception, discrimination, and taste, James was initially tempted to argue that the whole question of America's future was essentially bound up with the issue of moral and aesthetic (and, he could have added, social and political) values. The need in America, he predictably sensed, was simply for greater and different values than America itself could supply. But James was also by disposition a shrewd enough modernist to realize that this perception could generate very different responses. If some of America's citizens were likely to react to an inadequate supply of acceptable values by essentially trying to create new ones, others were quite capable of reasoning that if no acceptable values were available in America, then their appearance must somehow be faked.

In fact, much of what James reported himself confronting in the United States of 1904 and 1905 amounted to just such fakery, the simulation and not the substance of values. The question of assessing the American cultural experiment in a world where the image, likeness, or illusion of values was constantly being confused with their substance therefore tended to reduce itself to the ticklish issue he confronted at the very end of his book, the issue of what to make of the impression of "boundless immensity" that was framed for him by a Pullman car window when that very immensity was presumed by the culture of which the Pullman car itself was an expression to exist solely for the sake of its pretentious ability to impress. The rumble of the Pullman's wheels, as if speaking for America as a whole, seemed ready to plead, almost in apology, "See what I am making of all this—see what I'm making, what making" (463). But all James could think about, as he contemplated "the Margin," as he referred to it, "by which the total of American life, huge as it already appears, is still so surrounded as to represent for the mind's eye on a general view, but a scant central flotilla huddled as for very fear of the fathomless depth of water, the too formidable future, on the so much vaster lake of the materially possible" (410)—was what America had left unmade and perhaps forever unmakeable.

As was already apparent to many observers, what America was making was a society seeking through the shortcut of money to acquire those things that money alone cannot purchase, those things that come only with time, history, and experience. The challenge was to figure out what to make of this spectacle, how to interrogate it; and here James's genius took over when he decided to represent this spectacle as a kind of drama whose given, or *donnée*, might be described as "the great adventure of a society reaching out into the apparent void for the amenities, the consummations, after having earnestly gathered in so many of the preparations and necessities." While much of the interest in this drama, James reasoned, would naturally depend on whether the void was only apparent or actually real, and with what did or didn't lurk beneath the appearance of this vacancy, its chief interest lay in determining what the vacancy, as it were, cost, and how one was obliged to ante up—morally, emotionally, materially, aesthetically—to satisfy the needs of the spirit by means of the stratagems of cupidity and avarice. What had Americans been obliged to pay to use affluence and ostentation to fulfill what Emerson would have called the whole soul of the human self? It would all depend on whether the materials representing this case could be deciphered and read, but at this point James's interpretive efforts suddenly ran aground.

James had encountered such difficulties of interpretation in the United States before, as he had amply illustrated in his earlier book on Nathaniel Hawthorne, but now, some decades later, the problem was different. Here it was no longer a problem of finding his materials thin or opaque—or even, as his twenty years of European expatriation might have disposed him to feel, finding them trivial, weightless, or banal—but instead one of simply discovering them to be blank. Seeking to discern the buried significance, the hidden meaning, behind appearances, James was brought up short by the realization that many of the appearances he most wanted to understand in America lacked any buried significance at all, were simply void of inner content, and this produced a critical crisis of the first magnitude:

> To be at all critically or as we have been fond of calling it, analytically, minded [. . .] is to be subject to the superstition that objects and places, coherently grouped, disposed for human use and addressed to it, must have a sense of their own, a mystic meaning proper to themselves to give out: to give out that is, to the participant at once so interested and so detached as to be moved to a report of the matter. That perverse person is obliged to take it for a working theory that the essence of almost any settled aspect of anything may be extracted by the chemistry of criticism, and may give us its right name, its formula, for use. (273)

Yet James was to discover repeatedly that his material resisted his interpretive exertions. Appearances seemed to lack intrinsic meaning of any kind, to be devoid of content. If this resistance could have been explained by the mere absence of something, the critic, James reasoned, could have been asked to supply the wanted element. But in modern America this deficiency had already taken on an almost postmodern connotation. Given that there seemed to be nothing behind or beneath the materials of American life by means of which the discerning observer might infer their significance, some more richly interfused presence of the sort that used to be designated, say, by the term *tradition*, James was led to make two discoveries about America's unapproachability. The first was that in the absence of anything seemingly behind or beneath the most representative materials of American life, "the living fact" could be made to stand for almost anything. The second was that the value overriding all others in importance for Americans was their unwillingness to consent to any privation. Taken together, James was convinced that he had come up with "the theory of the native spirit," which was most evident in Americans' desire for things of whose existence or possibility they were as yet unaware (372). In such a social world, James realized, the purpose of culture quickly becomes reduced to the production and service of these future awakenings, but this service can only be performed, he reasoned, if the cultural medium is prepared to be stretched to an inordinate thinness. Thinness doing on America's side of the Atlantic what thickness once did on the other, James now found himself in a position to read the opacity and vacancy of his materials: simply refigure them pragmatically so that their incapacity to disclose any deeper import within themselves could be interpreted as the key to what might in truth be eventually made of them.

One can see the way this pragmatic refiguration was accomplished by noting how James "worked" his impressions to make sense of what was then, by the turn of the century, the new culture of the American hotel. While the outward elements of the new American hotel were plain enough for anyone to see, and required no going behind them, as in Europe, to infer the "multitudinous, complicated life" they obviously concealed, the innerness of the hotel in America appeared to James to be made up of nothing but its externalities, its manifest outward appearance constituting, for a very significant majority of the people who could afford to avail themselves of its benefactions, "the richest form of existence" (406). What in effect the hotel in America thus seemed to say was that its significance was written on its face and that, as a consequence, one was free to make of it whatever one can or will. But to this putative revelation, James could only reply: "Yes, I see how you are, God knows—for nothing in the world is easier to see, even in all the particulars. But what does it *mean* to be as you are?" (407).

By the time James completed his journey, he had found the answer to his question. America's unmindful, or, more accurately, mindless, quest for the materially possible not only made America unapproachable to itself but guaranteed that this unapproachability would prevent it from confronting the deeper elements of self-betrayal it contained within itself. Looking again out of his Pullman car window on his trip to the Far West, James was seized by a spectacle that continues to cast as dark a shadow over the American spiritual landscape now as it did then:

> You touch the great lonely land—as one feels it still to be—only to plant upon it some ugliness about which . . . you then proceed to brag with a cynicism all

your own. You convert the large and noble sanities that I see around me . . . to crudities, to invalidities, hideous and unashamed; and you so leave them to add to the number of the myriad aspects you simply spoil, of the myriad unanswerable questions that you scatter about as some monstrous unnatural mother might leave a family of unfathered infants on doorsteps or in waiting-rooms. . . . When nobody cares or notices or suffers, by all one makes out, when no displeasure, by what one can see, is ever felt or ever registered, why shouldn't you, you may indeed ask, be as much in your right as you need? But in that fact itself, that fact of the vast general unconsciousness and indifference, loom, for any restless analyst who may come along, the accumulation, on your hands, of the unretrieved and the irretrievable. (463–64)

James's jeremiad was provoked not simply by the way America had inured itself to the necessity of repaying the debts it had incurred on its own inherited ideals. It was also fueled by his perception that the country's "great grope of wealth" had insured its insensibility of, not to say indifference to, such obligations. This amounted to asserting that if the memory of such debts was likely to recede into still deeper mists of obscurity the more they were defended in a language of self-righteous entitlement, then the more their irretrievability would constitute the true meaning of America's exceptionalism, of its presumption, to recall Stanley Cavell, that it continues to lack any adequate language—for how could there be any?—to express its potential for yet still newer, more spectacular experience that it could boast it had still to achieve. Like Emerson before him, then, James gave America that language by using the terms of his pragmatist critique to suggest by contrast what America's mindlessness, its purported unapproachability, was attempting to efface: the costs entailed in failing to defend, much less to protect, that part of the whole human soul, to use the language of the religious imaginary, that can only be purchased in the coin, as the Enlightenment imaginary insisted, of rights, equality, freedom, and human dignity.

The Still Unretrieved and Irretrievable

This is one of the tasks that the pragmatic tradition in American writing and thought has tried to imagine for itself in the modern era. It was brought to richest early expression in the philosophy of John Dewey as well as George Herbert Mead, and has been continued by everyone from W. E. B. Du Bois, Alain Locke, and Kenneth Burke to Richard Rorty, Hillary Putnam, John McDermott, Richard J. Bernstein, Nancy Fraser, Cornel West, and numerous others. Though they might not put it this way, it is a tradition whose aim is to keep alive the pragmatist narrative as one way of resolving the relations between religion and the Enlightenment and is based on the assumption that this narrative cannot be terminated until all the voices implicated in it, all the parties with a vested interest in its outcome, have an opportunity to be heard in the language they believe best represents them.

But this task has been vastly complicated in the twentieth century by what American writers of color in particular have discovered and expressed about the racist basis of the still "unretrieved and irretrievable." When Henry James invoked this language to define what he believed had most consistently betrayed America's own religious and Enlightened sense of itself, he did not see the connection, as he should have, between America's rampant materialism and commercialism and its systemic racism. Had he done so, this could have been what Kenneth Warren has rightly described as "one of the signal moments in American literary history."[25] James had read W. E. B. Du Bois's *The Souls of Black Folk* and found it to be the best book to have come out of the South in many years, but he never put together its brilliant discussion of the "double consciousness" that black people were forced to adopt with whites—seeing themselves both through their own eyes and through the eyes of their oppressors—either with what he rightly perceived as the spectacle of white cruelty to blacks in the South, or with the other spectacle of ostentatious avarice that appalled him in the North. While his brother William had gone on public record to denounce lynching and other acts of violence against blacks, Henry felt that as a nonresident he should keep his own feelings about the horror of this situation to himself.[26]

What James did not manage to fathom was that the deepest source of the unretrieved and the irretrievable that he correctly identified as the sign of America's own self-betrayal was its history of inhumanity to its own, and that this history was founded on the interconnected rocks of material acquisition and racial and, latterly, ethnic and gender oppression. This oppression had begun with the demonization and displacement of Native American people and the enslavement of African American people, and it still constitutes down to the present day the real record of arrears that America has accumulated on its own debt to the future. This is a debt that America has refused to accept even when, at least since the Emancipation Proclamation in 1863, it has given lip service to it. And it is a debt that will never be settled until all the people who have been injured by it receive not only full recognition as fellow human beings but full rights as citizens, including rights of opportunity, from the rest of the people of the United States. Nothing makes America less approachable and more enigmatic to those outside its borders than the way it has rendered its professed benefits unapproachable to its minority populations, including women and the poor, within them.

If racism in America, whether explicitly or implicitly, has been the subject of entire traditions of writers and thinkers in America, beginning in the seventeenth century and continuing, as we have seen, down to the present, it has obviously not been confined to people of African descent. The collective achievement of all writers of color in America has been to expose the ideology of whiteness for the systemic prejudice it is, while giving voice to the distinctive terms of their own experience both of exclusion and of self-realization in the face of it.[27] However, few American writers have been more adamant than Toni Morrison about the urgent necessity to move this complex experience of oppression and resistance from the margins of the American imagination, where it has been confined, into the center of America's literature, where it belongs, and she has done so by declaring that the defining feature of America's history is the contrast between America's "claim to freedom" and "the presence of the unfree." What distinguishes America as a nation is that its people specifically "*decided* that their world view would combine agendas for individual freedom *and* mechanisms for devastating racial oppression" (italics Morrison's).[28]

This has left Morrison—and, for that matter, other writers who have had to grapple with the experience of living in a society so decisively and destructively racialized—with a formidable set of challenges. The first has been to map the history of racial exclusion and oppression in relation to their own specific perspectives on the experience of and resistance to it, in itself an exceptionally complex task in a culture where the markers of racism are as evident in the way whites have constructed themselves as unraced as it is in the way they have constructed others as racial. The second task has been even more daunting. This has required the placement of the map of American racial othering and oppression over the history of America itself so that America's own story can now be reread as a narrative of, in Morrison's work, black America, since its underside is a tale of how America's white imagination has been created in response to the Africanist and African American presences sedimented within it.

To accomplish this complicated cartographic redrawing or refiguration, Morrison and other writers have had to discover ways of telling a story that, on the one hand, compels its readers, many of whom think of themselves as race-free, to share in its processes of historical reconstruction while, at the same time, helping them realize that for those who have suffered its effects, whether directly or belatedly, this process of historical recollection is

simply never ending. Far from being able put it more or less aside as a process that has reached its termination, victims of slavery, as perhaps of any
forms of culturally systemic dehumanization, are now faced not only with
having to live with its memory but with actually having to live *by means of*
that memory.

Such a history thus entails a retrieval both of the unretrieved and of the
irretrievable. In Morrison's case, which might stand for so many others, the
racially unretrieved has involved, as in her second novel, *Sula,* what remains
still unspoken, unheard, unnameable about the experience of slavery itself
and its aftermath. By contrast, the racially irretrievable, as Morrison portrays in her fifth novel, *Beloved,* entails what in effect cannot be said, or
heard, or admitted about the experience of slavery itself, what remains un-
speakable, unbearable, almost unimaginable, though it must somehow still
be expressed, recognized, and acknowledged if the true horrendousness of
slavery is to be understood.

Beloved is loosely based on the actual decision in 1856 of a fugitive slave
mother named Margaret Garner to kill her infant daughter—she was also
apparently prepared to kill her remaining three children and herself—to
prevent her from being returned to slavery under the Fugitive Slave Act.
But Morrison's attention in the novel is not restricted to the self-torture of
her character Sethe, nor to the extreme desperation of her act, nor even to
the way she and others remain haunted and scarred by it and try not to remember it. Her attention is fixated rather, even in spite of Sethe's potential
redemption, on the fact that the descendants of slaves must live by means
of the memory of the racist crimes against their humanity even when they
have no specific recollection of them. For them the still unretrieved and
irretrievable are a particularly tragic reminder of what William Faulkner
noted in *Requiem for a Nun:* "The past is never dead. It's not even past."[29]

In Quest of the Normative

Such retrievals and, one hopes, potential repossessions serve to remind us
that the Enlightenment imaginary still lives if writers and their readers are
committed to telling or learning the truth no matter how great the cost to
the sensibilities of those already victimized by it as well as of those who
would prefer not to know it. By the same token, such retrievals should also
remind us that the religious imaginary still survives unless we are prepared
to concede that all experience is subsumable within some biological, graph-
ological, or ideological template that excuses us from being answerable. The

religious and Enlightenment imaginaries continue to endure just insofar as we continue to undergo experiences capable of being shared, of being communicated, that exceed our rational grasp precisely at the point where we need to explain what makes them, at least to and for us, so singular and salient, so distinctive and decisive.

But pragmatist philosophers like Richard Rorty and others have wondered why we need to associate such practices with the Enlightenment or with religion. By this, Rorty never meant to imply that we have derived no moral benefit from, say, Christianity and the Enlightenment but only that these benefits are no longer tied to the worldviews that were initially developed to express them and offer little further help to us so long as they continue to obscure or repress the contingency of their own origins. Despite the fact that this book has attempted to supply a good deal of information about the contingency of their origins and development in America, Rorty was convinced that the old contest between religion and the Enlightenment, just as the newer attempt to explore their relations and disjunctions, is either, in the first instance, essentially over or, in the second, inevitably futile, not because either side won, or that they both come to essentially the same thing, but because most intellectuals and artists no longer see themselves as actors in such productions.[30] The old problematics of their relationship, or what I am calling its new possibilities, have been not so much solved as dis-solved. And so the story ends, as the poet said, not with a bang but a whimper.

But the story for pragmatism and its relation to the formation of American literature—and particularly for pragmatism as one way of comprehending the continuing relevance of the relations between religion and the Enlightenment as spiritual imaginaries in that process—is clearly not over. The moral aim of the pragmatist narrative is not to reach closure so much as to suspend its achievement indefinitely, or at least until all the voices implicated in it with a vested interest in its outcome get to be heard. This is a world, so pragmatism maintains, whose evidence isn't all in yet and never can be until everyone with a claim on its meaning has their say.

Thus the story of the relations between the religious and Enlightenment imaginaries in America has less to do with reconciling their putative claims and practices than with realizing their potential for keeping alive a sense of the normative capacities of what might be called the ordinary, or what Emerson referred to as "the near, the low, the common."[31] "What would we know the meaning of?" Emerson had asked his audience in "The American Scholar," and famously answered: "The meal in the firkin, the milk in the pan, the ballad in the street; the news of the boat; the glance of the eye; the form and the gait of the body."[32] Emerson could make such a claim because of his confidence that "there is one design unites and animates the farthest pinnacle and the lowest trench," but his later pragmatist descendants are more likely to believe that experience requires no ground more transcendent than itself but can still furnish ways of negotiating its hazards if we can learn how to follow its own promptings and provocations.

Those promptings and provocations furnished by a recovery of a sense of the ordinary and its normative potential have typically taken one of two directions. The first is through its capacity for producing comic corrections, the other through its capacity for producing uncanny, untranslatable extensions. The first depends on the ordinary's ludic, iconoclastic ability to restore a measure of proportion and sanity to the distortions and inflations often caused by too much religion or too much Enlightenment. The second depends on the ordinary's imaginative, unpredictable, ineffable ability to represent itself in forms that resist incorporation within any of our traditional hierarchies of knowledge, our conventional forms of valuation. These capacities would appear less remarkable if they had not been so frequently overlooked or discounted in much philosophical criticism and underappreciated or dismissed in much pragmatist writing.

The Ordinary as Corrective and Curative

In its more vernacular, comedic, satirical mode, pragmatism exhibits itself in modern American writing as a wary but often bemused suspicion of anything that can be identified with what the sociologist Peter Berger once described as "the noise of solemn assemblies."[33] Assuming with Henry James that in an economy of relative moral and intellectual scarcity, cultural forms will always rush in to fill the vacuum by encouraging the development of a certain kind of spiritual pretentiousness, what Kenneth Burke described as an attitude of "Holier than Thou,"[34] this strain of American pragmatism typically attempts to resist the pull of such cultural pieties through its own form of pragmatist refiguration: by rhetorically negotiating a kind of transcendence downward in the hopes of restoring what Norman Mailer once described, in *Armies of the Night,* as "the hard edge of proportion to the overblown values that otherwise threaten to engulf each small [human] existence."[35]

It is no accident that this tradition of pragmatist comic correction has often found a target for its iconoclastic refigurations in one of the chief creations of the American Enlightenment itself. That creation is what is now known as American civil religion, which has traditionally defined itself not as a substitute for more conventional religious faiths like Christianity or Judaism but rather as a spiritual complement and sometimes an alternative to them. Drawing freely on such Jewish and Christian themes as the myth of the Chosen People, the New Jerusalem, and the Errand into the Wilderness, and applying them to America's own sacred occasions and consecrated sites, such as the Fourth of July and the Gettysburg battlefield, American civil religion has sought to resituate the nation's own cultural experience within a transcendent perspective at the risk of making a religion of America itself.[36]

So conceived, American civil religion comprises a system of national symbols and rituals that construe the American political experiment in representative government as a decisive event in modern spiritual history, and documents like the Declaration of Independence, the Constitution, Washington's Farewell Address, Jefferson's Second Inaugural, Lincoln's Gettysburg Address, and other presidential statements as the sacred scriptures of this social and political religion. If George Washington, who is often doubled with everyone from Jefferson to Theodore Roosevelt, Woodrow Wilson, John Fitzgerald Kennedy, and Ronald Reagan, is frequently cast in the role of an American Moses leading his people out of the bondage of English tyranny (or the threat of any other kind of foreign domination), the Promised Land is depicted as the New World of American liberty and independence.

Serving as a means of sanctifying the mythos of national consciousness, it is easy to see why American civil religion has drawn fire from representatives of the pragmatist tradition from Emerson himself, Whitman, Melville, Mark Twain, and Hemingway to popular humorists and public satirists. Much of their writing has been created in reaction to the public world of civic piety and has been devoted to deflating its pomposities. Often comic and earthy, even scatological, it specializes in questioning any attempts to sanctify the meaning of "America" itself and ethically valorize or dogmatically prescribe its practices. Exhibiting an impatience with all theological forms of cultural pretension, it is designed as a reminder that over against all the pretended virtues of our national imaginary, there is an "other," more profane world of the familiar, the mundane, and the commonplace that is capable, at least discursively, of by turns comic or ironic transgressions against their sanctimonious posturings. This more profane, suspicious, irreverent, even sacrilegious world is prepared to view all attempts to transform American civil religion into a legitimation of New World cosmologies and their sacred entitlements as just another conspiracy designed to bamboozle, if not indoctrinate, its citizens and therefore adopts a stance of wary skepticism of the sort expressed in the title of Aretha Franklin's great song "Who's Zoomin' Who?"

Kenneth Burke remains the master theorist of this pragmatist disposition by defining culture as a conspiracy of piety. Piety in Burke's terms is to be identified not exclusively with religion, or even with our broader sense of "what properly goes with what," but also with our "desire to round things out" and "fit experiences into a unified whole." No mere expression of preference or propriety, Burke viewed piety as "our chief system-builder," the source and servant of all zealotries.[37] Maintaining itself by means of a complicated network of interpretive symbolic associations (if something is held to be sacred, piety demands that some ritual act be performed to approach it with clean hands; clean hands demand preparation or initiation for the technique of cleansing; the need for cleansing is accompanied by some feeling of taboo)[38] that bring all the coordinates into play, it is equally difficult to maintain, much less to challenge, because it requires "a set of symbolic expiations to counteract the symbolic offenses involved" in displacing it.[39] The moral question thus raised by the ubiquity and sovereignty of piety is not simply how to keep from being seduced but how to escape its psychological mechanisms of control.

Burke was convinced that the challenge now is not only psychic but semiotic or, as he eventually put it, terminological. If we cannot wrench things loose enough from their conventional linguistic, symbolic, and axiological moorings to imagine them in new valuational configurations, then we are, indeed, prisoners of a closed system and there is nothing to be done. But Burke believed in symbolic refiguration, in terminological and critical metamorphosis, and was thus continually transforming himself into a kind of intellectual quick-change artist, trickster, magician whose disguises and improvisations were rhetorically designed less to hide his intellectual sleights of hand than to bring his readers into the game and show them how to play.

These ludic improvisations and performances give to much of Burke's writing an almost liminal quality. One is always in the process not only of exposing cultural shibboleths but also of transgressing against the boundaries of propriety that protect them. The moment of illumination for Burke comes in those intellectual maneuvers where one set of critical coordinates can be reconfigured or reimagined as another. Burke refers to such coordinates as providing a kind of "calculus" for mapping and charting experiences and events for the purpose of clarifying their potential implications and effects. Such mental gymnastics all depend on the fallibilist persuasion that every perspective is limited, every position susceptible to revision, Burke's favorite example being "the trout who becomes a critic when his jaw is ripped, learning then a nicer discrimination between food and bait."[40]

Burke's recourse to a discourse that is continuously colloquial, vernacular, even proverbial, reflects his belief that the wisdom of comedy is essentially cautionary. The key to its pragmatic wariness is a kind of critical humility that in contrast to "the modern tendency to look upon intelligence as merely a *coefficient of power* for heightening our ability to get things, be they good or bad" (italics Burke's)[41] helps teach us how "to get off before the end of the line."[42] Burke claims that this kind of humility serves as a corrective to the effects of pride, though its emphasis is not, as in tragedy, on pride's criminality and evil so much as its ignorance and stupidity. Comedy, which Burke regarded as the most enlightened and humane outlook yet attained by human beings, depicts people not as inherently vicious so much as mistaken. And "when you add," Burke goes on, "that people are *necessarily* mistaken, that *all* people are exposed to situations in which they must act as foolish, that *every* insight contains its own special kind of blindness, you complete the comic circle, returning again to the lesson of humility that underlies great tragedy" (italics Burke's).[43] Yet Burke would be the first to admit that without corrective discounting, the comic perspective can also be fetishized. Comedy remains a kind of critical cure-all that draws on the potential normativity of the ordinary only because it does not rest on the conclusions of its reductions and reversals but rather contains the seeds of its own counterstatements within itself.

But if the comic serves as a kind of curative for the inflations and infatuations of pride and piety, the critic's or intellectual's medicine is somewhat different from the artist's. The artist's method, as Burke puts it in one of his more famous analogies, is essentially homeopathic in that he or she tries to immunize us "by stylistically infecting us with the disease."[44] The critic's or philosopher's method, on the other hand, is allopathic, since he or she is out to combat the disease by providing us with remedies to counter its effects. Hence where the artist tries to cure us by inoculating us against the worst effects of some form or forms of piety, the critic or intellectual seeks to cure us by supplying us with a sufficient antidote of skepticism, or at least of circumspection, to ward off their aftereffects. Yet these two strategies eventually come to roughly the same thing: both are ways of preventing us from privileging, much less absolutizing, of our own limited and selected senses of what goes with what.

The Ordinary as Uncanny and Untranslatable

In its less suspicious, more elevated mode, this pragmatist tradition locates the ordinary's capacity for keeping alive a sense of the normative through its unexpected, seemingly gratuitous disclosure of the unimagined, the uncanny, the unlegible.[45] Such capacities and their relation to pragmatism have nowhere been described more effectively than by Richard Poirier. Starting with Emerson's statement that the poet "uses forms according to the life, and not according to the form," Poirier retrieved an Emerson who is the originator of a tradition of literary and intellectual pragmatism in American writing that constitutes an alternative to our conventional view of modernism and simultaneously casts modernism's relation to postmodernism in an entirely new light. Poirier sought to explain this in two different ways. In the first, the tradition initiated by Emerson is associated with the practice of a kind of humanistic self-erasure or, as Poirier termed it, "writing off the self."[46] In the second, it is defined in terms of a self-conscious linguistic skepticism that enables language to point beyond itself.

By the phrase "writing off the self," Poirier intended to describe a tradition where the vitality of the human presence is often discovered in forms so alien to its traditional interests and sites of valorization as almost to link it with energies that deny it.[47] As figured (for Poirier) in a group of writers that begins in America with Emerson and includes Thoreau and Whitman but also extends through William James and his brother Henry to such moderns as Gertrude Stein, Robert Frost, Wallace Stevens, and Marianne Moore from one generation, Robert Lowell, Elizabeth Bishop, Ralph Ellison, and John Berryman from another, Frank O'Hara, Audre Lorde, and Tony Kushner from still another, the possibility of self-evacuation from those inherited descriptions that define human beings at present is precipitated by, and leads to, moments whose transformative power have little to do with narratives of fulfillment and cannot be made available to ideology. In writers such as these—whose association with the intellectual assumptions and stylistic proclivities of American pragmatism is evident in everything from their faith in the materials of ordinary experience and their distrust of absolutes to their delight in process, action, and mutability, and their conviction that truth is made rather than found, fabricated not given—such moments are preceded neither by catastrophe nor by collapse. They are instead produced by the metaphorical capacities of language itself when those capacities that enable language to swerve away from its own inherited meanings, to resist tropologically the technology of its own traditional usages, are seen as a source of empowerment that needs no sanctions, religious or otherwise, for the sense of personal enhancement that accompanies them. In the moment when punning, joking, and troping break the grip of institutionalized terminologies, the emancipation of the self is effected simply by the way the writing calls attention to the performative presence of the self even in gestures of its own dissolution or effacement.

Poirier is fully cognizant of the fact that this possibility has long met with critical resistance. Even as works of literature have frequently entertained the idea that the human presence can be revealed in those very processes that apparently deny it, so traditions of scholarly assessment have typically denied or discounted this possibility. Critical thinking about such matters has been too often blocked because of its seduction by a false dualism, a simple either-or: either the Judeo-Christian notion of the self whose creaturely identity as a substantial and self-conscious entity is secured by such a metaphorical description as "child of God," or the view enunciated by Emerson in his essay "Circles," where every fact is seen as the beginning of another series for which there is no necessary circumference, causing the dissolution of any self seeking resolution through language, "since language has no fixed or ultimately rationalizing term."[48] Such an either-or assumes, in effect, that religion and the Enlightenment are utterly opposed in America.

Poirier counters this reductionism by arguing that there is an alternative possibility entertained by the pragmatist tradition in American writing that centers on "discovering a form of the human which emerges from the very *denial* of its will to become articulate, or of looking at a landscape from which the familiar human presence has been banished and of enjoying this vista without thinking of deprivation."[49] These are occasions when the ordinary becomes unexpected, exceptional, incomparable without being formulated as such. As in Walt Whitman's "As I Ebb'd with the Ocean of Life," or Wallace Stevens's "The River of Rivers in Connecticut," or Elizabeth Bishop's "At the Fishhouses," we become aware of how "it is possible to confer value on moments of transformation or dissolution without looking ahead toward a narrative of fulfillment. The moment is endowed with something as vague as wonder or beauty, empty of the desire to translate these into knowledge."[50]

Given the skepticism with which this possibility is still greeted in many critical circles, often being dismissed as just another attempt to smuggle religion into the discussion of art, it is not surprising that Poirier later decided to reconceive this literary practice of self-erasure as the expression of a kind of self-conscious linguistic skepticism.[51] This is a skepticism linked to the deconstructive mechanisms within language itself that enable language to resist the self-reflexivity of its own inherited meanings and thus point beyond them toward possibilities for personal or cultural renewal. To follow this movement within language, as it were, beyond language requires that we think very differently about words and the things that can be done with them. Where the conventional thinking about such matters associates words with things, language with reference, verbal signs with substantive entities, Emerson, anticipating the nomenclature that William James would later employ, was convinced more than a century before speech act theory that words have more to do with actions and events, language with processes and power, verbal signs with transitives and connectives.

William James formulated this possibility most simply when he said somewhere that what "[verbal] formulas express leaves unexpressed almost everything that they organically divine and feel." It was this element of the "unexpressed" and the verbally inexpressible—what James simply called "the vague" and its cognate "the superfluous"—that Poirier wants to reinstate in criticism, just as James before him wanted to reinstate it in philosophy. Vagueness, ambiguity, even undecidability, derive from the limitations that language continuously experiences in its efforts to represent its own understanding in words. But this failure, as Poirier, like William and Henry James, and Emerson before them, all attest is quickening as well as salutary. The words are there to point to—or, better, lead toward—insights, intuitions, intimations, implications that would be lost if in fact they were named.

If this linguistic skepticism were merely another way of maintaining that, as T. S. Eliot wrote in "Burnt Norton," "Words strain / Crack and sometimes break, under the burden, / Under the tension, slip, slide, perish, / Decay with imprecision, will not stay in place, / Will not stay still,"[52] such a demonstration would merely reinforce the appeal of deconstruction itself, with its summary rejection of the Eliotic quest for "the still point in the turning world" and its conviction that the instability of language points to the indeterminacy of its reference.[53] But Emerson and James, together with Poirier, intend to say something quite different. In opposition to Eliot's attempts to evade such issues by holding out the possibility of their transcendence in some larger "idea of order," and in contradistinction to deconstruction's frequent tendency to identify these problems with something flawed and treacherous about the nature of language itself, Poirier, James, and Emerson all insist that these obstacles that language places in the way of what Dewey

called the "quest for certainty" afford significant opportunities, both cognitive and affective, for further knowledge, deeper insight, richer awareness.

In this sense, vagueness is far more than a mere constituent of perception; it is also, as Poirier brings out more effectively than James ever did, the
only guarantee that perception contains within itself a potential for criticizing some of its own cognitive deliverances. Requiring, as Poirier calls it, "a
disciplined resistance" to the seductions of habit as well as to the desire for
closure, vagueness functions simultaneously both as a kind of counterforce
to dogmatization and as an incitement to the exploration of new truths.[54]
Often conveyed in writing by nothing more concrete than voice and sound,
vagueness derives, so Poirier maintains, from the failure that language continuously experiences in its effort to represent its own understanding in
words. If most postmodernist criticism typically reads this failure as the
death knell of logocentrism, pragmatism reads it as representing potentially
a "saving uncertainty."[55]

In this pragmatist understanding of language, the words are there—in
Charlotte Perkins Gilman's "The Yellow Wallpaper" or Ezra Pound's *Cantos,*
Gertrude Stein's *Tender Buttons* or Williams's *Spring and All*—to point to
or, better, to lead toward intimations, inferences, insinuations, implications,
situated on or just beyond the horizon of consciousness, or that lack any
placement within our current geographies of understanding but belong to
that "whole field" constituted by what James called "our full self" and from
which radiate "all those indefinitely subconscious possibilities of increase
that we can only feel without conceiving and can hardly begin to analyze."[56]
Thus, art is for pragmatism important not because it designates, as in the
monumentalist or hierarchic view, somewhere to get to, but rather because
it suggests, as in a more democratic or colloquial view, somewhere to depart
from. As Emerson said, the arts are not final but initial. It is not what they
reach that matters but rather what they aim at. Hence, even when they claim
to furnish their readers with what Thoreau described in *Walden* as "a hard
bottom and rocks in place, which we can call *reality,* and say This is, and no
mistake" (italics Thoreau's), that "bottom" or "reality"—as Thoreau characteristically added in further elaboration, and as pragmatist critics and intellectuals like Burke, Trilling, McDermott, Poirier, would agree—is merely
another *"point d'appui."*[57]

This pragmatist narrative thus transmutes the dialectic between religion
and the Enlightenment not into another "myth of eternal return," such as
the one T. S. Eliot envisioned at the end of "Little Gidding," where the end
of all our exploration is to arrive "where we started / And know the place

for the first time," but into a new access to otherness.[58] If this doesn't quite convert the philosopher into what Cavell touchingly describes as a "hobo of thought," it does transform the thinker into a kind of explorer whose primary intellectual ambition is to travel far enough out beyond the conventional boundaries of thought, past the traditional oppositions of the intellect, in search of a "somewhere" where we may "witness our own limits transgressed, and some life pasturing feely where we never wander."[59]

Is this how philosophy, like religion, should be practiced or how they are transcended? It scarcely seems to matter. The key to the meaning of being is still to be found, as Cavell, Poirier, Burke, Dewey, the Jameses, and Emerson would all agree, on what Whitman called "the open road of experience"—a road whose journeying can become edifying, enhancing, enabling, both personally and socially, only as we learn how to respond to moments when the ordinary becomes uncanny, the familiar strange, the habitual again "other" because it "is imagined as if it were not less but, because extemporized within and also against existent forms, immeasurably more than the result of some 'arrangements of knowledge.'"[60]

NOTES

Introduction

1. William James, *A Pluralistic Universe* (Cambridge, MA: Harvard University Press, 1977), 14–15.

2. See Arjun Appadurai's famous essay "Disjuncture and Difference in the Global Economy," in his *Modernity at Large: Cultural Dimensions of Globalization* (Minneapolis: University of Minnesota Press, 1996), 27–47.

3. Cornelius Castoriadis, *The Imaginary Institution of Society*, trans. Kathleen Blamey (Cambridge, MA: MIT Press, 1987); Benedict Anderson, *Imagined Communities: Reflections on the Origin and Spread of Nationalism* (London: Verso, 1983); Appadurai, *Modernity at Large*; Charles Taylor, *Modern Social Imaginaries* (Durham, NC: Duke University Press, 2004).

4. For an excellent discussion of the way the notion of the imaginary has worked itself out in contemporary social science and intellectual history, see Dilip Parameshwar Gaonkar, "Toward New Imaginaries: An Introduction," *Public Culture* 14.1 (2002): 1–19.

5. Lionel Trilling, *The Liberal Imagination* (New York: Doubleday Anchor Books, 1957), 200. Trilling goes on to note that such expressions of value, taste, and disposition are most often hinted at not by large actions but by small, "sometimes by the arts of dress or decoration, sometimes by tone, gesture, emphasis, or rhythm, sometimes by the words that are used with a special frequency or a special meaning" (200).

6. See Thomas Bender, and particularly chap. 1, "The Oceanic World and the Beginnings of American History," in his *A Nation among Nations: America's Place in World History* (New York: Hill and Wang, 2006), 15–60.

7. Ralph Waldo Emerson, *Selected Essays*, ed. Larzer Ziff (New York: Penguin Classics, 1985), 302.

8. Ibid, 303.

9. See Richard J. Bernstein, *The New Constellation: The Ethical-Political Horizons of Modernity/Postmodernity* (Cambridge, MA: MIT Press, 1992), 201.

10. See, e.g., John Bender, *Ends of Enlightenment* (Stanford: Stanford University Press, 2012); Sarah Rivett, *The Science of the Soul in Colonial New England* (Chapel Hill: University of North Carolina Press, 2011); Ann Taves, *Fits, Trances and Visions: Experiencing Re-*

ligion and Explaining Experience from Wesley to James (Princeton: Princeton University Press, 1999); Leigh Eric Schmidt's *Hearing Things: Religion, Illusion, and the American Enlightenment* (Cambridge, MA: Harvard University Press, 2002); John Lardas Modern, *Secularism in Antebellum America* (Chicago: University of Chicago Press, 2011); Maurice Lee, *Uncertain Chances: Science, Skepticism, and Belief in Nineteenth-Century American Literature* (New York: Oxford University Press, 2013); Tracy Fessenden, *Culture and Redemption: Religion, the Secular, and American Literature* (Princeton: Princeton University Press, 2007); James Delbourgo, *A Most Amazing Scene of Wonders: Electricity and Enlightenment in Early America* (Cambridge, MA: Harvard University Press, 2006).

11. Pierre Bourdieu, *Outline of a Theory of Practice*, trans. Richard Nice (Cambridge: Cambridge University Press, 1977), 79.

12. No one has to my knowledge brought out this critical, skeptical side of the European Enlightenment with more brilliance that Peter Gay in his classic two-volume study, *The Enlightenment: An Interpretation*, vol. 1: *The Rise of Modern Paganism*, and vol. 2: *The Science of Freedom* (New York: W. W. Norton, 1995, 1996).

13. William James, *The Varieties of Religious Experience* (1902; Cambridge, MA: Harvard University Press, 1985), 410.

14. Wallace Stevens, "An Ordinary Evening in New Haven," in *The Collected Poets of Wallace Stevens* (New York: Alfred A. Knopf, 1964), 473.

15. This phrase belongs to the title of an election sermon that Samuel Danforth delivered in 1670, and it subsequently furnished the title of a famous essay by Perry Miller and later the title of a well-known book of his essays under the same name: Perry Miller, *Errand into the Wilderness* (Cambridge, MA: Belknap Press of Harvard University Press, 1956).

16. Robert Frost, *Collective Poems of Robert Frost* (New York: Henry Holt, 1936), 329.

1. The Difficulty of Beginnings

1. Henry F. May, *The Enlightenment in America* (New York: Oxford University Press, 1976).

2. See Crane Brinton, *Ideas and Men* (Englewood Cliffs, NJ: Prentice-Hall, 1950), 369–408, and *A History of Western Morals* (New York: Harcourt Brace, 1959), 297–98, 306–7, 374–75, 450–79.

3. Jonathan Mayhew, "A Discourse Concerning Unlimited Submission," in *Pamphlets of the American Revolution*, ed. Bernard Bailyn (Cambridge, MA: Harvard University Press, 1965), 1:213.

4. Alan Heimert, *Religion and the American Mind from the Great Awakening to the Revolution* (Cambridge, MA: Harvard University Press, 1966).

5. Robert A. Ferguson, "We Hold These Truths," in *Reconstructing American Literary History*, ed. Sacvan Bercovitch (Cambridge, MA: Harvard University Press, 1986), 24.

6. For this formulation of the innermost assumption of Enlightenment belief, I am indebted to remarks made by Schubert M. Ogden at the symposium "Knowledge and Be-

lief in America," sponsored by the Woodrow Wilson Center for International Scholars at the Smithsonian Institution, April 18–20, 1990. This formulation also possesses a distant relation to Henry May's association of Enlightenment faith with all those who believe the following two propositions: "first, that the present age is more enlightened than the past; and second, that we understand nature and man best through the use of our natural faculties" (*The Enlightenment in America*, xiv).

7. Of the two, the Enlightenment is probably the easier to define simply because the historical movement to which it refers, however various its expressions, was confined to a much smaller group of people who were far narrower in interests and enjoyed such dominion as they achieved for a decisively shorter period of time. Thinking of a collection of intellectuals that included Voltaire, Locke, Hume, Moses Mendelssohn, Montesquieu, Rousseau, Diderot, Turgot, Helvetius, Condorcet, Adam Smith, Jefferson, and Paine, Isaiah Berlin has provided perhaps the most satisfactory summary of the consensus that linked their diverse views in the following statement, which must be quoted in its entirety ("Joseph de Maistre and the Origins of Fascism," *New York Review of Books*, 27 September 1990, 60):

But sharp as the genuine differences between these thinkers were, there were certain beliefs that they held in common. They believed in varying measure that men were, by nature, rational and sociable; or at least understood their own and others' best interests when they were not being bamboozled by knaves or misled by fools; that, if only they were taught to see them, they would follow the rules of conduct discoverable by the use of ordinary human understanding; that there existed laws which govern nature, both animate and inanimate, and that these laws, whether empirically discoverable or not, were equally evident whether one looked within oneself or at the world outside. They believed that the discovery of such laws, and the knowledge of them, if it were spread widely enough, would of itself tend to promote a stable harmony both between individuals and associations, and within the individual himself.

Most of them believed in the maximum degree of individual freedom and the minimum of government—at least after men had been suitably reeducated. They thought that education and legislation founded upon the "precepts of nature" could right almost every wrong; that nature was but reason in action, and its workings therefore were in principle deducible from a set of ultimate truths like the theorems of geometry, and latterly of physics, chemistry, and biology.

They believed that all good and desirable things were necessarily compatible, and some maintained more than this—that all true values were interconnected by a network of indestructible, logically interlocking relationships. The more empirically minded among them were sure that a science of human nature could be developed no less than a science of inanimate things, and that ethical and political questions, provided that they were genuine, could in principle be answered with no less certainty than those of mathematics and astronomy. A life founded upon these answers would be free, secure, happy, virtuous, and wise. In short they saw no reason why the millennium should not be reached by the use of faculties and the practice of methods that had for over a century in the sphere of the sciences of nature led to triumphs more magnificent than any hitherto attained in the history of human thought.

8. Richard Brodhead, "Literature and Culture," in *The Columbia Literary History of the United States,* ed. Emory Elliott et al. (New York: Columbia University Press, 1988), 472–73.

9. Henry Adams, *The Education of Henry Adams* (Boston: Houghton Mifflin, 1961), 7.

10. There is reason to believe that this lacuna is in the process of being significantly addressed in texts already mentioned by Sarah Rivett, Ann Taves, Leigh Eric Schmidt, John Lardas Modern, Maurice Lee, Tracy Fessenden, and James Delbourgo.

11. Serious objections to the primacy Miller accords the mind and the role of cognition in Puritan spirituality range from Alan Simpson's *Puritanism in Old and New England* (Chicago: University of Chicago Press, 1955) and later studies like Andrew Delbanco's *The Puritan Ordeal* (Cambridge, MA: Harvard University Press, 1989) down to the present day. Important challenges to Miller's focus on New England in early American cultural life can be found in numerous works, from Daniel J. Boorstin's *The Americans: The Colonial Experience* (New York: Random House, 1958) to, among many other seminal studies, Jack P. Greene's *Pursuits of Happiness: The Social Development of Early Modern British Colonies and the Formation of American Culture* (Chapel Hill: University of North Carolina Press, 1989), and David Hackett Fischer's *Albion's Seed: Four British Folkways in America* (New York: Oxford University Press 1989).

12. Kenneth Murdock, *Literature and Theology in Colonial New England* (New York: Harper and Row, 1949, 1963), 208.

13. Van Wyck Brooks, *America's Coming-of-Age* (Garden City, NY: Doubleday Anchor 1951), 3; and D. H. Lawrence, *Studies in Classic American Literature* (Garden City, NY: Doubleday Anchor, 1951), 26.

14. Herman Melville, "Hawthorne and His Mosses," in *Moby-Dick,* ed. Harrison Hayford (New York: W. W. Norton, 1967), 540.

15. Terrence Martin, *The Instructed Vision: Scottish Common Sense Philosophy and the Origins of American Fiction* (Bloomington: Indiana University Press, 1961), 60–76.

16. Richard Chase, *The American Novel and Its Tradition* (Garden City, NY: Doubleday Anchor, 1957). This trend has beginnings as early as F. O. Matthiessen's *American Renaissance: Art and Expression in the Age of Emerson and Whitman* (New York: Oxford University Press, 1941), and its persistence can be seen even in works that problematize an understanding of the form, such as Michael Davitt Bell's *The Development of American Romance* (Chicago: University of Chicago Press, 1980), or that seemingly address different traditions, such as Eric J. Sundquist's "The Country of the Blue," in *American Realism,* ed. Sundquist (Baltimore: Johns Hopkins University Press, 1982), 3–24.

17. Edmundo O'Gorman, *The Invention of America: An Inquiry into the Historical Nature of the New World and the Meaning of Its History* (Bloomington: Indiana University Press, 1961).

18. See Alan Taylor, *American Colonies* (New York: Penguin, 2002), 40.

19. Bernal Díaz, *The Conquest of New Spain,* trans. J. M. Cohen (Harmondsworth: Penguin 1963), 214–15.

20. Mircea Eliade, *The Sacred and the Profane: The Nature of Religion,* trans. Willard Trask (New York: Harcourt, Brace, 1959).

21. Michel de Montaigne, quoted in *Early Modern Writing,* ed. Giles Gunn (New York: Penguin Books, 1994), 58.

22. Chief Powhatan, quoted in ibid., 406.

23. Chief Logan, quoted in ibid., 409–10.

24. Thomas Jefferson, *Notes on the State of Virginia,* ed. William Peden (Chapel Hill: University of North Carolina Press, 1982), 63.

25. Chief Pachgantschilias, quoted in Gunn, *Early American Writing,* 411.

26. Chief Tecumseh, quoted in ibid., 413.

27. Chief Seattle, quoted in *New World Metaphysics: Readings on the Religious Meaning of American Experience,* ed. Giles Gunn (New York: Oxford University Press, 1981), 284.

28. "The Book of Chilam Balam of Chumayel," quoted in Gunn, *Early American Writing,* xxi–xxii.

29. I am indebted to Stephen Greenblatt for this insight. See his *Learning to Curse: Essays in Early Modern Culture* (New York: Routledge, 1990).

2. Puritan Ascendance and Decline

1. See Nathanial Philbrick, *Mayflower: A Story of Courage, Community, and War* (New York: Penguin, 2006).

2. The life and trial of Ann Hutchinson have been the subject of a number of studies. For a history of the problems within transatlantic Puritanism that gave rise to the Antinomian movement, see Theodore Dwight Bozeman, *The Precisianist Strain: Disciplinary Religion and Antinomian Backlash in Puritanism to 1638* (Chapel Hill: University of North Carolina Press, 2012). For studies of Ann Hutchinson and her relationship to the Antinomian movement, see Louise A. Breen, *Transgressing the Bounds: Subversive Enterprises among the Puritan Elite in Massachusetts, 1630–1692* (New York: Oxford University Press, 2001); and Michael P. Winship, *The Times and Trials of Anne Hutchinson: Puritans Divided* (Lawrence: University Press of Kansas, 2005).

3. See Edmund S. Morgan, *Roger Williams: The Church and the State* (New York: W. W. Norton, 2007); and John M. Barry, *Roger Williams and the Creation of the American Soul: Church, State, and the Birth of Liberty* (New York: Penguin, 2012).

4. For a more specific treatment of the relation between religion and race in Massachusetts and elsewhere during the Puritan era, see Heather Miyano Kopelson, *Faithful Bodies: Performing Religion and Race in the Puritan Atlantic* (New York: New York University Press, 2014).

5. Mary Rowlandson, *A Narrative of the Captivity and Restauration of Mrs. Mary Rowlandson,* quoted in Gunn, *Early American Writing,* 219.

6. Hector St. John de Crèvecoeur, quoted in Sebastian Junger, *Tribe: On Homecoming and Belonging* (New York: Twelve, 2016), 9–10.

7. Edmund S. Morgan, in *The National Experience: A History of the United States,* by John Blum et al., 2nd ed. (New York: Harcourt, Brace & World, 1968), 61.

3. Enlightenment and a New Age Dawning

1. Alexander Whitaker, from *Good Newes from Virginia,* quoted in Gunn, *Early American Writing,* 105.

2. Robert Beverley, from *The History and Present State of Virginia,* quoted in ibid., 288.

3. Thomas Jefferson, from *Notes on the State of Virginia,* quoted in ibid., 437.

4. Ibid., 439.

5. Thomas Jefferson, from *Autobiography,* quoted in ibid., 435.

6. J. Hector St. John de Crèvecoeur, from *Letters of an American Farmer,* quoted in ibid., 476.

7. Ralph Waldo Emerson, quoted in ibid., 390.

8. Abigail Adams, quoted in ibid., 504.

9. John Quincy Adams, *Letters of John Adams, Addressed to His Wife,* ed. Charles Francis Adams, vol. 1 (Boston: CC Little and J. Brown, 1841), 97.

10. Hannah Webster Foster, from *The Coquette; or, The Life and Letters of Eliza Whitman,* Letter 12, quoted in Gunn, *Early American Writing,* 599.

11. Max Horkheimer and Theodor Adorno, *Dialectic of Enlightenment,* trans. John Cumming (New York: Herder and Herder, 1972).

12. However defined, the ideas with which the Enlightenment was associated were to meet with bitter resistance in America. Much of that story, particularly its intellectual roots, is brilliantly told by Jonathan I. Israel in *Enlightenment Contested: Philosophy, Modernity, and the Emancipation of Man, 1670–1752* (New York: Oxford University Press, 2006).

13. A. R. Ammons, "Corson's Inlet," in *Selected Poems* (Ithaca: Cornell University Press, 1965), 137.

14. See Sidney Mead, *The Lively Experiment* (New York: Harper and Row, 1963).

15. Benjamin Franklin, from *The Autobiography of Benjamin Franklin,* quoted in Gunn, *Early American Writing,* 364.

16. Ibid., 63–64.

17. Benjamin Franklin, *The Autobiography and Other Writings,* ed. Kenneth Silverman (New York: Viking Penguin, 1986), 101.

18. The Bible was also changing in other important ways during the eighteenth century with even larger cultural implications. See Jonathan Sheehan, *The Enlightenment Bible: Translation, Scholarship, Culture* (Princeton: Princeton University Press, 2007).

19. Benjamin Franklin, from Letter to Ezra Styles, in Gunn, *Early American Writing,* 373.

20. The origins of republicanism and its effect on the creation of a new political order in America have been under discussion for many years, but one can obtain a sense

of the modern shape of that discussion from the following texts: J. G. A. Pocock, "Machiavelli, Harrington, and English Political Ideologies in the Eighteenth Century," *William and Mary Quarterly* 22 (October 1965): 549–83; Gordon S. Wood, *The Creation of the American Republic, 1776–1787* (1969; New York: W. W. Norton, 1972); Joyce Appleby, *Capitalism and a New Social Order: The Republican Vision of the 1790s* (New York: New York University Press, 1984); Patricia U. Bonomi, *Under the Cope of Heaven: Religion, Society, and Politics in Colonial America* (New York: Oxford University Press, 1986); and Bernard Bailyn, *The Ideological Origins of the American Revolution* (Cambridge, MA: Belknap Press of Harvard University Press, 1992).

21. Thomas Paine, from *Of the Religion of Deism . . .* , quoted in Gunn, *Early American Writing,* 490.

22. Thomas Paine, from *Introduction to Common Sense,* quoted in ibid., 489–90.

23. Thomas Jefferson, from *Autobiography,* quoted in ibid., 433.

24. Richard Wright, quoted in *The Harper American Literature,* vol. 2, ed. Donald McQuade (New York: HarperCollins, 1987), 200.

4. The Pragmatist Refiguration of American Narratives

1. Henry Adams, *The Education of Henry Adams* (1918; Boston: Houghton Mifflin, 1961), 457–58.

2. Alfred Kazin was the first American critic to make this claim with conviction, in *American Procession* (New York: Knopf, 1984).

3. One can hear the strong echo of the Enlightenment in Channing's explanation of what spiritual freedom means: "I call that mind free which jealously guards its intellectual rights and powers, which calls no man master, which does not content itself with a passive or hereditary faith, which opens itself to light whencesoever it may come, which receives new truth as an angel from heaven, which, while consulting others, inquires still more of the oracle within itself." See William Ellery Channing, "Spiritual Freedom," in *The Works of William Ellery Channing in Six Volumes,* vol. 1, ed. Joseph Baker (London: Chapman, 1844), 105–6.

4. Ralph Waldo Emerson, *Selected Essays,* ed. with an intro. Larzer Ziff (New York: Viking Penguin, 1982), 36.

5. Ralph Waldo Emerson, from *Nature,* ibid., 38–39.

6. Chase, *The American Novel and Its Tradition,* 11.

7. Tony Tanner, *City of Words* (New York: Harper and Row), 15.

8. Henry James, *The Portrait of a Lady,* ed. Robert D. Bamburg (New York: Norton, 1975), 175.

9. Herman Melville, *Moby-Dick,* 392.

10. Tanner, *City of Words,* 15.

11. Nathaniel Hawthorne, *The Scarlet Letter,* ed. Sculley Bradley, Richard Croom Beatty, and E. Hudson Long (New York: W. W. Norton, 1962), 126.

12. For an example of the first characterization, see Quentin Anderson, *The Imperial*

Self (New York: Knopf, 1971); for an example of the second, see Nina Baym, "Melodramas of Beset Manhood: How Theories of American Fiction Exclude Women Authors," in *The New Feminist Criticism*, ed. Elaine Showalter (New York: Pantheon, 1985), 63–80.

13. Jane Tompkins, *Sensational Designs* (New York: Oxford University Press, 1985); and Cathy N. Davidson, *Revolution and the Word* (New York: Oxford University Press, 1986). A related but somewhat different narrative emerges from the study Tania Modleski has made of models of feminist self-description and ideological resistance offered by popular art forms such as gothic novels, Harlequin romances, and daytime soap operas in *Loving with a Vengeance: Mass-Produced Fantasies for Women* (New York: Methuen, 1982).

14. Ann Douglas, *The Feminization of American Culture* (New York: Knopf, 1977).

15. Elizabeth Fox-Genovese, "American Culture and New Literary Studies," *American Quarterly* 42 (March 1990): 21.

16. Ibid., 22.

17. Frederick Douglass, *Narrative of the Life of Frederick Douglass, an American Slave, Written by Himself,* ed. John W. Blassingame et al. (New Haven: Yale University Press, 2001), 35–36, 54.

18. Harriet Jacobs, in *Harriet Jacobs, a Life,* by Jean Fagan Yellin (New York: Civitas Books, 2005), 16, 30.

19. May, *The Enlightenment in America,* 360.

20. David S. Reynolds, *Beneath the American Renaissance: The Subversive Imagination in the Age of Emerson and Melville* (New York: Knopf, 1988).

21. I am indebted to my late colleague and eighteenth-century literary specialist Professor Everett Zimmerman for this insight.

22. An excellent discussion of the cultural metaphysics of this tradition can be found in John McWilliams, "Poetry in the Early Republic," in *Columbia Literary History of the United States,* 156–67.

23. See Giles Gunn, *The Interpretation of Otherness: Literature, Religion, and the American Imagination* (New York: Oxford University Press, 1979), 161–74.

24. Melville, *Moby-Dick,* 144; and Charles Feidelson, *Symbolism and American Literature* (Chicago: University of Chicago Press, 1953).

25. See D. H. Lawrence, *Studies in Classic American Literature* (Garden City, N.Y.: Doubleday Anchor Books, 1951).

26. Daniel Hoffman, *Form and Fable in American Fiction* (New York: Oxford University Press, 1965), 233–78.

27. Melville, *Moby-Dick,* 314.

28. Ibid., 400.

29. All the poems of Emily Dickinson quoted here are taken from *The Complete Poems of Emily Dickinson,* ed. Thomas H. Johnson (Boston: Little, Brown, 1960).

30. Charles R. Anderson, *Emily Dickinson's Poetry: Stairway of Surprise* (New York: Holt, Rinehart and Winston), 197.

31. The intellectual movement of which pragmatism was an expression was not limited to America or confined to philosophy. See James T. Kloppenbrg, *Uncertain Victory: So-*

cial Democracy and Progressivism in European and American Thought, 1870–1920 (New York: Oxford University Press, 1986).

32. William James, *The Writings of William James,* ed. John J. McDermott (Chicago: University of Chicago Press, 1977), 45.

33. Cited in Richard Poirier, *The Renewal of Literature: Emersonian Reflections* (New York: Random House, 1987), 45.

34. May, *The Enlightenment in America,* 109.

5. The Jamesian Component

1. William James, *Pragmatism and Other Writings,* ed. Giles Gunn (New York: Penguin Books, 2000), 112.

2. Ibid.

3. Ibid., 194.

4. George Santayana, "A Brief History of My Opinions," in *The Philosophy of Santayana,* ed. Irwin Edman (New York: Charles Scribner's Sons, 1936), 16.

5. George Santayana, *Persons and Places* (London: Constable, 1944), 249.

6. For a further discussion of these assumptions, see Henry F. May, *The End of American Innocence* (1959; Chicago: Quadrangle Paperbacks, 1964), 3–51.

7. Wallace Stevens, *Opus Posthumous* (London: Faber and Faber, 1957), 237.

8. Wallace Stevens, *The Palm at the End of the Mind,* ed. Holly Stevens (New York: Vintage Books, 1972), 175.

9. H. S. Thayer, *Meaning and Action: A Critical History of Pragmatism* (Indianapolis: Hackett, 1968), 6.

10. C. S. Peirce, "How to Make Our Ideas Clear," in *Philosophical Writings of Peirce,* ed. Justus Buchler (New York: Dover, 1955), 30, 31.

11. C. S. Peirce, "The Essentials of Pragmatism," in ibid., 261.

12. Peirce, "How to Make Our Ideas Clear," 38.

13. William James, "A Pluralistic Universe," in *Essays in Radical Empiricism and a Pluralistic Universe,* ed. Ralph Barton Perry (Cambridge, MA: Harvard University Press,) 222.

14. James, *Pragmatism and Other Writings,* 27.

15. William James, "Philosophical Conceptions and Practical Results," in *William James, Writings, 1879–1899,* ed. Gerald Myers (New York: The Library of America, 1992), 1080.

16. James, *Pragmatism and Other Writings,* 25.

17. William James, "Some Problems of Philosophy," in *William James, Writings,* ed. Bruce Kuklick (New York: The Library of America, 1987), 1013.

18. James, *Pragmatism and Other Writings,* 28; further citations to this work are in the text.

19. William James, *Essays in Radical Empiricism and A Pluralistic Universe,* ed. Ralph Barton Perry (Cambridge, MA: Harvard University Press, 1976), 131–32.

20. Hilary Putnam, "James's Theory of Truth," in *The Cambridge Companion to William James,* ed. Ruth Anna Putnam (New York: Cambridge University Press, 1997), 183.

21. William James, "Interview," *New York Times*, 3 November 1907.

22. William James, "Does Consciousness Exist?" in *The Writings of William James*, ed. McDermott, 178.

23. William James, "The Continuity of Experience," in ibid., 296.

24. The most important exception to this is Richard A. Hocks's *Henry James and Pragmatistic Thought: A Study in the Relationship between the Philosophy of William James and the Literary Art of Henry James* (Chapel Hill: University of North Carolina Press, 1974). I also treat this relation at some length in my *Thinking across the American Grain: Ideology, Intellect, and the New Pragmatism* (Chicago: University of Chicago Press, 1992), 143–44.

25. F. O. Matthiessen, *The James Family* (New York: Alfred A. Knopf, 1961), 343.

26. Ibid., 345.

27. My view of this subject has been most deeply informed by Ross Posnock, *The Trial of Curiosity: Henry James, William James, and the Challenge of Modernity* (New York: Oxford University Press, 1991), esp. 80, but there are other thoughtful discussions of this subject that are threaded throughout Matthiessen's *The James Family* and are brilliantly discussed at length in R. W. B. Lewis, *The Jameses: A Family Narrative* (New York: Farrar, Straus and Giroux, 1991).

6. Religion and the Enlightenment
under the Sign of the Modern and Beyond

1. Loc Wacquant, "Habitus," in *International Encyclopedia of Economic Sociology*, ed. J. Becket and Z. Milan (London: Routledge, 2005), 316.

2. John Peale Bishop, *The Collected Essays of John Peale Bishop*, ed. Edmund Wilson (New York: Charles Scribner's Sons, 1948), 93.

3. Ernest Hemingway, *Farewell to Arms* (New York: C. Scribner's Sons, 1929), 184–85.

4. Paul Fussell, *The Great War and Modern Memory* (New York: Oxford University Press, 1975), 30.

5. Northrop Frye, *Anatomy of Criticism* (Princeton: Princeton University Press, 1957), 345.

6. Ibid., 346.

7. T. S. Eliot, *Selected Essays of T. S. Eliot*, new ed. (New York: Harcourt, Brace & World, 1950), 124–25.

8. Ernest Hemingway, *Death in the Afternoon* (New York: Charles Scribner's Sons, 1932), 2.

9. Wallace Stevens, *The Collected Poems of Wallace Stevens* (New York: Alfred A. Knopf, 1964), 10.

10. Ezra Pound, *The Spirit of Romance* (London: J. M. Dent, 1910), 5.

11. Robert Frost, "The Most of It," in *The Poetry of Robert Frost*, ed. Edward Connery Lathem (New York: Holt, Rinehart and Winston, 1969), 338.

12. See Wayne C. Booth, *A Rhetoric of Irony* (Chicago: University of Chicago Press, 1974).

13. David Foster Wallace, "An Interview with David Foster Wallace," interview by Larry McCaffery, *Review of Contemporary Fiction* 13 (Summer 1993): 134.

14. Philip Roth, *Reading Myself and Others* (New York: Farrar, Straus and Giroux, 1975), 120.

15. Postmodernism is, in any case, far from the only style employed by contemporary American writers.

16. William Butler Yeats, "The Circus Animals' Desertion," in *Selected Poems of William Butler Yeats,* ed. with intro. M. L. Rosenthal (New York: Macmillan, 1962), 185.

17. It should be noted that Foucault's so-called antihumanist sentiments were restricted primarily to the 1960s and should not be confused with his overall philosophical project as a thinker, which was not to reflect on what he believed to be true or false, right or wrong, but rather on our relations to whatever we deem or construct as true and how, accordingly, we should act.

18. Stanley Cavell, *This New Yet Unapproachable America: Lectures after Emerson after Wittgenstein* (Albuquerque: Living Batch Press, 1989), 116.

19. It is worth observing that Cavell disputes the view that Emerson was himself pragmatist, or even a precursor of pragmatism in any strict philosophical sense. See Paul Grimstad, *Experimental Writing: Literary Pragmatism from Emerson to the Jameses* (New York: Oxford University Press, 2013), 3–11.

20. Cavell, *This New Yet Unapproachable America,* 116.

21. Ibid.

22. Ibid., 90.

23. Ibid., 92.

24. Henry James, *The American Scene,* ed. Leon Edel (Bloomington: Indiana University Press, 1968), 465; in the following discussion, further citations to this work are in the text.

25. Kenneth Warren, *Black and White Strangers: Race and American Literary Realism* (Chicago: University of Chicago Press, 1993), 112.

26. This is not to overlook the fact that James was elsewhere guilty of certain of the prejudices associated with America's systemic racism, as when he commented with condescension about how ill suited African American porters and waiters were for positions of personal service, or wondered what effect the new presence of Yiddish on the streets of New York would have on the English language.

27. I do not mean to imply that they have done this in the same way, any more than I wish to overlook the fact that the phrase "people of color" can as easily be used not merely to gloss crucial differences between and among racialized communities but also to dismiss them.

28. Toni Morrison, *Playing in the Dark: Whiteness and the Literary Imagination* (Cambridge, MA: Harvard University Press, 1992), xiii.

29. William Faulkner, *Requiem for a Nun,* in *Novels 1942–1954,* ed. Joseph Blotner and Noel Polk (New York: Library Classics of America, 1994), 535.

30. Richard Rorty actually defined the issues still associated with these two legacies somewhat differently, as the need to preserve great scope for the freedom of personal self-redescription with the necessity of maintaining a sense of solidarity with the pain and suffering of others. I have responded to the way Rorty formulated these issues most famously in his book *Contingency, Irony, and Solidarity* (Cambridge: Cambridge University Press, 1989), in, most recently, Giles Gunn, *Ideas to Live For: Toward a Global Ethics* (Charlottesville: University of Virginia Press, 2015), 54–75, 115–29.

31. Emerson, *Selected Essays* (Penguin Classics, 1985), 101.

32. Ibid., 102.

33. Peter Berger, *The Noise of Solemn Assemblies* (New York: Doubleday, 1961).

34. Kenneth Burke, *Counter-Statement* (Berkeley: University of California Press, 1968), 51.

35. Norman Mailer, *Armies of the Night* (New York: New American Literary, 1968), 47; Leo Marx has turned the narrative that furnishes Norman Mailer with this exemplum into what is the most incisive literary critique ever made of American civil religion in his brilliant essay entitled "Noble Shit: The Uncivil Response of American Writers to American Religion," *The Pilot and the Passenger: Essays on Literature, Technology, and Culture in the United States* (New York: Oxford University Press, 1988), 261–90.

36. Robert Bellah, *The Broken Covenant: American Civil Religion in a Time of Trial*, 2nd ed. (Chicago: University of Chicago Press, 1992).

37. Kenneth Burke, *Terms for Order*, ed. Stanley Edgar Hyman (Bloomington: Indiana University Press, 1964), 51.

38. Ibid.

39. Burke, *Counter-Statement*, 48.

40. Kenneth Burke, *Permanence and Change* (Los Altos, CA: Hermes, 1935), 5.

41. Burke, *Terms for Order*, 86.

42. Quoted in Stanley Edgar Hyman, *The Armed Vision* (New York: Vintage, 1955), 381.

43. Kenneth Burke, *Attitudes toward History* (Los Altos, CA, 1959), 334.

44. Burke, *Terms for Order*, 86.

45. I have borrowed the phrase "the uncanniness of the ordinary" from Stanley Cavell, who means by this pregnant phrase something rather different from what is intended here. For Cavell, "the uncanniness of the ordinary is epitomized by the possibility or threat of what philosophy has called skepticism, understood (as in my studies of Austen and of the later Wittgenstein I have come to understand it) as the capacity, even desire, of ordinary language to repudiate itself, specifically to repudiate its power to word the world, to apply to the things we have in common, or to pass them by" (*In Quest of the Ordinary: Lines of Skepticism and Romanticism* [Chicago: University of Chicago Press, 1988], 154).

46. Richard Poirier, *The Renewal of Literature: Emersonian Reflections* (New York: Random House, 1987).

47. For Cavell, see his *In Quest of the Ordinary*; for Poirier, see his *The Renewal of Literature*.

48. Poirier, *The Renewal of Literature*, 203.

49. Ibid.

50. Ibid., 202.

51. See Richard Poirier, *Poetry and Pragmatism* (Cambridge, Mass.: Harvard University Press, 1992).

52. T. S. Eliot, *The Complete Poems and Plays, 1909–1950* (New York: Harcourt, Brace, 1952), 121.

53. Ibid., 119.

54. Poirier, *Poetry and Pragmatism*, 42.

55. Ibid., 4.

56. William James, "The Continuity of Experience," in *The Writings of William James*, ed. McDermott, 296.

57. Henry David Thoreau, *Walden*, ed. J. Lyndon Shanley (Princeton: Princeton University Press, 1973), 98.

58. Eliot, *The Complete Poems and Plays*, 145.

59. Thoreau, *Walden*, 318. Thoreau used this phrase in a very different way to express Nature's ability to absorb the loss of myriad species without putting at risk its own plentitude and abundance.

60. Poirier, *The Renewal of Literature*, 202.

INDEX

RECENT BOOKS IN THE STUDIES IN RELIGION AND CULTURE SERIES

Also by Giles Gunn

F. O. Matthiessen: The Critical Achievement

The Interpretation of Otherness: Literature, Religion, and the American Imagination

The Culture of Criticism and the Criticism of Culture

Thinking Across the American Grain: Ideology, Intellect, and the New Pragmatism

Beyond Solidarity: Pragmatism and Difference in a Globalized World

Ideas to Die For: The Cosmopolitan Challenge

Ideas to Live For: Towards a Global Ethics

Books Edited by Giles Gunn

Literature and Religion

Henry James, Senior: A Selection of His Writings

New World Metaphysics: Readings on the Religious Meaning of the American Experience

The Bible and American Arts and Letters

Church, State, and American Culture

Redrawing the Boundaries: The Transformation of English and American Literary Studies (with Stephen J. Greenblatt)

Early American Writing

Pragmatism and Other Writings by William James

War Narratives and American Culture (with Carl Gutiérrez-Jones)

A Historical Guide to Herman Melville

America and the Misshaping of a New World Order (with Carl Gutiérrez-Jones)

Global Studies: A Historical and Contemporary Reader